THE FAILURE OF POLITICAL ISLAM

The Failure of Political Islam

❖ ❖ ❖

OLIVIER ROY

Translated by Carol Volk

HARVARD UNIVERSITY PRESS

Cambridge, Massachusetts

Originally published as *L'échec de l'Islam politique;* © Editions du Seuil, 1992

First Harvard University Press paperback edition, 1996

Library of Congress Cataloging-in-Publication Data

Roy, Olivier, 1949–
[Echec de l'islam. English]
The failure of political Islam / Olivier Roy; translated by Carol Volk.
p.   cm.
Includes bibliographical references (p.   ) and index.
ISBN 0-674-29140-9 (cloth)
ISBN 0-674-29141-7 (pbk.)
1. Islam and politics—Middle East.   2. Islam and politics—Africa, North.
3. Middle East—Politics and government—1979–
4. Africa, North—Politics and government.   I. Title.
BP63.A4M537313   1994
322'.1'0917671—dc20
94-18782
CIP

❖ *Contents* ❖

❖ *Preface* ❖

THIS BOOK IS neither about Islam in general nor about the place of politics in Islamic culture. It is about contemporary Islamist movements—the activist groups who see in Islam as much a political ideology as a religion, and who are therefore breaking with a certain tradition themselves. These are the movements that for several decades, and particularly during the last decade, have mounted challenges against both the West and the regimes in place in the Middle East.

Does contemporary political Islam offer an alternative to Muslim societies? This is the subject of the pages that follow.

It strikes me as intellectually imprudent and historically misguided to discuss the relationships between Islam and politics as if there were one Islam, timeless and eternal. In saying as much, I diverge as far from the prevailing discourse among Islamic intellectuals as from the mirror vision that still dominates a part of Western Islamic studies, or more precisely what I will refer to here as "Orientalism": the perception of Islam and of Muslim societies as one global, timeless cultural system. Not that I wish to deny fourteen centuries of remarkable permanence in dogma, religious practice, and world vision. But concrete political practices during that time have been numerous and complex, and Muslim societies have been sociologically diverse. We often forget as well that there is a broad range of opinion among Muslim intellectuals as to the correct political and social implications of the Quranic message. Western Orientalists, however, tend either to cut through the debate by deciding for the Muslims what the Quran means or to accept the point of view of a particular Islamic school while ignoring all others.

I have limited my inquiry to the Islamist current—without taking up the other visions of Islam and without studying the texts of the Quran or the Sunna—because of its considerable impact on the contemporary world: I am taking at its word what Islamism says about Islam. Thus, when I speak about Islamic politics or economics, I am referring not to Muslim society in general, but to the thought and actions of the movements of contemporary political Islam. I use the term "Muslim" to designate what is based on fact (a "Muslim country" is a country in which the majority of the population is Muslim; a "Muslim intellectual" is an intellectual of Muslim origin and culture), and the term "Islamic" for the result of an intention (an "Islamic state" is a state that bases its legitimacy on Islam; an "Islamic intellectual" is an intellectual who consciously organizes his thought within the conceptual framework of Islam).

To reduce all the problems of the contemporary Muslim world—from the legitimacy of existing states to the integration of immigrant workers—to the residual effects of Islamic culture seems to me tautological, in that by imposing the grid of a culturalist reading upon the modern Middle East, we end up seeing as reality whatever was predetermined by the grid, notably with regard to what I call the "Islamic political imagination," to be found in generic statements such as "In Islam, there is no separation between politics and religion." Of course, this political imagination must be taken seriously, in the sense that it permeates and lends structure to both the leaders' discourse and the subjects' revolt. But it is never directly explanatory and in fact conceals all that is rupture and history: the importation of new types of states, the birth of new social classes, and the advent of contemporary ideologies.

Beginning in the 1930s, Hasan al-Banna, the founder in Egypt of the Muslim Brotherhood, and Abul-Ala Maududi, the creator of the Indo-Pakistani Jamaat-i Islami party, introduced a new movement of thought that endeavored to define Islam primarily as a political system, in keeping with the major ideologies of the twentieth century. But they brought legitimacy to this new vision by the theme of a "return"—a return to the texts and to the original inspiration of the first community of believers. We will thus be examining the historical actuality of a movement that rejects its own historicity. In keeping with the terminology used by others, I will refer to the contemporary movement that conceives of Islam as a political ideology as "Islamism."

What is of interest to us in this movement? Its novelty, its effect on the West—which has been paralyzed for ten years by the "Islamic threat"—and, ultimately, its failure: aside from the Iranian revolution, Islamism has not significantly altered the political landscape of the Middle East. Political Islam does not pass the test of power. In the early 1990s the regimes of 1980 are still in place, and the Gulf War has established American hegemony. A strange Islamic threat indeed, which waged war only against other Muslims (Iran/Iraq) or against the Soviets (Afghanistan) and caused less terrorist damage than the Baader-Meinhof gang, the Red Brigade, the Irish Republican Army, and the Basque separatist ETA, whose small-group actions have been features of the European political landscape longer than hizbullahs and other jihad movements.

Not that Islamism is disappearing from the political scene. On the contrary, from Pakistan to Algeria it is spreading, becoming commonplace, being integrated into politics, leaving its mark on mores and conflicts. It will probably come to power in Algeria. But it has lost its original impetus. It has "social-democratized" itself. It no longer offers a model for a different society or a brighter future. Today, any Islamist political victory in a Muslim country would produce only superficial changes in customs and law. Islamism has been transformed into a type of neofundamentalism concerned solely with reestablishing Muslim law, the *sharia,* without inventing new political forms, which means that it is condemned to serving as a mere cover for a political logic that eludes it—a logic in which we ultimately find the traditional ethnic, tribal, or communal divisions, ever ready to change their discourse of legitimization, hidden beneath the new social categories and regimes. As for the "Islamic economy," it is mere rhetoric, masking either a form of Third World state socialism (Iran in the era of Khomeini) or an economic liberalism geared more toward speculation than toward production.

Why didn't it succeed? The failure is primarily an intellectual one. Islamic thought rests on an initial premise that destroys its own innovative elements: on the one hand, as the logic goes, the existence of an Islamic political society is a necessary condition for the believer to achieve total virtue; but on the other hand, such a society functions only by the virtue of its members, beginning with its leaders. In short, the development of Islamist thought, which is political par excellence, ends up dissociating itself from the very components of politics (institutions, authorities, an autonomous sphere separate from the private realm), seeing them as mere instruments for raising moral standards and thereby returning, by a different route, to the traditional perception of the ulamas and the reformists, in whose eyes Muslims need only be virtuous for society to be fair and Islamic.

Second, Islamism is a failure historically: neither in Iran nor in liberated Afghanistan has a new society been established. The failure of Islamism does not mean that parties such as the Algerian FIS (Islamic Salvation Front) will not achieve power, but only that those parties will not invent a new society. After the revolution, moral order will reign. For the rich the Islamic model is Saudi Arabia (revenue plus *sharia*); for the poor it is Pakistan, Sudan, and, tomorrow, Algeria: unemployment plus *sharia*.

Political Islam is no longer a geostrategic factor; it is at most a societal phenomenon. Throughout the Muslim world, nation-states are easily resisting the calls for the unity and reforging of the Islamic community. While it is true that North–South tensions will long remain vital, fueling a resentment that can easily take on the colors of Islam, the Islamic revolution is behind us.

Yet the crisis still remains. It lies in the weak legitimacy of regimes and states, even in the very idea of a nation. It is manifest in the permanence of autocratic regimes and the influence of tribal, ethnic, and religious segmentation. It is inherent in population growth, the destitution of the middle classes, the unemployment of the educated, the growing ranks of the masses who live in cities but are poorly integrated there. The crisis is also a problem of models: secularism, Marxism, nationalism. Hence the popularity of the illusion of the "return to Islam."

The crisis of the state in Muslim countries, however, is not the result of Islamic political culture: from Zaire to the Philippines, we find patrimonialism (confusion of the public and private sectors), segmentation, weak democratic demand, nonintegration of the society into a state logic. These are the symptoms of state crises in all the countries of the Third World. Islam is not a "cause." Could it have been a cure? I believe that the Islamist moment closed a door: that of revolution and the Islamic state. Only the rhetoric remains.

In the following chapters I first examine the sociology of the Islamist movement and its conceptual matrix. There seems to be a close connection between Islamist ideology, which is obsessed with the state, and the diminished status of the modern intelligentsia. Next I trace the drift of political Islamism toward a more conservative neofundamentalism, in which the ethical model takes precedence over political philosophy. I then survey the cluster of contemporary Islamist groups. The exercise reveals that despite their ideological proximity, these movements never coalesced into an Islamist International: on the contrary, state logic has dominated the geostrategic checkerboard of the Middle East. Finally, I look at two concrete cases: that of Afghanistan, to show how the ideologies of jihad and Islamism have been unable to overcome traditional segmentations, instead providing a framework for their return; and that of Iran, where the revolution was as much a Third World movement as an Islamic one. Although its revolutionary project was the only one to succeed, Iran immediately locked itself into the Shiite ghetto and is today reverting to a conservative "Saudi" model of society.

THE FAILURE OF POLITICAL ISLAM

❖ *Introduction* ❖

MANY IN THE West seem to view the end of our century as the era of the "Islamic threat." The irruption of Islam into the political landscape is often perceived as an anachronism; how is it possible, late in the twentieth century, to return to the Middle Ages? We envision bearded mullahs everywhere, surging forth from mosques and villages to attack the modern-day Babylons, seeking to create a reactionary, irrational, and violent world. Yet history has taught us that barbarity is inherent in cities and has never signaled a return to what came before. It is not that the Middle Ages are invading our modern world, but rather that modernity itself produces its own forms of protest.

In our prevailing outlook we remain prisoners of the old schema of the Enlightenment whereby there is only one form of Progress: as we see it, political modernity, embodied in parliamentary democracy, goes hand in hand with economic development, the easing of moral codes, and secularization. In this respect our memory is short and selective. How many revolutions have been fundamentally puritanical, even profoundly religious, from Cromwell to Robespierre? How much industrial modernization has occurred under dictatorships, from Napoleon III to Mussolini? How many dictatorships have been secular, even antireligious, from Mexico to the Soviet Union?

Islamism as a Third World Movement

The Islamist sphere of influence spans the entire spectrum of activist groups who, in the second half of the twentieth century, see their actions as an extension of the concepts elaborated by the founder of the Muslim Brotherhood in Egypt, Hasan al-Banna (1906–1949),

1

and by Abul-Ala Maududi (1903–1978), the creator of the Jamaat-i Islami party on the Indian subcontinent. Revolutionary Shiite political thought shares many elements with the Muslim Brotherhood but remains distinct (both more leftist and more clerical): it has drawn inspiration from the Ayatollahs Khomeini, Baqir al-Sadr, and Taliqani, as well as from the secular Ali Shariati.

From the outset, then, we find Islam divided into three geographic and cultural tendencies: the Sunni Arab Middle East, the Sunni Indian subcontinent, and Irano-Arab Shiism; Turkey, isolated from the Arab world, has its own organizations. These groups are as distinct politically as they are geographically, which is why it is more appropriate to speak of an Islamist sphere of influence than of an international union. The largest organizations are those of the Arab world's Muslim Brotherhood (MB), vaguely dependent on their Egyptian leadership but in reality organized on a national basis; several dissident and minority groups, generally influenced by the most radical ideas of the MB's Sayyid Qutb (1906–1966), have branched off from this common base (Hizb al-Tahrir in 1952, the Islamic Jihad in the 1970s, and so on). Next we find organizations on the Indian subcontinent (the various Jamaat-i Islamis of Pakistan, India, and Bangladesh), the Afghan *mujahidin* (Hizb-i Islami, Jamaat-i Islami), and, more recently, the North African Islamists (the Algerian FIS, or Islamic Salvation Front; the Tunisian Nahda party) and the Islamic Renaissance Party in the former Soviet Union. This bloc has recently tended to merge with older, apolitical fundamentalist movements (the Saudi Wahhabis, the Pakistani Ahl-i Hadith), thus somewhat losing definition. As for the revolutionary Shiite movement, it is the only one to have taken power by way of a true Islamic revolution; it has therefore become identified with the Iranian state, which used it as an instrument in its strategy for gaining regional power, even though the multiplicity of Shiite groups reflects local particularities (in Lebanon, Afghanistan, or Iraq) as much as it does the factional struggles of Tehran.

Colonel Qaddafi's Libya, despite its activism (which in fact was more financial than ideological), has been outside the Islamist sphere ever since Qaddafi outlawed the Libyan Muslim Brotherhood in

1973 and effected the disappearance of the charismatic head of the Lebanese Shiites, Musa al-Sadr, in 1978.

The Islamist movement has developed over half a century, beginning more or less in 1940. Concepts have of course evolved, historical circumstances have changed, and splits and differences have brought diversity. Nevertheless, there are a conceptual matrix and a sociological base common to all the groups.

Indeed, as much from a sociological as from an intellectual point of view, these movements are products of the modern world. The militants are rarely mullahs; they are young products of the modern educational system, and those who are university educated tend to be more scientific than literary; they come from recently urbanized families or from the impoverished middle classes. Islamists consider Islam to be as much a religion as an "ideology," a neologism which they introduced and which remains anathema to the ulamas (the clerical scholars). They received their political education not in religious schools but on college and university campuses, where they rubbed shoulders with militant Marxists, whose concepts they often borrowed (in particular the idea of revolution) and injected with Quranic terminology (*da'wa,* designating preaching/propaganda). Emphasis is placed on the organization, a framework reminiscent both of Leninist-type parties (in which the amir replaces the secretary-general and the *shura*—the advisory council—the central committee) and of Sufi brotherhoods. For them, taking control of the state will allow for the spread of Islam in a society corrupted by Western values and for a simultaneous appropriation of science and technology. They do not advocate a return to what existed before, as do fundamentalists in the strict sense of the word, but a reappropriation of society and modern technology based on politics.

The masses who follow the Islamists are not "traditional" or "traditionalists" either: they live with the values of the modern city—consumerism and upward social mobility; they left behind the old forms of conviviality, respect for elders and for consensus, when they left their villages. These followers are fascinated by the values of consumerism imparted by the shop windows of the large metropolises; they live in a world of movie theaters, cafés, jeans, video, and sports, but they live precariously from menial jobs or remain unemployed in immigrant ghettos, with the frustration inherent in an unattainable consumerist world.

The Islamist adaptation to the modern, urban setting is striking—from the use of modern weapons and communications technology to the organization of large demonstrations. Their militant actions exist in symbiosis with their urban environment: except in Afghanistan and Kurdistan, the guerrillas of the contemporary Muslim world are city-dwellers.

Thus, far from being a strange irruption of an irrational, archaic phenomenon, the Islamist movement is in keeping with two pre-existing tendencies. One, of course, is the call to fundamentalism, centered on the *sharia:* this call is as old as Islam itself and yet still new because it has never been fulfilled. It is a tendency that is forever setting the reformer, the censor, and the tribunal against the corruption of the times and of sovereigns, against foreign influence, political opportunism, moral laxity, and the forgetting of sacred texts. The other tendency, more recent and therefore more difficult to see, is that of anticolonialism, of anti-imperialism, which today has simply become anti-Westernism—from Cairo to Tehran, the crowds that in the 1950s demonstrated under the red or national flag now march beneath the green banner. The targets are the same: foreign banks, night clubs, local governments accused of complacency toward the West. The continuity is apparent not only in these targets but also in the participants: the same individuals who followed Nasser or Marx in the 1960s are Islamists today.[1] There is an abundance of coming and going and of connections between Marxist groups and the Islamist sphere (the secular Palestinian Ahmad Jibril, for instance, has close ties with the Lebanese Hizbullah). Without question the Shiites have provided the best bridge between the two Third World movements: Ali Shariati, an ideologist of the contestant Shiite movement, was a great reader of Frantz Fanon. And of course it is the Islamic revolution in Iran that has best embodied the Third World continuity of the Islamist movement by expressing the North–South opposition in religious terms.

The secular, Marxist, and nationalist revolutionary movements of the Third World were caught off-guard by their victories, and their ideals were corrupted by the practice of power. Islam has taken up the torch of the Third World, but with slogans that can no longer be shared by Western leftists or by other Third World movements: religious universalism has killed universalism plain and simple.

The parallels between the Muslim and Christian worlds are nonetheless striking with regard to recent history, no doubt because the two intelligentsias shared common political references. The 1950s and 1960s were years of communion: the Algerian guerrilla fighter and the Palestinian activist seemed the brothers of progressive Western militants. Their violence made sense. The divorce occurred in the 1970s: one could no longer understand the new militants of political Islam. Yet in their social origins, their relationship to knowledge, and even in the values that replaced their Marxist-leaning universalism, they are still the cousins of the Western "militants" of the 1970s: they have in common the cult of the return to the past, of authenticity and purity; the concern with dress, food, and conviviality; the rebuilding of a "traditional" way of life in a context and by methods that presuppose that the tradition is obsolete; the shift into terrorism for the most radical fringe. For the most sectarian, *hijra*, hegira, in the caves of Egypt[2] is akin to a return to the countryside. There are analogies between the Italian Red Brigade and the new extremist Muslim intelligentsia: its members, "microintellectuals" whose social integration falls short of their expectations, hurl themselves into political violence on the basis of self-taught Marxist (or elsewhere Islamist) dogma. The hair-splitting logorrhea of the communiqués of the French "Action directe" movement is a good example of this relationship.

The connection between the two Third World tendencies is stronger than it seems: previously, in the Marxist-leaning sphere of influence, we found the same synthesis between revolution and Christian theology ("liberation theology"), the same voluntarist activism, and the same quest for an "authenticity" that would break with Western, including Soviet, models. The Marxist-leaning revolutionary currents of the 1970s—Hafizullah Amin in Afghanistan,

Pol Pot in Cambodia, the Shining Path in Peru—all sought, beneath a dogmatic Marxist line, to invent a new "national" model built around a "lumpenintelligentsia," particularly the "indigenous" or traditional sectors of the population (tribes, peasants, Indians). Curiously, whereas the Marxist guerrillas were peasants, the Islamists were urban, and thus *sociologically* more modern. The parallel between Islamism and Third World movements extends to their decomposition and the shift of their most radical sectors into terrorism, which is a product of the 1970s and not an Islamic invention. But we have lost the common frame of reference, the Third World Marxist vulgate that allowed some to "understand" the Baader-Meinhof Gang or the Red Brigades, even the Palestinian hijackers, but not the Hizbullah hostage-takers.

Not that we have heard the last of the Third World. The collapse of the Soviet Union and of communism makes it likely that Islam will long remain the dominant force in the mobilization of the Muslim world's masses in times of crisis, and the Third World is still in crisis. But unlike Marxism, Islam cannot reach beyond its cultural sphere: the age of converting entire peoples is past. Religious universalism spreads only through individual conversion and defines a community separate from others: it thus draws its own limits and produces a "culture war" effect that makes it difficult to see the relationship between Third World contestation and Islamist self-assertion. Today's Islamist activists are obsessed with conversion: rumors that Western celebrities or entire groups are converting are hailed enthusiastically by the core militants. Indeed, even as a political ideology Islamism cannot evade the issue of individual belief, whereas Marxism allowed one to explain and thus to influence a social movement on the basis of group determinisms. Religion requires individual conversion, transforming the dynamic of conversion to Islam among Christians into a matter of simple arithmetic rather than a mass sociopolitical phenomenon: you keep adding until the number of converts shifts the balance of the society. But here is where the difficulty lies: anyone in a Christian environment who converts to Islam is psychologically choosing a sect structure, which generally indicates a marginalized person, a fanatic, or a true mystic—in other words, a loner, which thus precludes desire for a mass movement.

Where Does Political Modernity Come From?

That said, comparisons don't prove anything. To show the modernity, and thus the deep historicity, of Islamist movements is interesting in terms of political sociology, but goes against the Islamists' own arguments. For them, there is only one Islam, that of the age of the Prophet, which has since lost its way, for modernity is loss. But this vision of Islam as possessing a single essence is not unique to the Islamists, since we find it both among traditionalist ulamas and among many Western Orientalists, who are in turn adopting Max Weber's reading of Islam: a culture, a civilization, a closed system. Islamist and Orientalist thinkers are in disagreement, of course, as to what constitutes the essence of Islam, but all speak in terms of a global, timeless system—a mirror effect that no doubt explains both the violence and the sterility of the polemics. The pages that follow will seem at times to accept this presupposition, by the mere fact that we take at their word the arguments of the actors: to which conceptual configuration are they referring when they conceive of Islam as a political system? To what extent does this configuration function in their political action?

The "Orientalist" presupposition consists, among Western specialists or essayists, in defining a timeless "Islamic culture," a conceptual framework that structures both political life and urban architecture, the thought of the ulamas and of their detractors, and whose consequence would be the nonemergence of capitalism (M. Weber) and the absence of an autonomous space for politics and institutions (B. Badie). A timeless civilization in which everything is interrelated and reflects a same structure, from the stucco arabesque to the legal treatise, but a civilization brutally confronted with the challenge of a modernity arisen from outside. According to this view, "Islamic culture" is the major obstacle prohibiting access to political modernity.[3]

What is this presupposition of political modernity? We find

today under the bylines of many authors, after the Third World moment during which the West masochistically beat its breast, the Weberian idea according to which a single civilization—that is to say, Europe—invented a true universalist culture.[4] In the political domain, the invention of modernity lies in the emergence of an autonomous political space, separate from both the religious and private spheres and embodied in the modern, law-based state. Secularity and politics are born of a closing in of Christian thought onto itself. This is not to deny that there has been some remarkable historical and political research addressing the birth of politics and the modern state.[5] But the consequence of this work has been to posit that there is no salvation (no modernity) outside of the Western political model. The "popularized" argument that is put forth, based on these works and aimed at Muslim intellectuals, is twofold: (1) parliamentary democracy, the ideology of human rights, and the law-based state are ethically desirable and economically more efficient; (2) historically, this configuration comes out of Christian Europe. In postcolonial settings this argument is very badly received, and not only in Islamist or traditionalist circles. The Gulf War showed that even among secular, Westernized, and "democratic" Muslim intellectuals there was a conscious choice, whether tortured or enthusiastic, in favor of Saddam Husayn, who all agreed was a dictator . . . a bad Muslim. This passionate reaction implies an admission of failure: the absence of an alternative aside from a miracle, a sign from God. It is this absence of an alternative thought that we should examine without anchoring it to "Islamic culture," which we imperceptibly tend to transform into a psychological category, especially since the self-satisfied defense of the Western model proposed for the benefit of the Third World (and which also serves as a form of self-therapy after the Third-Worldism of the 1960s) has been divided, internally, by increasingly virulent debate about the crises of politics and values in Western societies. We therefore need to break away from these mutually defensive arguments.

The problem is comparativism. Comparativism tends to take one of the elements of the comparison as the norm for the other, finding that there is either a resemblance or a lack of one, but never questioning the original configuration. Comparativism thus risks isolating the two entities, ignoring not only their individual dynamics, but particularly the dialectic of the relationship between one and the other: this dialectic tends both to fix in the imagination differences that are more emblematic than real and to obscure their factual specificity. While there is definitely an Islamic political corpus, from the traditionalist ulamas to the Islamists, it is difficult if not downright specious to posit a simple equivalency between a civilization and a history on the one hand and this corpus on the other.

In comparativism, one is constantly moving between the Islamic corpus (the texts produced by scholars and intellectuals) and the concrete sociological reality: the "lack" of modernity in Muslim countries is explained at times by the effects of the absence of a conceptual category that is present in Western thought (for example, since the concept of a state based on territory is absent from the corpus of Islamic politics, it is impossible to achieve a modern state, which is by definition territorialized); at times by the existence of a sociological category not reflected in the corpus (the patrimonial state, the segmentation into "solidarity groups," *asabiyya*).[6] The first approach confirms the impossibility of the emergence of an autonomous political authority within the framework of "Islamic culture"; the second, in contrast, highlights the autonomy of the political authority—albeit a premodern political authority (a patrimonial state)—with respect to Islamic thought.

But far from being inherently and originally marked by a lack, Islamic political thought is inscribed within a different configuration of the relationship between power and the law. That this configuration is in turn a source of difficulties is not in doubt, but one must measure it in relation to its original meaning, not in relation to the Western state. What is original is the place of the *sharia,* Muslim law, with respect to power. The *sharia* has two characteristics: its autonomy and its incompletion. The *sharia* does not depend on any state, on any actual, positive law, on any political decision; it thereby creates a space that is parallel to the political space, to power, which, it is true, can circumvent the *sharia* or manipulate it (hence the strong theme of the corruption of the judge), but which cannot make it into something other than what it is: an autonomous, infinite commentary. For the *sharia* does not depend on any official body, church or clergy; the *fatwa*, formal legal opinions that decide matters not mentioned in the text, are always pronounced in the here and now and can be annulled by a subsequent authority.[7] The *sharia* is never closed, for it is based not on a core of concepts, but rather on an ensemble of precepts which is at times general, at times precise, and which expands to include the totality of human acts through induction, analogy, extension, commentary, and interpretation. While the basic precepts, as they are explicitly formulated, cannot be called into question, their extension is a matter of casuistics. The work of the judge is not to apply a principle or a concept, but to bring the case before him back into the realm of what is already known.

These two "weaknesses" in the *sharia* (no institutional closure, no conceptual closure) also make totalitarianism, understood as the absorption of the entirety of the social realm into the political realm, foreign to Islamic culture: its warning symptoms appear only when this culture is in shambles (Iraq). At the same time, no one can lay claim to Islam and simultaneously contest the *sharia:* secularity can result only from violence (Ataturk's Turkey) or from escheat, through a change in lifestyles and customs.

The excess of state, which is latent in the place the state occupies in the West, is totalitarianism. It is not surprising that Western contemporary thought on the birth of the state would also be a reflection on and against totalitarianism.[8] In Islam, it is because there is a weakness in the political space that totalitarianism does not occur, which naturally does not mean that there is no state or arbitrary violence, which, when it occurs, is considered to be "unjust tyranny," *zulm:* the opposite of tyranny, in the Islamic political imagination, is not liberty, but justice. Ethics, and not democracy, is the watchword of protest, clearing the way for every kind of populism. This is how one must interpret the weakness of democratic demand in a Muslim country. It is not that there is an acquiescence in dictatorship, but that a different demand is made: first of all, the respect for privacy, for the family space, the home, honor *(namus);* next, the demand for justice (the recurrence of the theme of the good sovereign). Liberty is demanded in the sphere of the family, in the private sphere, and not in the political domain, where the value expected is justice.

These brief reflections aim to show that there are different configurations and problematics in the relationships between the state and society in Islamic and Western cultures. To investigate the first culture on the basis of the concepts of the second, elevated to the level of universality, can only bring to light an absence, a lack—the lack of a modern state—without making it clear that what prevents the emergence of this state (the *sharia* and the horizontal bonds of solidarity groups) is also what makes Islamic totalitarianism impossible. This doesn't mean that I am equating the *sharia* with Western democracy: simply that comparativism must be viewed as a conclusion and not as a premise. It is a question of methodology.

The Muslim responses to the "Orientalist" discourse are often stereotypical and can be sorted into three categories: (1) the nostalgia argument ("it was Islam that brought civilization to the West"); (2) rejection of the hypothesis ("in what way are Western values superior?"), combined with a denunciation of Western doubletalk, which applies its strict requirements only to others; (3) the apologia for Islam ("everything is in the Quran and the Sunna, and Islam is the best religion"). The first two are defensive: they evade the question while accepting as fact that there is a modernity that produces its own values. The third constitutes the topic of this book.

In fact both Islamism and the traditional fundamentalism of the ulamas have difficulty posing the real question: why does Western Orientalism study Islam *sub specie aeternitatis,* while approaching Western civilization as a "socio-historical configuration"?[9] The reason is simple: the Islamic political imagination accepts and even demands the presupposition according to which Islam exists *sub specie aeternitatis.* The dominant corpus in Sunni Islamic culture, that of the ulamas, as well as those of the Salafist reformists and contemporary Islamists, conceive of Islam as timeless, ahistorical, and beyond criticism.[10] We must therefore understand the reasons for the hegemony of the argument for "oneness" among Muslim scholars and intellectuals, a hegemony that entails the marginalization of other points of view; it is interesting to see that it is "Western" researchers who uncover the atypical thinkers of the Muslim world (such as Ibn Khaldun), whose thought then becomes, in turn, suspect to many Muslim intellectuals. But is it legitimate, considering the nonhistoricity that Islamic thought attributes to itself, to infer that Muslim societies are incapable of achieving political modernity?

The Islamic Political Imagination

We refuse to allow ourselves to establish a relationship of causality between, on the one hand, the manner in which the Islamic tradition thinks of politics and, on the other, the reality of the regimes and institutions in Muslim countries, or even to consider that one is a direct expression of the other. Yet this tradition cannot help but have an effect. There exists unquestionably what one might call an "Islamic political imagination" (in the sense of a horizon of thought), which recurs in the corpus of the ulamas and is explicit in the texts of the Salafists (nineteenth-century reformers) and the Islamists. This "imagination" is not "Islamic culture," for we must be wary of unruly generalizations. There is another classical corpus (philosophy); there are other thoughts, other practices; there are intellectuals who think outside this horizon. But one need only skim the literature of the ulamas or the Islamists, or listen to the sermons in the mosques, to admit that there is an Islamic political imagination dominated by a single paradigm: that of the first community of believers at the time of the Prophet and of the first four caliphs.

Independently of its historical reality, this model offers the militants of political Islam an ideal for Muslim society. Islam was born as a sect and as a society, a political and religious community in which there existed neither institutions nor clergy nor specialized functions, and in which the Prophet Muhammad was the sole narrator and interpreter of a divine and transcendent law that governed all human activities. An egalitarian, undifferentiated society, placed under the auspices of a man who didn't legislate, but who stated the revelation: this oneness *(tawhid),* extends to the individual, whose practices are considered in the aggregate and not classified according to the area in which they are implemented (the social, private, devotional, political, or economic sphere). This paradigm would definitively mark the relationships between Islam and politics even if the original community, nostalgia for which haunts Islamic political reflection, was never to be rebuilt. This paradigm of the original community, which rejects any internal segmentation (ethnicities, tribes) and derives its unity from a charismatic leader, would even be reinterpreted in secular fashion and included in Arab nationalist ideology.[11]

From this paradigm result a certain number of recurring themes in Islamic political thought. The nonseparation of the religious, legal, and political spheres is affirmed. The *sharia* should be the sole source of law as well as the norm for individual behavior, both for the sovereign and for the simple believer. The definition of an autonomous political space, with its own rules, its positive laws, and its own values, is prohibited. Finally, the state is never considered in terms of a territorialized nation-state: the ideal is to have a power that would rule over the entirety of the *umma,* the community of the faithful, while actual power is exercised over a segment of the *umma* whose borders are contingent, provisional, and incomplete.

It is thus commonplace to say that in the Islamic political imagination, no distinction is made between the religious and the political orders. This idea is one of the deep convictions of the political actors in contemporary Islam: on the basis of this fact alone, independently of any theological analysis of its validity, it should be taken seriously. We therefore should study the effect it produces on thought and political practice, and not consider it a necessary fact in the history and the actual political practice of Islam, which would mean an absence of a specifically political authority.

The Debate on the State in Muslim Society

According to the Orientalist perspective, the intellectual configuration described above has been an obstacle to the appearance of a political space and to the emergence of a modern state. This is not the place to revisit a historical debate. But there are two problems we cannot circumvent: the appearance of a political space in the practice of power in classical Islam, and the nature of contemporary states in Muslim countries.

In reality, since the time of the original community there has always been a de facto autonomous political space in the Muslim world: what has been lacking is a political thought regarding the autonomy of this space, which has therefore been perceived by the traditionalists as contingent and by the Islamists as deviant. As early as the end of the first century of the hegira, a de facto separation between political power (sultans, amirs) and religious power (the caliph) was created and institutionalized. But this separation always resulted from a division that was different from the one that developed in the West. No positive law emanates from the center of power: the sovereign reigns in the empirical, the contingent. Any intervention into the private sphere is perceived as arbitrary, precisely because social relationships, regulated by the *sharia,* are not supposed to be subject to arbitrariness and violence, contrary to the image of the capricious despot that Western chroniclers often sent home. It is because Islam occupies the sphere of law and of social regulation that the power of the sovereign, even of a fair and good sovereign, cannot help but seem contingent and arbitrary, for he can intervene only in what is outside the domain of the *sharia,* and thus only in nonessential matters. There is, in Islam, a civil society indifferent to the state. There is no "Oriental despotism."[12]

Yet according to the tradition, the sovereign has a "religious" function: to defend Islam and the *sharia.* The state, too, has a goal: to enable Muslims to live as good Muslims.[13] The state is an instrument and not an end in itself. Thus treatises on Muslim law contain a section devoted to the exercise of power. The good sovereign is one who fulfills this function; the bad, one who exercises an "unjust tyranny" *(zulm).* "Justice" *(adala)* is at the center of this ethic of the good prince. The sultan (power in fact) is not the caliph (a successor to Muhammad), and yet the Muslim must obey the sultan if he institutes the *sharia* and defends the Islamic community against its enemies. The sultan is a sword (*sayf al-din,* the "sword of religion," an often conferred title), not an ethical model, but his virtue is none-theless important. Similarly, his legitimacy is indirectly religious, in that he ensures the public good *(maslaha),* enabling the believer to observe his religion: this legitimacy is symbolized by the right to coin money and to have the Friday prayer *(khutba)* said in his name.

This configuration is meaningful for the "classical" period. There is no question that it marks the imagination and beliefs of traditionalist mullahs. But if we look at recent history and at the nature of existing Muslim states, "Islamic culture" as applied to pol-itics tends to lose a good deal of its pertinence: there are genuine historical developments in Muslim societies and the emergence of modern state tendencies in the early nineteenth century.

In the post-Weberian critiques of the state in Muslim countries, we find two analyses explaining its precariousness, its lack of legitimacy, and its seizure by solidarity groups *(asabiyya).* The one (Badie), as we saw earlier, views this as a consequence of "Islamic culture": the absence of an autonomous political sphere and the confusion between public and private spaces bring about a kind of neopatri-monial state. The other (M. Seurat) explains it by the imported and recent nature of the modern state in the Middle East: "The modern state in the Middle East . . . is a successful *asabiyya,*"[14] which is to say that a solidarity group, generally a clan or a minority, seizes control of the state apparatus and turns it into an instrument for the economic exploitation of the society; such a state is predatory and lives off unearned income (oil proceeds, money extorted from rich countries by threat of harm, proceeds from influence peddling and speculation). Seurat's analysis applies perfectly to Syria and Iraq: a minority group (the Alawis in Syria, the Sunni Takritis in Iraq) first infiltrates the army, then takes over the state, which it turns against its own society (dictatorship and massacres); this state in fact lives from external predatory practices (direct in the case of Lebanon, and, for a few months, of Iraq in Kuwait; indirect in the case of Syria, which cashes in on its power as a potential menace to obtain Saudi subsidies), from oil dividends (Iraq), and from taxes on foreign trade (sale of export licenses, "farming out" sources of private revenue to dignitaries: drugs, customs, technical ministries). But as Seurat emphasizes, Syria and Iraq are secular states, engaged in bloody battle with the Islamists. M. Seurat's work, which refers constantly to Ibn Khaldun and not to the corpus of the ulamas, shows that the position of the state in the political configuration of the Middle East is not necessarily a consequence of "Islamic culture," but rather a "Third World" type of phenomenon, resulting from the brutal importation of the European model into a segmented and unstructured society. In fact, the patrimonial state, employed as a source of revenue by a group or a family, is a phenomenon that exists in every culture, from the Marcoses' Philippines to Mobutu's Zaire.

But can we generalize and say that the Middle Eastern state is simply an optical illusion?

The contemporary Muslim world is no more the medieval Muslim world than the European state according to Machiavelli was that of Thomas Aquinas. There is a genuine history of the state in the Middle East, but this history is inseparable from the encounter with the West, which figures into the political makeup of the current Islamic world for better or for worse, just as it figures into Islamist thought and the consumer values of today's societies.

There is a historical process to the construction of states, dating from before colonialism (Morocco, Egypt, Iran, and even Afghanistan). In the nineteenth century, the latter three countries and the Ottoman Empire began a transformation of the state from the top down, based on the model of enlightened despotism and beginning with an army and the construction of a modern state sector (schools, universities, and so on). It is true that Europe continually broke the wings of these states, which were poorly implanted in any case. Military operations (Egypt in 1840, Iran in 1907, the coup against Musaddiq in 1953), growing indebtedness, the arbitrary erection of borders (in 1918 and at other times) have always shattered the impulse toward the construction of stable states. The most recent war, the Gulf War, was not followed by an effort to restructure the political landscape: the same actors and the same regimes were used to reenact the same play according to a different strategic power relationship. In short, from Disraeli to Bush, by way of Clemenceau and Kissinger, the West has never been concerned with encouraging political modernization in the Middle East.

Nevertheless, as cynical as this policy is and as acerbic as the critiques of Arab intellectuals have been regarding the role of the West, one fact is undeniable: the nation-states currently existing in the Middle East have held up, with or without legitimacy. After each crisis, they again become the keys to negotiations; the longer they last, the more reality they acquire. These states have resisted all the "pan . . . ism" crises: pan-Arabism and pan-Islamism. Arab nationalists have secularized the notion of the *umma* and in theory reject the territorialized state: Egypt (whose official name from 1958 to 1972 was the "United Arab Republic"), Syria, and Iraq consider themselves to be parties, "regions," in a future Arab nation. And yet all the plans to unite (the most serious of which was the Syrian-Egyptian union of 1958) have failed: each time there is a return to the preexisting states. Similarly, the exaltation of the Arab combat against Israel cannot hide the fact that each state pursues its own interests, to the detriment of the Palestinians if need be. The same is true of pan-Islamism: the Iraqi masses, who as Shiites are victimized by their own state, did not join the Iranian revolutionaries during the first Gulf conflict. The latest Gulf crises saw the same states, the same leaders, the same borders reemerge, now legitimized by the peace proceedings.

Since the Iranian revolution, the countries of the Middle East have experienced great stability in their regimes and leaders. Is this proof of the patrimonial nature of the state? Perhaps, but this is an insufficient explanation. For even if these states hold together by the great personalization of their leaders, by the absence or weakness of a democratic space, by the disdain for rules of law, even if they have often been taken over by factions, by an *asabiyya,* and are based on an overabundant and corrupt bureaucracy, they exist. There are state mechanisms, sectors of the economy tied to the existence of the state, strata of the population (in particular the new intelligentsia) that live solely from the state, modern armies. The last Gulf war, for example, showed the capacity of the Iraqi state apparatus, which survived a military defeat, to remain in place. Even if these states maintain themselves mostly because of the weakness of the opposition, the lack of democratic "demand," or the separateness of the civil society, their persistence shows that there is a "state fact" more resistant to analysis and to events than was formerly believed. Regimes can change, but the states remain.

The existence of these states is also fixed by the globalization of politics: the great powers and the United Nations guarantee the world map, thus the borders, thus the territories, and thus, ultimately, the states that incarnate them. Territorialization, characteristic of the modern state, may not be inherent in the thought either of the "Islamic imagination" or of Arabism, but it is part and parcel of the balance of international forces. The Kuwaiti identity might have been weak before the Gulf War; now it is very real, especially since Kuwait is certain to subsist under the American umbrella. Today's political globalization operates in favor of the consolidation of the existing states. Inclusion in a world order gives these states a sociopolitical consistency as well, no doubt, as a psychological reality in the minds of their "nationals."

Yet these states are not revolutionary. Their politics cannot be explained, as Seurat aptly demonstrates, without reference to the concept of the *asabiyya,* to segmentation and esprit de corps, which is to say to the establishment of clientele networks more concerned with their own prosperity than with that of the state. But these networks do not represent the permanence of a tradition behind a mere facade of modernity. The structures of the traditional *asabiyya* were dismantled by urbanization, by the shuffling of society, by ideologization: they rebuilt themselves along different lines (political patronage and economic mafias), but they may also disappear. The modern *asabiyya* are recompositions of the esprit de corps based on the fact of the state and the globalization of economic and financial networks; they are translations of a traditional relationship of solidarity into the modern realm.[15] It is still important to know who is from which village, who married whom, but also who is of what rank at the military academy or who studied with which theology professor. The modern *asabiyya* are not merely the permanence of tribalism or religious communalism: they may be reconstituted on the basis of modern sociological elements (the new intelligentsia versus the old families), but they function as predators and perpetuate themselves through matrimonial alliances. Their space is no longer the grandfather's village but the modern city. The militia of Beirut may function as old urban *asabiyya*—the *futuwwa,* brotherhoods of bad boys who ensure order and "protection" in the areas poorly patrolled by the palace—while political parties may function as patronage networks around important notables, but these militia and these parties are still something other than the continuation of an old tradition: the stakes they represent, the type of activities they engage in with regard to international conflicts, the insertion of the bazaar into a globalized economy—all this makes them into something other than surviving remnants, the residue of tradition in modern times. Even in a traditional society such as Afghanistan, the network that develops around a smalltime local commander, himself plugged into an "international" network for the circulation of goods (arms, and sometimes drugs), is no longer the clan that existed before, but a recomposition of the traditional segmentation around a new political elite and the globalized flow of wealth.

Challenging the Orientalist vision of the state in Muslim countries are critics from three milieus in the Muslim world: the "Westernized" intellectuals (those who accept the values of the modern state), the ulamas, and the Islamists.

The first denounce not the Western model of the state, but the doubletalk by which the West does everything in its power to prevent the universal model it proposes from becoming reality. This argument, which is often well founded, nonetheless carries with it an intellectual danger: that of blaming the foreigner for all one's problems. Segmentation is seen as a Western plot (Berberism, Kurds . . .) and charismatic dictators as the best response to Western duplicity. The worse legacy of the West was no doubt to offer the Muslim people a ready-to-wear devil: conspiracy theory is currently paralyzing Muslim political thought. For to say that every failure is the devil's work is the same as asking God, or the devil himself (which is to say, these days, the Americans), to solve one's problems.[16] Between the miracle that doesn't happen and the pact in which one loses one's soul, there is plenty of room for discontent.

Among the ulamas, mullahs, and their followers, the historical evolution of the Muslim world has had little effect on the political imagination derived from the paradigm of the "Islamic society," a paradigm that also recurs in Islamist movements. The "Islamic political imagination" has endeavored to ignore or disqualify anything new. Not that the ulamas have always fought innovation: on the contrary, by allowing sovereigns to render *fatwa* they legitimated the establishment of a new state order (for which they would later be reproached by the Islamists); however, aside from a segment of Shiite clergy, they simply neither developed a new form of thought nor integrated the new facts into their discourse. The atemporality of the mullahs' and ulamas' discourse is striking to this day. History is something that must be endured; whatever is new is contingent and merits only a *fatwa* from time to time. Modernization exists side by side with the old discourse.

As for Islamist thought, it sees itself as a response to the problematics of the imported state and of segmentation: it has something to say about the Muslim world's backwardness by comparison with Europe, about industrialization, about the Islamic economy, and so on. It notes, rightly, that secularity and nationalism are not *ipso facto* modernization.[17] The seizing of power by *asabiyya* in the secular and nationalist states of Syria and Iraq, the role of tribalism and patronage, and the formation of social strata born of and parasite to the state are constant themes of Islamist propaganda. Islamist protest occurs in the name of the universality of the social body (conceived of as the religious community) against the particularism of the state, against segmentation, against both the new state-managed and the old tribal societies. Islam is seen as the introduction of a universal outlook and the common good against particularism and communalism.[18]

The modernity of Islamist thought is in this quest for a universal state. The Islamists' reference to the original society and their rejection of history are not enough in and of themselves to mark their thought as archaic. Another fundamentalist mode of thought, the Protestant Reformation, was, as we know, one of the best instruments for access to economic and political modernity. Referring to the Tradition (with a capital T) of the Prophet allows one to evade the tradition issued from history and thus to integrate a modernity which is no longer a purely external phenomenon, as it is for the Salafists, but which is a fact of Muslim society.

But does Islamist thought fulfill its program? This is the subject of our inquiry. In my view, it has failed because Islamist thought, at the end of an intellectual trajectory that tries to integrate modernity, ultimately meets up with the "Islamic political imagination" of the tradition and its essential premise: politics can be founded only on individual virtue.

The Internalized West

With respect to the effect of Western domination, it is necessary to examine not only the economic and political structures of the contemporary Muslim world (political backwardness would thus be an effect of neocolonialism, evoking emotional identification with the *umma* even at the price of secular dictators such as Saddam Husayn) but also the thought of this world, the conceptual framework of Islamist intellectuals. One thing is indeed striking: most Islamists were educated in a "Westernized" environment, yet they hold to the corpus of the ulamas (whom they accuse in passing of having poorly managed this corpus). All their literature insists on the rationality of religious prescriptions; this militant rationalism is a sign that modernity has worked its way into the very heart of Islamist discourse, which is so rationalist that it ends up denying its own religious practices.

But does Islamist discourse truly dominate the Muslim world? In addressing this question we should consider neither the number of books published nor the opinions of professors or journalists, but the networks through which these works are distributed, and the places and languages in which they are written—in other words, the public that is touched by them. The publication and distribution networks are financed today by conservative, often Saudi milieus. The Islamists have their own public which cannot or does not want to read Westernized intellectuals. Aside from some ephemeral Marxist writings, and at least with respect to the Arab world, it is as if the only audience for Westernized Muslim intellectuals writing within the framework of the modern social sciences were in fact within the Western world. On the Indian subcontinent, "modern" Muslim intellectuals write in English, leaving the writings for the masses, whether Islamist or neofundamentalist, in Urdu. We will no doubt witness the same phenomenon in central Asia, where Russian will long remain the language of the social sciences. The Maghreb is divided into three languages (French, literary Arabic, and Arabic dialect): in choosing a language, one chooses an audience. Only Turkey, Iran, and Egypt produce social science texts in the vernacular. In France, and especially in the United States, we are witnessing an astonishing "brain drain" of non-Islamist intellectuals, particularly in the social sciences. With the elite gone, the world of thought has been inhabited by "new intellectuals."[19] And as we shall see, these new intellectuals have a "religious" relationship to their own knowledge. They will not be the ones to open up the ulamas' corpus. The modernity they brought to the reading of Islam exhausted itself in a repetitive, uncritical and undemonstrative defense of Islam, which for them has answers to all the problems of the modern world.

But Islamism's ultimate failure in its attempt to address modernity doesn't prevent modernity from turning into sociological facts and movements. Modernity creeps into Muslim countries regardless of Islam, and the Islamists themselves play a part in this secularization of the religion. They are a stage toward the "disenchantment of the world."[20] By rejecting a Westernization that is already in place, they express the myth of authenticity in a borrowed, inauthentic language. For they borrow from this modernity the refusal to return to the real tradition in the name of an imaginary Tradition: they reject popular religious practice, the village, Sufism, philosophy. They themselves deny and undermine what is and was Muslim civilization and ensure the triumph of fast food (*halal*, of course—religiously correct), of jeans, Coke, and English. The urban culture (in the ethnological sense) of the Islamists strikingly resembles that of any modern Western suburb. And the reinvention of a vestiary tradition that never existed (raincoats, gloves and scarves for women, beards and parkas for men) will not bring about a new authenticity. The Tehran of the mullahs has a very American look.

Modernization occurred, but outside any conceptual framework: it happened through rural exodus, emigration, consumption, the change in family behavior (a lower birthrate), but also through the cinema, music, clothing, satellite antennas, that is, through the globalization of culture. It also occurred through the establishment of states that, fragile, corrupt, and clientele oriented though they may be, are nonetheless profoundly new in their method of legitimation, their social base, and their division into territories frozen by international agreements. Protest against the West, which includes contesting the existing states, is on the same order as Western ecology or anti-immigrant arguments: they are arguments one propounds when it is too late. Just as France will never return to a preindustrial society, and its immigrants are there to stay, so Muslim cities will never return to the harmony of the bazaar and of guilds. It is a hybrid world, a world of nostalgia. Only when it is too late do we dream of the past, and then our dreams incorporate everything we want to deny. The tradition of which the nostalgic dream, like the tradition condemned by modernists, never existed.

The Failure of Islamism

In retrospect, it appears that the political action of the Islamists, far from leading to the establishment of states or of Islamic societies, falls in either with the logic of the state (Iran), or with traditional, if reconfigured, segmentation (Afghanistan). No matter what the actors say, any political action amounts to the automatic creation of a secular space or a return to traditional segmentation. Herein lies the limit of the politicization of a religion, of any religion. Our problem, then, is not to survey to what extent Islam allows for a secular space in its texts and age-old practice (this would pose considerable problems of methodology and amounts to returning to the conceptual categories of those whom one is critiquing), but to study a coherent ensemble, limited in time and space, of texts, practices, and political organizations that deeply marked the political life of

Muslim countries and their relationships with the countries of the North, while tending to alter the Muslims' perception of Islam in a stricter moral direction.

The thought of the movements we are studying oscillates between two poles: a revolutionary pole, for whom the Islamization of the society occurs through state power; and a reformist pole, for whom social and political action aims primarily to re-Islamize the society from the bottom up, bringing about, *ipso facto,* the advent of an Islamic state. The split lies not on the question of the necessity of an Islamic state, but on the means by which to arrive at one and on the attitude to adopt with respect to the powers in place: destruction, opposition, collaboration, indifference. The entire spectrum of attitudes is possible: the Jordanian MB participated in parliamentary elections, the Jamaat-i Islami of Pakistan and the Sudanese MB supported military putsches, the Egyptian Islamic Jihad launched a campaign of assassinations of government personalities. Can the two poles be placed on a chronological scale that would move from Islamization from the top down (Islamism) to Islamization from the bottom up (neofundamentalism)? Yes and no. On the one hand, there is no systematic correspondence between intellectual radicalism and political extremism: the Jamaat-i Islami of Pakistan, which is radical in its demand for a fully Islamic society, has always remained within a legal framework, even when its results in elections were laughable; in Afghanistan, it is often difficult to comprehend the ideological differences between the Hizb-i Islami and the Jamaat-i Islami, although the first has carried out sectarian and quite violent actions, and the second has always proved to be a party of openness. What is more, the Islamist movements themselves constantly oscillate between political activism and neofundamentalism, that is, between primacy accorded the political struggle and that given to the Islamization of the society. Al-Banna, for one, has at times advocated the rejection of compromise, at times called for collaboration. Certain things have remained constant, of course, over the last fifty years: the Ayatollah Khomeini has always advocated a radical break (but in language that is at times traditionalist, at times revolutionary); the Arab Muslim Brotherhoods stepped over the line into armed confrontation only when forced into it by external repression (Syria); the Jamaat-i Islami of Pakistan has continued to act legally; the revolutionary movements—the Iranian sphere of influence, the Afghan Islamists, and radical Arab groups (Jihad, Takfir wal-Hijra)—emerged only later, after the 1967 Arab-Israeli war.[21]

The revolutionary path was a failure: the Iranian revolution got bogged down in internal struggles and the economic crisis, the activism of the MB dissident groups never managed to achieve a change in regime in an Arab country. The Sunni extremist groups marginalized themselves, the Shiites, on the contrary, became pawns in state strategies (the manipulation of terrorism by Syria and Iran). But Islamism has profoundly marked the political landscape and contemporary Muslim society.

Toward the end of the 1980s, the failure of the Islamist revolutionary idea brought about the drift of a revolutionary, political, Third World type of Islamism, incarnated in the Iranian revolution, toward a puritanical, preaching, populist, conservative neofundamentalism, financed until recently by Saudi Arabia but violently anti-Western, particularly since the end of the East–West confrontation has ceased to cast communism as a foil. The Algerian FIS (Islamic Salvation Front) is the prototype for this sort of group: a conjunction of the political heritage of Islamism, Saudi money (until 1990), and the influence of a more pious than political return to Islam. Yet the distinction that we are exploring here between Islamism and neofundamentalism has no chronological cutoff point; it is a difference in emphasis. Islamist militants did not suddenly become neofundamentalists starting in 1984 or 1985. On the other hand, the shrinking prospects for political revolution, the growing influence of Saudi money, the inability of Islamist thought to go beyond the founding texts, the appearance of a new generation of militants less politically educated and more concerned with the *sharia* and respecting rituals than with an Islamic revolution, all this set a different tone for the Islamist movement and confused, without erasing, what differentiated it from traditional fundamentalism. This is why it is important, on a given point, to note the differences between Islamism and neofundamentalism (the inversely proportional place accorded the *sharia* and women, the concept of revolution) and, on other points, to note the similarities (the relationship to knowledge, the critique of the official ulamas, the definition of the economy).

Islamist ideas have spread throughout broad sectors of Muslim societies, losing part of their political force in this popularization. An obvious re-Islamization is occurring in high places and on the street. Since the end of the 1970s, the states have reintroduced principles from the *sharia* into their constitutions and laws; secularity is receding in the legal domain (family statute in Algeria in 1984). From below, one may note the increased visibility of fundamentalist Islam (in attire: the wearing of beards by men, and of veils or scarves by city women) and a greater externality of practice, with the sprouting of neighborhood mosques uncontrolled by the state.

Yet basically, the influence of Islamism is more superficial than it seems. The *sharia* has been put only partially into practice in the most conservative states (Saudi Arabia, Pakistan, Sudan). The existing regimes have proved stable in the face of Islamist contestation; the leaders have experienced great political longevity: in the 1980s, from Morocco to Pakistan (with the exception of Lebanon, Sudan, and Afghanistan), the only heads of state who disappeared did so as a result of illness or death (Bourguiba, Khomeini, Zia ul-Haqq); all the others (Hasan II, Chadli Benjedid, Mubarak, Husayn of Jordan, Asad of Syria, Fahd of Saudi Arabia, Saddam Husayn, Jabir al-Sabah of Kuwait, Qabus of Oman, Abdallah Salih of North Yemen) remained in place the entire decade.

Re-Islamization has in no way changed the rules of the political or economic game. The geostrategy of the Middle East is connected to the existing states, not to the popular or international Islamist movements. The victory of Islamist movements such as the FIS in Algeria will not give rise to a new pan-Islamism, but on the contrary to "Islamo-nationalisms." Everywhere, even within the Islamist sphere of influence, the repressed is resurfacing: ethnic and tribal segmentation, political maneuvering, personal rivalries, but also evil . . . corruption, speculation. These mechanisms are not thought out.

The essential premise of the Islamist movement is that the political model it proposes presupposes the virtue of individuals, but that this virtue can be acquired only if the society is truly Islamic. All the rest is plot, sin, or illusion.

The vicissitudes that marked the minds of so many during the 1980s have ultimately had little influence on the facts and history: in the end we find the countries, states, regimes and borders that existed ten years earlier. After the second war in the Gulf, the dependence of Muslim countries on the North has never been greater.

Nonetheless, the socioeconomic realities that sustained the Islamist wave are still here and are not going to change: poverty, uprootedness, crises in values and identities, the decay of educational systems, the North–South opposition, the problem of immigrant integration into the host societies. The Islamic revolution, the Islamic state, the Islamic economy are myths, but we have not heard the last of Islamist protestation. The coming to power of movements such as the FIS will only make more apparent the emptiness of the phantasm of the "Islamic state."

❖ 1 ❖

Islam and Politics:
From Tradition to Reformism

Mullahs and Ulamas

WE KNOW THAT there is no clergy in Islam. Yet there is a body of lettered men, doctors of law—the ulamas— whose corpus and curriculum display remarkable stability in space and time, and who have had a quasi-monopoly on intellectual production and teaching, at least between the end of the great period of philosophic creativity in the Middle Ages and the emergence, in the nineteenth century, of intellectuals of secular culture. The places where they perpetuate themselves are called *madrasa,* theological schools or universities. The homogeneity of this body results from the teaching that is dispensed there and from the techniques used for the transmission of knowledge (repetition, access to texts through commentary, loyalty to a master).[1] But ulamas can fulfill various functions: teachers, judges *(qadi),* imams in mosques. They do not have a monopoly on houses of worship: many mosques, especially village or neighborhood mosques, are served only by simple mullahs, who have no higher religious preparation and are basically "ritual practitioners"; they do not answer to any higher authority (except in Iran). These mosque mullahs are referred to by terms that vary depending on one's location in the Muslim world (mullah in Iran, Turkey, central Asia, and the Indian subcontinent; imam in the Maghreb and therefore among immigrants to France).

The trend toward creating an institutionalized clergy is recent and derives from the states and not from the clerics (except in Iran). This incomplete clericalization begins at the top: the state controls the large *madrasa,* names a mufti or *shaykh al-islam* and tries to gives these authorities a monopoly on the nomination of mullahs (or mosque imams) and judges (who might issue *fatwa*). Official, bureaucratized clergy have emerged in Tunisia, Morocco, Egypt, and . . . in the Soviet Union (in 1941).

The primary demand of ulamas and mullahs is the complete and total implementation of the *sharia,* without regard to the nature of the political system; this is fundamentalism *stricto sensu,* which as a corollary also entails a secular space: the place of power. Classical Islamic thought is overflowing with treatises on governing, advice to sovereigns, and didactic tales. They do not reflect on the nature of politics, but on the nature of the good ruler and of good government (advice, techniques, paradigms, anecdotes).[2] The issue of ethics is at the heart of classical Muslim political philosophy. Obviously, within this body of thought there is no lack of nuance and controversy: Must one obey a sovereign who is himself a bad Muslim? Can one resign oneself to living in a state conquered by infidels? and so on. But the general framework remains the same. The fundamentalist clergy want the sovereign to apply the *sharia* and to defend the Muslim community. His legitimacy lies therein. In the Sunni tradition, there is neither a transcendent source of political legitimacy nor a requirement that a particular type of state exist. The political demand of the fundamentalist clergy is that the law conform to the *sharia;* it claims the right to censure, not to exercise power. This traditional fundamentalism, which has been the object of much theoretical reflection by the ulamas, is the spontaneous ideology of most mullahs and other clerics, yesterday as today.

The permanence of traditional religious teaching throughout the Muslim world, conveying this vision of the relationship to power, has often been obscured by the emergence of Islamism. Not only does this teaching continue to perpetuate itself, but it is also expressed in what one might call not popular Islam—often confused with Sufism, magic and customs that are pre-Islamic in origin—but the "popular knowledge of Islam," which is to say the elements of an orthodox body of knowledge that circulate in nonclerical milieus. In the region in which I did field research (Afghanistan, Soviet Central Asia), this circulation is obvious: in the village mosques and among families (including urban families) I found a corpus composed of lithographed brochures (generally written in Persian, even among Turkish- and Pashto-speakers), the originals of which often date from the last century and contain both reports on religion (the pillars of faith, prayer rituals), moral advice (anecdotes, fables), and excerpts from classical works (Saadi), all presented in rhymed prose or verse. Children learn these texts by heart under the guidance of their father or the mullah.[3]

Even in Iran, until Khomeini the ulamas were content to have control over the laws voted by Parliament. It was Khomeini who first defined the conditions for the exercise of power by the clergy (theory of the *vilayat-i faqih*), a position that would ultimately be adopted by only a minority of the Iranian high clergy.

Although the ulamas and mullahs are potentially fundamentalist, they are never the ones who take power to implement a policy of "shariatization," with the exception of Iran in 1979. There has never been a theocracy in Islam; clergy have never served as heads of state. From the Great Moghul Awrangzeb, the sovereign of India (1656–1707), to General Zia ul-Haqq (the head of state of Pakistan from 1977 to 1988), by way of the Saudi dynasty, all are secular figures—kings, generals, or presidents—who undertook to realize the fundamentalist ulamas' program.

Two currents can be distinguished within this fundamentalism: one traditionalist, the other reformist. The traditionalist one accepts the continuity between the founding texts and their commentaries; it takes as its basic principle imitation *(taqlid)*, that is, refusal to innovate, while accepting what was said before; its adherents follow one of the great legal schools (Shafiism, Malikism, Hanafism, Hanbalism); its vision of the *sharia* is essentially legalistic and casuistic. It is sometimes connected to the popular forms of Sufism (hence the Barelvi school in Pakistan).[4]

There also exists a reformist fundamentalism, which criticizes the tradition, the commentaries, popular religious practices (maraboutism, the cult of saints), deviations, and superstitions; it aims to return to the founding texts (eighteenth-century examples are Shah Wali Allah in India and Abd al-Wahhab in the Arabian Peninsula). This reformism generally developed in response to an external threat (the influence of Hinduism on Islam, for example).

It is in keeping with this reformist line that a fundamentalist current, the *salafiyya*, appeared in the nineteenth century, marking a phase between fundamentalism and Islamism.

Salafist Reformism

In the nineteenth century, for the first time, the Muslim world felt structurally on the defensive, faced with a technical-minded, conquering Europe. The symmetry that had existed for centuries between Muslim and Christian crusaders, between Ottoman and imperial armies, had vanished.

Why was Islam unable to compete with European colonialism? Outdatedness? Distraction? Divine punishment? The question arises with regard to the constant retreat of the Ottoman Empire, the arrival of the French in Algeria (1830), the disappearance of the Moghul Empire in India (1857), the Russian incursions into the Caucasus (1857) and Central Asia. Two means of resistance emerged during the nineteenth century: the one of peasant and religious origin, the other urban and nationalist. On the one side charismatic leaders, generally ulamas or leaders of religious orders, launched the call for jihad and formed tribal coalitions. To unify the tribes, they imposed the *sharia* in defiance of the local common laws; the fundamentalism of the mullahs became a political force because the *sharia* was used against *asabiyya*, against tribal and ethnic segmentation, which in contrast was exploited by the colonizers. This group included Abd al-Qadir in Algeria, the Mahdi in Sudan, Shamil in the Caucasus, the Sanusis in Libya and in Chad, Mullah-i Lang in Afghanistan, the *akhund* of Swat in India, and, later, Abd al-Karim in Morocco. These movements failed despite spectacular victories (destruction of the British army in Afghanistan in 1842, the taking of Khartoum in 1885). The anti-imperialist banner was in turn raised, after the war of 1914–1918, by movements that were more nationalistic than religious, even though the tradition of the fundamentalist jihad continues to our day (the Afghan *mujahidin*). The second mode of resistance lay in the constitution of modern states (Egypt, Iran, Turkey) by members of the urban, Westernized elite. The modernization was authoritarian and ordered from above, following the model of the enlightened despot; it was oblivious or opposed to Islam and shied away from democratization (the dissolution of the Ottoman Parliament in 1878, the repression of the constitutionalist movement in Iran in 1907). Without any direct colonization, these regimes came under Europe's, and particularly Britain's, thumb, as a result of debt.

These historical antecedents continue to haunt the Muslim, and in particular the Arab, imagination. The "backwardness" with respect to the West is now called underdevelopment, enlightened despotism is called "ba'thism" and fundamentalism is resurfacing in all its forms (traditionalist in one part of the Afghan resistance, Islamist in the other, neofundamentalist in the Algerian FIS).

During the second half of the nineteenth century, a current of thought within the framework of Islam endeavored to address the backwardness of the Muslim world: it was the *salafiyya*, the "return to the ancestors," typified by its three canonical authors, Jamal al-Din al-Afghani (1838–1898), Muhammad Abduh (1849–1905), and Rashid Rida (1865–1935). Like all other fundamentalist reformist movements, it rejected common law *(adat, urf)*, maraboutism (belief in the powers of intervention of certain individuals blessed with *baraka,* or divine charisma), and rapprochement with other religions. But it went even further than its successors in rejecting the tradition of the ulamas (the textual commentary, *tafsir,* which is followed to the letter, *taqlid*), as well as the body of additions and extensions, whether relating to systematization of the religion (the *madhahib*—the four legal schools), culture (philosophy), theology (Sufism), or institutions (the clergy). Reform *(islah)* did not entail adopting modernity, but returning to the Tradition of the Prophet, which would enable one to conceptualize this modernity. Salafism pushed the logic of reformism to its extreme: it demanded the right to individual interpretation *(ijtihad)* of the founding texts (the Quran and the Sunna) without regard to previous commentaries. The reopening of the right to *ijtihad* marked a significant rupture with ten centuries of orthodoxy.

Al-Afghani was concerned less with developing a new corpus than with generating political and cultural activism, with wrenching Muslims away from the tyranny of a dead and deadening system of transmitting knowledge, with "bringing consciousness" to the people and the elite, to the point that others have wondered whether Islam was for him an end in itself or only a means of fighting imperialism.[5]

The demand for a resumption of *ijtihad* also aimed to destroy the ulamas' monopoly on the religious corpus. The Salafists, like the Islamists, were not of clerical origins. But their thought would touch a chord among certain reformist ulamas, such as Sheikh Ibn Badis in Algeria (1889–1940) who fought against maraboutism and the traditionalism of the great *madrasa.*[6]

Politically, Salafist thought remained traditional. There was no wholesale condemnation of existing Muslim governments. The state, as the political authority, was accorded little value:[7] it was instrumental, distinct from the *umma,* whose sphere was both smaller (civil society) and much larger (the community of all Muslims). Its only role was to apply the *sharia.* But Salafist thought was obsessed with the reconstitution of the Muslim *umma,* and in particular with the restoration of the caliphate. At the beginning of the twentieth century the Ottoman caliphate, though long in decay, experienced a surge of popularity in Muslim non-Arab milieus.[8] In fact, the split between the Arab and non-Arab world was conspicuous on the issue of the caliphate: the Arabs, dreaming of the reconstitution of a great Arab empire, fought the Ottoman Empire, which all other Muslims at the time regarded as the best defense against imperialism and the starting point for a reconstruction of the *umma*.[9] The suppression of the caliphate in 1924 forced the *salafiyya* to abandon the myth, especially since the personality of Ataturk and his role in the struggle against the West earned him the sympathy of ulamas—who were never suspected of secular complacency—such as Ibn Badis.

Although the *salafiyya* never became a political movement, it left its mark on all twentieth-century fundamentalist reformists, particularly since Sheikh Abduh served as Grand Mufti of Egypt from 1899 until his death.

❖ 2 ❖

The Concepts of Islamism

THE ORIGINS OF today's Islamist thought and organizations
today can be traced to the Society of the Muslim Brotherhood,
created by the schoolteacher Hasan al-Banna in Egypt in 1928,
and the Jamaat-i Islami of Pakistan, established by Abul-Ala Maududi in 1941.[1] Although the two movements developed independently, the overlapping of their themes was striking, and intellectual
contacts were soon established: it was a disciple of Maududi, the
Indian Abul Hasan Ali Nadvi, who undertook the translation of
Maududi into Arabic and who met with Sayyid Qutb.[2] On the Indian
subcontinent the Jamaat-i Islami received little challenge from more
radical movements, while in Egypt the MB spawned radical Islamist
groups in the 1970s, inspired by the thought of Sayyid Qutb (an MB
himself, executed by President Gamal Abdel Nasser in 1966).

We will therefore study the common matrix, in terms of ideas
and of organization, of contemporary political Islamism.

Islamism was created both along the lines of and as a break
from the *salafiyya*. The Islamists generally adopt Salafist theology:
they preach a return to the Quran, the Sunna, and the *sharia* and
reject the commentaries that have been part of the tradition (the

gloss, the philosophy, but also the four major legal schools, the *mad-hahib*). They therefore demand the right to *ijtihad*, individual inter-pretation. But they don't stop there.

Three points clearly separate the Islamists from the fundamen-talism of ulamas: political revolution, the *sharia*, and the issue of women.

Islamists consider that the society will be Islamized only through social and political action: it is necessary to leave the mosque. The Islamist movements intervene directly in political life and since the 1960s have attempted to gain power. The economy and social relationships are no longer perceived as subordinate activ-ities that grow out of pious acts or the *sharia*, but are considered key areas.

The Islamists pose the question of politics starting from the principle that Islam is a global and synthesizing system of thought. It is not enough for society to be composed of Muslims; it must be Islamic in its foundation and its structure: a distinction is therefore introduced between what is "Muslim" and what is "Islamic," a dis-tinction that legitimates the use made here of the word "Islamism."[3] From there it follows, but only for the most radical of the Islamists (disciples of Sayyid Qutb and of Khomeini, but not of Maududi), that one has a duty to revolt against a Muslim state judged to be corrupt: it was over the duty to excommunicate *(takfir)* the sovereign considered apostate and to move into violent action (terrorism and revolution) that a considerable rift would develop within the Islamist movement between revolutionaries and "neofundamentalists."

The Islamist movement is not led by clerics (except in Iran), but by young secular intellectuals, who openly claim to be "religious thinkers," rivals of or successors to a class of ulamas who have com-promised themselves with respect to those in power: "Because all knowledge is divine and religious, a chemist, an engineer, an econ-omist, or a jurist are all ulamas."[4] There is an Islamist anticleri-calism,[5] which led the most radical elements to assassinate ulamas judged to be too close to power (such as the Egyptian minister of the Waqf, Muhammad al-Dhahabi, in 1977; and the director of the Waqf in Aleppo, Syria, Muhammad al-Misri, in 1979). The Sunni

Islamists reject both the bureaucratized clergy and the clerical state in which ulamas have power.[6] Even among the Iranian Islamists, an anticlerical tendency has always existed (Ali Shariati adopted the term *akhund,* which in the Iranian tradition is a pejorative way of referring to the mullahs). The Islamist movement was created outside the body of ulamas and the large religious universities, such as Al-Azhar in Egypt, which it opposed with extensive polemics, although over time moderate Islamists have gained ground within these establishments and recruited from among the ulamas. The demand for the right to interpretation and the condemnation of the nitpicking legalism of the mullahs who specialize in *fiqh* (Islamic jurisprudence), which is timeless and indifferent to the social and political context, is also a means for the Islamists to contest the very foundation of the ulamas' and mullahs' legitimacy: their religious knowledge and their function as judges.

The Islamists reproach the ulamas for two things. One is their servility to the powers in place, which leads them to accept a secular government and laws that do not conform to the *sharia.* The other is their compromise with Western modernity: the ulamas have accepted modernity where the Islamists reject it (acceptance of the separation of religion and politics, which necessarily leads to secularization) and maintained the tradition where the Islamists reject it (indifference to modern science, rigid and casuistic teachings, rejection of political and social action).

Islamism adopts the classical vision of Islam as a complete and universal system, one, therefore, that does not have to "modernize" or adapt. But it applies this model to a "modern" object: to society, or more exactly, to a society defined in modern terms (that is, one in which the distinction among social, political, and economic authorities is recognized). Whether the Islamist ideal aims to bring these different segments of society together to recreate the unity of the original community, or whether it views history as decadence and not as an agent of modernity, the Islamists make modern society the focus of their actions, a society of which they themselves are products. Consequently one finds an important body of literature concerning social problems (*ijtima*, the social) and economics (*iqtisad*, the economy): the Ayatollahs Baqir al-Sadr and Taliqani both wrote Islamic economic treatises, Sayyid Qutb wrote a book titled *Social Justice in Islam (Al-adala al-ijtima'iyya fi al-islam)*, which was also the title of a series of radio broadcasts by the Syrian MB M. al-Siba'i in 1950.[7]

Two other issues divide Islamists and fundamentalists *stricto sensu*: the *sharia* and women. Islamists generally tend to favor the education of women and their participation in social and political life: the Islamist woman militates, studies, and has the right to work, but in a chador. Islamist groups include women's associations. The Iranian constitution recognized the right to vote for women without provoking much debate among constituents.

Islamist movements insist less on the application of the *sharia* than do the fundamentalist ulamas. Whereas moderates and neo-fundamentalists see the application of the *sharia* as a key to the Islamization of society,[8] the radical Islamists, without questioning the principle of the *sharia*, tend to consider it more a project than a corpus.[9] Indeed, for radical Islamists, institution of the *sharia* pre-supposes a transformation of society if it is not to be sheer hypocrisy. The real gamble is to redefine the social bond itself on a political basis, and not simply to apply the *sharia*. Imam Khomeini, in a famous declaration of January 1989, affirmed, in opposition to the president of the Khamanei Republic, that the logic of the revolution took precedence over the application of the *sharia*. Sayyid Qutb spoke of an "Islamic law in motion" (*fiqh haraki*), resulting from the interpretation of those who fight for Islam and established in accordance with social conditions—as opposed to the fixed, rigid and casuistic law of the ulamas. This concept was adopted by the Moroccan Islamist Yasin.[10] Islamic law—beginning with punishment by amputation—cannot be applied in a society that is not yet Islamic. The same issue is addressed by Iranian militants, particularly by Islamist women.[11] On the other hand, in a truly Islamic society, the state can innovate on technical subjects not provided for in the *sharia* or make use of the right to interpretation by its leaders on other questions, such as the creation of taxes and all ad hoc legislation.[12] For Islamists, to recognize the current states' right to innovate, as do the ulamas, is to recognize a secular space; on the other hand, to recognize this right to innovate in a true Islamic state is to inscribe the *sharia* in a broader whole: that of the Islamization of the entire society and not only of the law. For Islamists, Islam is more than the simple application of the *sharia:* it is a synthesizing, totalizing ideology that must first transform society in order that the *sharia* may be established, almost automatically. The Islamic nature of the state is more important than the strict application of the *sharia,* which is meaningful only in a truly Islamic society—a society that can then move beyond this application, even to the point of innovation.

These three elements (the place of politics, women, and the *sharia*) are good criteria for distinguishing radical Islamists (such as Imam Khomeini) from conservative fundamentalist regimes (Saudi Arabia, Pakistan) or even from modern neofundamentalist movements (the Algerian FIS), although the definition, at this point, lacks detail and nuance.

The Islamist movement thus conceives of itself explicitly as a sociopolitical movement,[13] founded on an Islam defined as much in terms of a political ideology as in terms of a religion. One proof of this is the symmetrical comparison the Islamists regularly make between their thought on the one side and, on the other, not other religions, but the major ideologies of the twentieth century (Marxism, fascism, "capitalism").[14] It is within this framework that we will study their vision of society and politics.

A Political Reading of the Quran

The Islamists fill a conceptual matrix borrowed either from Marxism or from categories of Western political science with Quranic terminology or neologisms meant to Islamize the grid.

From the Quran come the terms: *shura* (advisory council), *hizb* (party), *tawhid* (oneness), *mustadaf* (oppressed), *umma* (community of believers), and *jahiliyya* (ignorance), which are interpreted in a modern political context (democracy, political parties, a classless society, social classes, and so on). We also find neologisms (the roots exist, but not the meaning): *hakimiyya* (sovereignty),[15] *thawra* and *inqilab* (revolution); and, finally, words that are simply borrowed terms or calques: the word "ideology" is abundantly used either as a borrowed term (*ideolozhi* in Persian), or as a calque (*mafkura* in Arabic and Persian, *fikra* in Arabic), as if the term "religion," *din*, were perceived as insufficient.[16]

The Islamists engage in a political and social rereading of the Quran, made possible precisely by the distortion of Muslim tradition. Maududi and Hassan al-Turabi, for example, are careful to classify the concepts of political Islam as functions of areas of law and of Western political science, as if they were universal.[17] The Iranian ideologues, such as Bani Sadr, equate *tawhid* with a classless society and *mustadaf* with the proletariat; in the work of Ali Shariati, Shiite eschatology drifts toward a revolutionary mold. But at the same time, Islamists refuse to strike the defensive, conciliatory, and apologist note of many Muslim "modernists," who aim to demonstrate Islam's modernity by the yardstick of Western values and concepts. For Islamists, it is a matter of showing not that Islam perfectly realizes universal values, but on the contrary that Islam is the universal value and need not be compared with other religions or political systems.

Islam as an "Inclusive Order" and an Ideology

Islamism begins with a theological concept that is the very foundation of the Muslim religion: divine oneness or *tawhid*, which says that God is transcendent, unique, and without associates. The Islamist contribution (or rupture) with respect to the tradition consists in applying this theological concept to society, whereas previously it was related exclusively to God.[18] Society is, or rather must be, a reflection of divine oneness, of *tawhid*.[19] While "oneness" is the basic fact of divine essence, in a human society it is something that must be constructed, created. A *tawhidi* society (an adjective in use among Iranian ideologues) cannot tolerate either intrinsic segmentation (social, ethnic, tribal, or national) or a political authority that is autonomous with respect to the divine order, even in a contingent manner. God's absolute sovereignty, *hakimiyya,* will then prevail, governing all aspects of the life of the individual as well as of society.[20]

Islam is thus not only an ensemble of beliefs but an "inclusive order," a "total order," *nizam:*[21] "Islam is an inclusive order that pertains to all aspects of life."[22] This new order excludes any secular space, even a contingent one.

From Rupture to Revolution

But how can an Islamic society be established? Disagreement between moderate and radical Islamists has existed on this point throughout the history of Islamism. All acknowledge the necessity of controlling political power. The moderates are partisans of re-Islamization from the bottom up (preaching, establishing sociocultural movements) while pressuring the leaders (in particular through political alliances) to promote Islamization from the top (introducing the *sharia* into legislation): this was the politics of the founding fathers, al-Banna and Maududi,[23] who accepted the notion of revolt only if the state took a resolutely anti-Islamic stance and if all means of peaceful protest had been exhausted: "If the government should become so alien as to transcend the *sharia,* then [the individual] has the right and obligation to revolt. This is the revolutionary element in Islam."[24]

Meanwhile, the radicals consider that no compromise with current Muslim society is possible: they advocate political rupture and introduce the concept of *revolution,* another borrowing from the century's progressive ideologies. It was Sayyid Qutb, an Egyptian Muslim Brother (executed in 1966), who fashioned himself as the theoretician of rupture and inspired the revolutionary groups of the 1970s. His analysis turns upon two concepts: *jahiliyya* and *takfir.*

Jahiliyya, a Quranic term, refers to the condition of pre-Islamic society, combining ignorance and savagery. Islamists assert that current Muslim societies have reverted to *jahiliyya,*[25] a theme that is also present in revolutionary Iran in the expression *taghuti:* society, spirit, or individual, the *taghuti* (the name of an idol in the Quran) is everything that denies the divine order. In such a case, jihad against governments who are Muslim only in name is lawful.[26] Their leaders can be declared to be in a state of infidelity: *takfir*, or excommunication, is the act of declaring that someone who professes Islam is in fact an infidel, *kafir*. Moderate Islamists reject the concept of excommunication, considering, in the tradition of the ulamas, that an unjust power is preferable to division of the community *(fitna)*.[27]

Whereas moderate Islamism maintains a reformist position, radical Islamism reappropriates the idea of revolution: the forceful overthrow of a political regime in order to replace it with a system founded on a different ideology.

The State and the Institutions of Islamist Thought

"The Quran Is Our Constitution" is the slogan encountered from the Egyptian Muslim Brotherhood to the Afghan Islamists. But what institutions are to be derived from this generality? Two concepts recur constantly among most Islamist theoreticians: that of the leader (amir) and that of the advisory council *(shura)*, around which both the Islamic political party and the future Islamic society are structured.

The terms that designate the leader vary: *murshid* among the MB; amir for Tunisians, Pakistanis, Afghans, and Soviet Muslims; imam in Iran (but this concept has specifically Shiite connotations). The term *khalifa,* caliph, sometimes used in the 1950s, has practically disappeared. The amir is both the political and religious leader of the community. For Islamists, the challenge is to end the division of power that has traditionally existed in the Muslim world between the de facto sovereign and a class of ulamas who oversee the law without involving themselves in matters of power.

Early on, Islamists replaced the concept of the caliphate (surviving mainly in the writings of Hasan al-Banna) with that of the amir. One reason for this is that according to the classical authors, a caliph must be a member of the tribe of the Prophet (the Quraysh), which would not correspond to the emergence of a new elite; moreover, caliphs ruled societies that the Islamists do not consider to have been Islamic (the Ottoman Empire). Next, Islamists wish to establish a political organization that can become visible at once in the first country in which an Islamic revolution succeeds, without waiting for a hypothetical reconstitution of the political *umma*. Finally, before being society's guide, the amir has the advantage of being a party leader, a new concept that is entirely unrelated to the medieval debates on the nature of the caliphate.

Who designates the amir? Little is said in Islamist literature about concrete procedures for designating the amir or about the extent and limits of his power. To many Islamists (with the exception of the Iranians), the idea of voting and of elections seems to weaken the unity of the *umma* and to relativize, "humanize," that which proceeds from God alone. The ideal solution, which runs throughout the debate, would be for the amir to be *index sui,* his own indicator; that is, by merely appearing he would be instantly recognizable. Hence, no doubt, the incessant quest for a charismatic chief, which is transformed in political life into a quest for a leader. The only criterion for designating an amir would therefore be the man himself, his virtue, his personality.

The quest for the amir is often reduced to a description of the qualities he should exhibit. Thus, for Maududi, who generally is very concerned with inscribing political Islam into a modern constitutional framework, the political leader must meet the following conditions: he must be a Muslim, a male, an adult, healthy, and have performed *hijra*, that is, he must belong to the community of followers who have separated themselves from a corrupt society; he must fear God, be wise, worthy of trust, and . . . he must not aspire to the position.[28] According to the Afghan Hizb-i Islami's program, the amir must abstain from sin and from all that is "religiously forbidden," must incarnate "sincerity, equity, justice, purity" and "surpass all members of society in the qualities that are required of a believer."[29] Although the amir is obviously never equated with the Prophet, it is clear that he is considered a model for behavior. He is as much a religious chief as a political leader; many theoreticians accord him the right to *ijtihad,* which places him above the ulamas, although no Islamist text requires that he come from the ulamas' milieu.

In general, the more radical the party, the more central is the figure of the amir. In the program of the Hizb-i Islami, which often simply paraphrases the texts of Hasan al-Banna, it is written that the director must be considered "a spiritual leader" by party members.[30] The amir is thus a "doctor of law," a political leader, as well as a model of behavior. One must pledge him allegiance *(bay'a)*.[31] The right to interpretation is explicitly accorded to the amir in the program of the Afghan Hizb-i Islami, although the current leader, Gulbadin Hikmatyar, is an engineer with no particular religious training; the primacy of politics over religion is clearly apparent here, as is the resulting paradox: the amir is supposed to have greater religious competency than the ulamas. Meanwhile the more moderate groups limit the right to interpretation to an amir who has actual religious training, at the risk of reintroducing the preeminence of the ulamas that the Islamists have so decried.[32]

Nevertheless, there has been a weakening of the figure and the concept of the amir among recent Islamist movements, which tend to be more neofundamentalist (the Algerian FIS, the Soviet Islamic Renaissance Party).

Elections and the Advisory Council

Since sovereignty belongs only to God, the Islamists reject the notion of popular sovereignty and accord only contingent value to the elective principle. If no individual comes forward as the evident amir, then he can be elected by an advisory assembly (the *shura*) or even by universal suffrage, both of which, in this case, do not express sovereignty, but simply the principle of community consensus *(ijma)*.[33]

The *shura* only "counsels": sovereignty effectively emanating from God alone, the only power the community has is to advise (and admonish) the amir in the name of Islamic principles. In short, the *shura*'s function is redundant: to reiterate divine principles, to help the amir make decisions in the name of these principles, and ultimately to censure the amir if he strays from them. The *shura* can take the form of a parliament.[34] What matters is that the function of "counseling" (and not legislation, since God alone legislates) be provided for, whatever the concrete modalities may be: "This consultative process . . . could very well be formulated through a parliament, a council, or a *majlis-i-shura'* [consultative council]."[35] This is a good indication of the indifference of Sunni thought to the concrete form that institutions may take. Once the principles are agreed upon, the details can be worked out when the time comes.

But who sits on the *shura?* Here we find the same problem as for the designation of the amir. Islamist thought refers to those who, following a Quranic verse, are called the *ahl al-hall wal-aqd,* that is, "those who have the power to bind and unbind." Three groups, in contemporary writings, are in competition:

The clergy, that is, the ulamas, which reintroduces the dichotomy that the Islamists have always wanted to abolish between clerics and the society

The entire community, which justifies universal suffrage but which today implies a reference to the "Western" democracy reviled by many Islamists

"Islamist intellectuals," that is, the intellectuals and militants of contemporary Islam, who are almost always secular from a sociological point of view[36]

The debate forms a vicious circle, since the choice of those who decide the question implies the answer to the question. As for the amir, it is expected that "good men" will emerge through a natural process, which may or may not take the form of elections.[37]

All Sunni Islamist thought in fact expresses a strong repugnance for translating the notions of the amir and of the *shura* into terms of autonomous institutions capable of effectively producing a stable political practice independent of the individuals who compose it: in other words, into the form of a constitution. The Sunnis stop at the slogan "The Quran Is Our Constitution." What specific form the executive and "legislative" branches will take does not appear essential, for, as Turabi notes, "Whatever form the executive may take, a leader is always subject both to the *shariah* and to the *ijma* [the consensus] formulated under it."[38] Unlike the Iranians, the Sunni Islamists remain wary of the state in general. (In fact in this same text Turabi speaks of the Islamic state as a very limited government.)

Association, Party, or Sect?

Unlike the ulamas and the Salafists, Islamists give precedence to political action. They have established movements that operate outside the framework of mosques and strictly religious activities, the form of which oscillates among three models:

A Leninist-type party presenting itself as an avant-garde aiming to conquer power and denying the legitimacy of all other parties; the Hizb-i Islami in Afghanistan is an example.

A Western-style political party, seeking, within an electoralist and multiparty framework, to get the maximum number of elements in its program adopted; an example is the Prosperity Party in Turkey.

A religious militant organization, aiming to promote Islamic values and to modify society and mentalities by giving rise to associations and by penetrating the elite, but without direct political ambitions; examples include the Egyptian Muslim Brotherhood, which insists on mass action; and the Jamaat-i Islami of Pakistan, more given to infiltrating the elite. The two parties occasionally present their own candidates at elections.

There is constant vacillation among these three forms. For example, in Egypt, when the decree of September 9, 1952, invited political parties to register themselves, the current head of the MB, Hudaybi, opposed registration as a party but was vetoed by the Advisory Council. The Algerian FIS has successively claimed to fit each of these molds, depending on whether it is denouncing or playing the political game. Generally, words suggesting the notion of a "society" *(jama'a, jam'iyya)* tend to be used by moderates, while the radical groups more readily call themselves parties *(hizb),* under the influence, no doubt, of Marxist-leaning movements (Hizb al-Tahrir, Hizb-i Islami, Hizbullah). If the choice is difficult, it is because for the Islamists the party is both a means of political action and a countersociety in which the militant can begin to live right away according to the true Islamic model.

The very notion of a party is problematic to Islamists. In the *umma* there is "no other party than the Party of God": *la hizb illa hizbullah* was the chant of the Iranian militants as they attacked other parties' headquarters and demonstrations during the first year of the

Iranian revolution. Hasan al-Banna asked King Farouk to dissolve the *hizbiyya,* that is, the very fact that political parties could exist.[39] The radical Egyptian leader Farag criticized those who wanted to establish an Islamic party as a party among others to compete in the political arena.[40]

The Islamists' difficulty in situating their party within the framework of politics can be explained by the party's very specific nature. A reading of the statutes of the different movements makes it clear that the Islamist party prefigures the Islamic society, first in that it demands an individual "re-Islamization" of its members (what one might call a born-again Muslim), and then because the institutions it provides for within itself (the amir, the *shura*) are identical with those of the future Islamic state. The party is a cross between a Leninist structure and a mystical order based on personal initiation under the auspices of a Guide. The vocabulary can be read in two ways: guide/secretary-general, brother/comrade, council/central committee, advisory duties followed by allegiance, *bay'a*/democratic centralism, and so on.

Most of the movements adopt the model instituted by the Egyptian MB. The chief (amir, guide . . .) is elected but then becomes quasi-irremovable unless disqualified by the *shura*. He is backed up by an executive committee or council, over which he generally has supervisory authority. The party has at its disposal an administration in the form of specialized committees, including those of preaching and propaganda *(da'wa)*. Specialized sections cover the professional sectors (peasants, workers, students, and so on). The party sometimes also includes a secret paramilitary or special service organization. Almost all Islamist parties include a women's association.

It is significant that there is almost never a council of ulamas in Islamist parties (with the exceptions, in central Asia, of the Afghan Jamaat-i Islami and the Soviet Islamic Renaissance Party).

Thus despite the difference in emphasis between moderates and radicals, Islamist movements offer a coherent doctrine and a new organizational model. As we shall soon see, they have taken root in areas that are sociologically modern, breaking cleanly with the intellectual and social universe of the traditionalist ulamas.

❖ 3 ❖

The Sociology of Islamism

BEGINNING IN THE 1960s, demographic growth and rural exodus in the countries of the Middle East swelled the population of cities, where the state was unable to ensure the functioning of public services or even simple urbanization. At the same time, the development of education, combined with budgetary restrictions, and thus a relative decrease in jobs offered by the state, increased the number of intellectuals forced into the lower classes. Not only were there no jobs to meet their hopes, but conditions at the universities worsened, disposing them to participate in various forms of protest.[1]

The educational systems follow a Western style of teaching. They are generally coed (except of course in Saudi Arabia) and experienced considerable development between 1950 and 1980, followed by stagnation and decline. If one considers the case of Egypt, the cradle of the extremist groups of the 1960s, one notices that during this decade the number of students doubled,[2] while demographic growth was at 2.8 percent a year. Today in Egypt there is one doctor for every 770 inhabitants: in most cases their status is that of underpaid bureaucrats (the equivalent of about thirty-five dollars a month for someone starting out in 1989); similarly, the country produces more engineers (3,000 per year in 1989) than it needs. Literacy is at around 50 percent. In Iran, at the time of the revolution in 1979, 65 percent of the urban population was literate, climbing to 83 percent for men aged fifteen to thirty[3]—the main participants in the revolution. In 1988 in Tunisia, 54 percent of the population was literate.

At the same time, these hard-won diplomas were devalued for want of openings. The states were incapable of absorbing the new graduates, despite a kind of "right to employment" policy (in Egypt, in Afghanistan before 1978, and in Saudi Arabia) by which the state systematically offered jobs to graduates; but this policy had another perverse consequence: the state became the graduate's sole horizon. An intellectual was a bureaucrat. In the meantime, the various policies of liberalization and government cuts instituted in the 1970s under pressure from the International Monetary Fund (the policy of *infitah*—opening up—in Egypt, beginning in 1971; the policy of President Chadli Benjedid in Algeria) led to devalued status for the intellectual-bureaucrat. Liberalization of the economy essentially favored the private sector; salaries were eaten away by inflation and declined relative to the new rich; the bureaucrat had to take a second job to survive (taxi driver, night watchman at an international hotel . . .); the business sector became politically more important than the intellectual one. The state forgot the intellectuals, and they could not adapt. Indeed, university education is essentially bookish, even in medicine, and out of synch with the social and economic realities. A graduate sees himself as a member of a caste; he assumes that he should no longer be subjected to physical labor, or even to physical contact; he strives to mark his difference on his physical person, in his clothing for instance. He is therefore not very receptive to his new proletarian status, to which he responds by ideologizing his condition and dreaming of a revolution and a new, strong, centralized state.

The Cadres of the Islamist Party

The cadres of the Islamist parties are young intellectuals, educated in government schools following a Westernized curriculum and in many cases from recently urbanized families. At the university, the

Islamists recruit more from engineering than from philosophy departments, with one exception: the teachers' training colleges. The prototype of the Islamist cadre is an engineer, born sometime in the 1950s in a city but whose parents were from the country. Some, the elite, have even completed their studies in the West. The Council of Iranian Ministers is a good example of this sociological tendency (Vilayati, the minister of foreign affairs, is a pediatrician educated in the United States; Nabavi, formerly minister of industry, is an engineer also educated in the United States). This is equally true of the former Turkish president Turgut Özal: although he has now settled down, he once militated for an Islamist party, Erbakan's National Salvation, after studying engineering at the Massachusetts Institute of Technology; in the 1970s, one-fourth of the deputies in this party were engineers.[4] Abd al-Salam Yasin, the Moroccan Islamist leader, is an inspector for French language teaching in the national education department.

Thus the advent of contemporary political Islam is in no way the return of a medieval, obscurantist clergy crusading against modernity. Muslim revolts today are urban: Tehran in 1978–1979, Hama (Syria) in 1982, Asyut in a recurrent manner in Egypt, Gaza in Palestine, Algiers, and, in Lebanon, southern Beirut and Tripoli. The only recent armed peasant uprising in the name of Islam occurred in Afghanistan and owes its strength to the need to repel foreign invaders; but its cadres also came from the city and in many cases match the profile of the Islamist militant: Ahmad Shah Masud, the great leader from the north, is a former student of the Kabul Polytechnic; Gulbadin Hikmatyar, director of the Hizb-i Islami, is a former student of the engineering school. In Algeria, the spokesperson for the FIS in 1991, Abd al-Qadir Hashani, was an oil engineer. All sociological studies of the Islamists lead to the same conclusions:[5] they recruit from intellectual, urban milieus. It is a group that is sociologically modern, issued from the modernist sectors of the society. Rather than a reaction against the modernization of Muslim societies, Islamism is a product of it.

Beginning the 1970s, however, a new generation of Islamists emerged, less intellectual than the first. Student overpopulation, the

weakening of the general standards of education, and the replace-
ment of colonial languages (English and French) with national languages, which in some places are under the disadvantage of not being
the normally spoken language (like modern Arabic in Algeria, as
opposed to the dialect), brought about the emergence of a young
"lumpenintelligentsia"; they've spent enough time in school to consider themselves "educated" and not to want to go back to the
country or work in a factory (if these possibilities existed, which isn't
the case), but they haven't pursued higher education. Spending on
education declined in the Maghreb in the years 1980–1985 as compared with 1975–1980,[6] while in Algeria 100,000 young people leave
secondary school each year without being able to continue their
studies.[7] Meanwhile, in the 1980s the Islamist movements recruited
more from secondary schools than from universities: the change was
observed in 1983 in Pakistan.[8] Unemployment among the educated
is undoubtedly the main resource of the Islamist movements: the
policies of "Arabization," like the one implemented in Algeria in the
1970s, accentuates the phenomenon in that young "Arabists" no
longer even have the possibility of emigrating. This new generation
is more neofundamentalist than Islamist, for it is intellectually less
"Westernized" than the preceding generation.

The Islamists made headway everywhere, first on campuses and
then, more solidly, among the recently urbanized masses. University
elections show an Islamist breakthrough on campuses beginning in
the early 1970s in Egypt, Pakistan, and Afghanistan.[9] During the
1980s it was the Palestinians and the three North African countries
that were most affected by the re-Islamization of student milieus: a
certain delay can be noted generally in the Maghreb with respect to
the Middle East proper in the development of the movement.

One of the reasons for this success is that the ideologies or
groups (secular, nationalist, or Marxist) that fulfilled the need for
protest were losing momentum. Militant Arab nationalists, who are
often socialist leaning, were absorbed by the state bureaucracies,
from Algeria to Egypt to Iraq. The Palestine Liberation Organization
embarked on a process of international negotiation and recognition
that brought no results for local people. The communist parties were

unable to break out of their ghettos among the newly formed working classes, ethnic and religious minorities, or on campuses. Paradoxically, the communist or secular (ba'thist) parties have a more rural than urban base (Hafiz al-Asad and Saddam Husayn are from the country). In Afghanistan, Iraq, South Yemen, and Syria, the armies, vehicles of secular state coups, have officers of peasant origins.

Islamist gains in intellectual milieus can also be explained by a crises in ideology. The general loss of prestige of progressive ideologies and the failure of the "Arab socialist" model have left room for new protest ideologies to emerge in destructured societies in which the notions of roots and identity have suddenly resurfaced, in a quest not for a return to the past but for the readaptation of modernity to a newly rediscovered identity. That is why the Islamists everywhere favor industrial development, urbanization, education for the masses and the teaching of science. What they offer the oppressed *(mustadafin)* of all countries is the dream of access to the world of development and consumption, from which they feel excluded. Islamism is the *sharia* plus electricity.

But the young Islamists are blocked by often archaic political systems in societies that are for the most part modern. Power resides in patronage networks, in which nepotism and corruption are the norm. In a country as developed as the Shah's Iran, for example, the summits of power functioned in the archaic ways of the seraglio and the court. In Syria and Iraq, power is held by *asabiyya*, solidarity groups founded on ethnicity, clan, and family. After the riots of October 1988 in Algeria, the sole strategy of the party in power, the FLN (National Liberation Front), was to stay in power, which it did through multiple manipulations of electoral law. In Pakistan, both the conservative party and the Bhutto family's People's Party were arms of large families with industrial and land holdings. In Afghanistan and Lebanon, Islamism is entering into open struggle with the great tribal families: the Amal movement, founded by Imam Musa al-Sadr, established itself in the Lebanese Beka Valley against the powerful Jaffar clan and assembled the new generation of educated youth around two religious families, the Musawis and the Husaynis. Finally, in countries such as Lebanon, Iraq, Afghanistan, and Pakistan, not to mention the oil monarchies, the simple fact of being a Shiite made a career in the army or government nearly impossible.

Deprived of a political future within the framework of the system, young intellectuals have little hope of finding a post equal to their ambitions either in an overcrowded state bureaucracy or in a national capitalist system less concerned with development than with shady business and financing. For them the revolution means social integration and upward mobility. The revolution is being waged in the name of civil society, of the Muslim *umma,* that is to say, for the universal good, against a state perceived as particularist, issuing from and hostage to an individual group.

The Islamist Masses

You can't create a revolution solely with party cadres. You need masses. The masses of revolutionary Islam are also a product of modern society. Islamist themes resonate little in the countryside, where people are often faithful to a popular, marabout-type Islam that includes few clergy. The modern masses are the new urban arrivals, the millions of peasants who have tripled the populations of the great Muslim metropolises in the past twenty years (Tehran's population increased from three to nine million between 1970 and 1990). It is not by chance that the Iranian revolution took place the very year the proportion of city-dwellers in Iran passed the 50 percent mark.[10] By 1988, 44 percent of the populations of Algeria, Morocco, and Egypt were urbanized; in Tunisia, 54 percent. Urbanization and social problems are exacerbated by population growth, which exceeded 3 percent annually in many countries (Algeria, Iran, Pakistan). It is true that the fertility rate (number of children per woman) is falling today (from 7.4 to 4.8 in Algeria between 1965 and 1987), following the dissemination of the Western cultural model, but it will take two decades for this decline to affect the rate of population growth. There is thus a mass of young people with little prospect for social mobility.[11]

But these urban populations are different from the inhabitants of the traditional Muslim city, contrary to a common analysis that sees Islamism as the bazaar's reaction against active industrialization. The traditional Muslim city defined by the bazaar, the old city, the palace, professional organizations and trade guilds, neighborhoods, and the absence of public space has disappeared.[12] The Kasba in Algiers is crumbling; the old city of Fès is collapsing from overpopulation. Everywhere the important families are leaving the bazaar and the center; they are being replaced by an uprooted class that does not possess an urban culture. The traditional city is dead even though its memory still structures the surface appearances, as in the case of the bazaar in Tehran, which seems to be organized according to guilds, each with its own street and mosque; but what counts is the telephone that connects the store to New York and to the circle the shop owner frequents when he goes home at night, to the neighborhoods in the north of the city, far from all the pollution. A new space is being created, divided by avenues and squares where mass demonstrations can occur; these cities are organized along social lines (in Tehran, north versus south; elsewhere, suburbs versus the inner city) or denominational divisions (in Beirut, west versus east).[13] The urban explosion is causing a housing and transportation shortage. In Algeria in 1990, 80 percent of youth aged sixteen to twenty-nine still lived with their parents, with an average of eight inhabitants to a room.[14] The distant suburbs are connected to the center by overcrowded buses. The city no longer offers places for socializing.

These new populations are squeezing into an urban space that the state has been unable to organize either with respect to infrastructures (water, sewers, transportation) or in terms of cultural or political structures. New neighborhoods spring up in a mixture of squatting and real estate speculation, while the state is unable or unwilling to impose a strategy for urban development.[15] They are not really shantytowns, but a juxtaposition of small houses built with makeshift materials, reproducing as well as possible the traditional Muslim home (rooms opening onto a small interior courtyard). The old clan or ethnic solidarities, the clout of the elders, and family control are fading little by little in the face of changes in the social structure: uprootedness, absent fathers (emigration, long commutes, straining of the family fabric and a divorce rate unparalleled in the country), population explosions, unemployment, and so on. The crisis is only getting worse: in 1990 in Algeria, for example, economic growth was lower than population growth (2.4 percent versus 2.7 percent), unemployment affected 23 percent of the active population, but especially the young. The repayment of foreign debt and the demands of the International Monetary Fund are leading to a considerable increase in the price of staples, which had previously been subsidized. Salaried workers and bureaucrats are growing poorer and must often take on second jobs, which naturally leads to a degradation in public services, beginning with education, and to the spread of corruption.

The unions and leftist movements, which are more bourgeois, have been unable to penetrate these new locales, where small trades and odd jobs are more common than true working-class jobs, considered the domain of the privileged.

Between Consumption and Frustration

The cultural models of consumption in these modern cities are those of Western society: people dream of videos and cars, signs of success, ways of ostentatiously displaying one's place in a new social hierarchy based on money. Shops and black markets are obliged to offer Western or Japanese "musts." Even the forms of leisure tend to be a compromise between the traditional way of life (centered upon the family) and a modern mode of consumption. The traditional society no longer furnishes a model for pleasure, aside from that of the ostentatious banquet, which in any case requires significant funds (and which the wealthiest segments of the population hold in large international hotels). Fast-food restaurants are flourishing, especially in places where cafés are banned (Iran). Modernization involves the juxtaposition of ostentatious consumption on the part of the new rich with the new needs of the poor. Hence the riots over prices and the attacks against symbols of wealth and Westernization that began in the 1970s: the "bread" riots in Cairo in January 1977, with attacks on the famous nightclubs of Pyramids Street; the Casablanca riots in 1983.

One minor but important aspect of the success of Islamism is precisely that it offers frustrated youth a justification for their frustration. Western acculturation has not freed up mores, or else has made pleasure financially inaccessible.[16] Value is still attached to a girl's virginity, but age at marriage is rising, and the young are more promiscuous than they ever were in traditional society: everything is coed, from schools and universities to housing and transportation; temptation is reinforced by the model of sexual freedom conveyed through television, films, and magazines, but also by experiences of and stories about life in the West. Impoverishment and overpopulation make it difficult for young people to have independent lives. Pleasure is only for the rich. The Islamists present a defense of chastity and virtue, a defense that is in fact widely divergent from a certain *art de vivre* inherent in Muslim civilization. They transform what was previously a reflection of one's degraded self-image into a source of dignity.

Implantation and Preaching

The Islamists have endeavored to "resocialize" these new urban spaces. In Iran, as in south Beirut and the Shiite sections of Baghdad, it was the Shiite clergy, often aided by young Islamist militants, who performed this work of resocialization, using the mosques as their bases of operation with sports clubs, mutual aid cooperatives, foundations to provide dowries for destitute young girls, reading circles, political sermons, and so on. All this occurred in an ambiance of puritanism that highlighted the alleged corruption of the ruling classes. All revolutions are puritanical (which is why May 1968 in Paris was not a revolution): the advent of Islamic dress is merely a sign of this puritanism and of the anxiety of the neo-urbanized faced with the sudden and apparent degradation of values incarnated in the city. Only in Iran has there been a revolution, because only in Iran could the *mustadafin* ("those who have fallen on earth," a category that corresponds to the newly urbanized) be incorporated into this new framework, owing to the autonomy and free rein given to a well-organized Shiite clergy.

Militancy strictly speaking results more from religious preaching than from political training: the term used is *da'wa*, "call," "invitation," in fact "militant preaching"; Hasan al-Banna wrote a tract titled *Da'watuna* (Our militant preaching). We find here the old tradition of the Ismaili *da'i* or of the Sufis, preachers of combat. But in this case the preaching emanates from the mosques, although it reflects a sensitivity to social questions and the influence of the Marxist model. It is addressed to specific groups (peasants, students, workers, members of the military). Social differentiation is taken as a basic fact, even if it is supposed to disappear in the ideal Islamic society. "Cells" are created at universities, in factories, in administrations. A socialization process that was derailed by the weakening of the traditional solidarity networks is reinvented: clubs, libraries, night classes, mutual aid. In the 1940s, the Egyptian Muslim Brotherhoods developed a network of schools, clinics, and even small industries. They created student and professional sections, geared in fact toward modern professions (lawyers, engineers, doctors, teachers, bureaucrats), as well as worker sections in which they encouraged unionization. In south Lebanon, Imam Musa al-Sadr also developed social action to detach the Shiite population from the patronage of the powerful families. The Islamists take into consideration the rural exodus and the break with traditional village, clan, or family allegiances.

But the resocialization is based on popular values, on a social rereading of Islam and the use of a language of moralization and solidarity accessible to the people. No mention is made of the proletariat, but of the little person—the poor, the humiliated—to whom dignity and pride must be restored.

The Islamists take advantage of a popular religiosity that the ulamas do a poor job of exploiting, while condemning its "deviations" (cults of saints). Young militants come to play the role of the benevolent imam or mullah in the poorly served or improvised mosques of newly urbanized areas. We find here the "implantation" so dear to the French Maoists of 1968. The lines grow hazy between low-level clergy habitually co-opted by the base communities, and militants turned self-proclaimed mullahs, who delineate and appropriate the new social spaces abandoned by the state (suburbs, university campuses, the new intelligentsia . . .) and by the traditional mullahs. The problem then becomes one of expressing an often abstract discourse and radical practice in terms of a popular religious practice at times tainted by the very beliefs the Islamists condemn (Sufism, maraboutism), especially since this popular religious practice is presided over by a body of mullahs generally hostile to Islamism.

Thus the Islamists come to reassume certain functions that traditionally belong to ulamas and mullahs, despite their latent anticlericalism. Maududi created his own *madrasa* in Mansura, in the suburbs of Lahore, which would gain the official recognition of the Pakistani state. In Afghanistan the government school of theology, created in 1951 by the monarchy to check the traditionalism of the *madrasa,* would become the training ground of the Islamists. Products of secular milieus, the Islamists would first rally and then produce their own ulamas, who would generally form or rejoin the moderate currents of the Islamic movements (Rabbani in Afghanistan, Hudaybi and Talmasani among the Egyptian MBs), while the radical sphere would lie in secular hands (Hikmatyar in Afghanistan).

Women

The Islamists have often recruited among women, especially in Iran. The issue of women, as we have seen, is one of the points on which Islamism breaks with traditionalist fundamentalism. The Islamists consider women's role to be essential to education and the society. They see women as people, and no longer as mere instruments of pleasure or reproduction.[17] They are opposed to excessive dowries and divorces of convenience. Islamist organizations include entire women's sections, the "sisters," the first of which was created in Egypt in 1944 (*al-akhawat al-muslimat,* "the Muslim sisters"). As early as 1933, al-Banna opened a school for "the mothers of believers." Observers have all noted the presence and activism of women in the Islamist movement: recall the demonstrations of armed and veiled women in Iran. Both Iran and Egypt boast an elite class of Islamist intellectual women who write and are published.[18]

The Islamist woman militates and studies; she enters into politics, although she is excluded from specific posts: she cannot be a judge or a head of state. The Islamists' obsession is not that women should return to the home, but that the sexes be separated in public. The Islamists designate specific areas for women in mosques and public places. The invention of a new mode of dress (scarf, raincoat, gloves—basically a nunlike attire) allows women to achieve two contradictory objectives: to come out of reclusion (*purda* in the Irano-Indian world) and to maintain a sense of modesty (through *hijab,* wearing the veil). *Hijab,* then, is not a modern adaptation of the traditional veil; it marks a new place for women in the social order, where the Western model would entail renunciation of all traditional values. It is true that the position of women is still secondary: Islamists always speak of the weakness of women as inherent in their nature ("her sensibility is greater than her reasoning power; she is physically weaker"); similarly, they insist that family and motherhood are the natural spheres of women.[19] But the true taboo is that of coeducation *(ikhtilat).* Remember that in Iran women vote and drive cars, which would be unthinkable in traditionalist fundamentalism of the Saudi variety. Those most radical in their politics are often the least inegalitarian.[20]

The drift of Islamism toward neofundamentalism has translated into a regression on the issue of women: the Algerian FIS disputes women's right to vote and presented no female candidates for the 1991 elections.

We see then that as much by the sociology of their origins as by the manner in which they are attempting to construct a new urban space, in which relationships would no longer be mediated solely by family or guild bonds, the Islamists are products of and actors upon the modern urban space. But what has their political project achieved?

❖ 4 ❖

The Impasses of Islamist Ideology

THE ISLAMIST THEORETICAL model has broken down. It has broken down, first, in terms of texts: since the founding writings of Abul-Ala Maududi, Hasan al-Banna, Sayyid Qutb, Mustafa al-Siba'i (Syrian MB), Ali Shariati, Ruhollah Khomeini, Baqir al-Sadr, Murtaza Mutahhari, all before 1978, in all the languages of the *umma* there are nothing but brochures, prayers, feeble glosses and citations of canonical authors. It has broken down, next, in terms of concepts, which are reaching a dead end: for the Islamists, Islamic society exists only through politics, but the political institutions function only as a result of the virtue of those who run them, a virtue that can become widespread only if the society is Islamic beforehand. It is a vicious circle. Finally, it has broken down in terms of action, the success of which might have enabled people to forget the impoverishment of the discourse; but neither the Islamic revolution in Iran, mired in economic crisis and infighting among factions, nor the liberated zones of Afghanistan, torn apart by clannish and ethnic conflicts, furnish a model for what an Islamic society should be. And the FIS's Algeria will do nothing more than place a chador over the FLN's Algeria.

The Impossible Islamic State
Virtue, the Sole Foundation for Institutions

Aside from the Iranian revolution, which developed a complex and effective constitution, the poverty of Islamist thought on political institutions is striking, considering the emphasis Islamism places on politics. On the one hand, all Islamists agree on one point: political power is indispensable to the establishment of an Islamic society. "The reforms that Islam wants to bring about cannot be effected by sermons alone. Political power is also essential to achieve them," writes Khurshid Ahmed;[1] Maududi is entirely of this opinion, stating that it is impossible for a Muslim to observe successfully "an Islamic pattern of life" under the rule of a non-Islamic system of government.[2] But on the other hand, the plans for the creation of institutions are terminated while still on the drawing board in favor of a discussion of the qualities and virtues of their leaders.

How can one translate into concrete political institutions the concepts of the amir and the *shura,* which, as we have seen, are the basis for the Islamist vision of politics? The question is explicitly rejected as irrelevant. Maududi affirms right from the start: "Islam does not prescribe any definite form for the formation of the consultative body or bodies for the simple reason that it is a universal religion meant for all times and climes."[3] He maintains that the principles of political Islam can be embodied in a variety of constitutional formulas (including something that resembles Western democracy, with a parliament and elections). What counts is neither the form nor the strength of the institution, but rather the manner in which the institution effaces itself before the establishment of Islamic principles, which then must govern the hearts and actions of men. The key to politics is in a "social morality."[4]

Neither the people nor the parliament nor the sovereign can be sources of law. The state has no positive power in and of itself. What is the point of precisely defining political institutions, when in any case the executive, legislative, and judicial powers have very little room to maneuver? Sovereignty lies with God alone, and the law has already been given. "Whatever human agency is constituted to enforce the political system of Islam in a state will not possess real sovereignty in the legal and political sense of the term, because . . . its powers are limited and circumscribed by a supreme law which it can neither alter nor interfere with."[5]

Thus the important thing is that men, beginning with the leaders, efface themselves before the divine law. For Islamists, a discussion about institutions quickly turns into a discussion about determining the virtues and personal qualities of those qualified to fulfill the various functions. Aside from a certain number of "objective" criteria (the head of state must be male, a Muslim, sane and an adult),[6] the qualities are purely subjective, for they rest entirely on virtue, faith, and knowledge. The priority accorded to personal qualities over the definition of duties prevents the emergence of any thought on the subject of institutions. Institutional functions are only as good as the virtue of those who exercise them.

In speaking of "those who bind and unbind" (ahl al-hall wal-aqd), that is, of political personnel, Maududi writes, "they should be such whose sincerity, ability and loyalty [are] above reproach in the eyes of the public."[7] Turabi builds on this: "The prevailing criteria of political merit for the purposes of candidature for any political office [center] on moral integrity as well as on other relevant criteria."[8] The discussion of who should be the leader consists in sketching the portrait of the ideal sovereign according to Quranic norms.[9] Similarly, reflections on administration are reduced to discussion of the virtues and honesty of the functionary.

Institutions exist to oblige the individual to be a good Muslim (it is the duty of "ordering the good and chasing the bad"); once the members of the community are truly virtuous, there will be no need for institutions. Islamist authors evade any definition of institutions, which they essentially mistrust, in favor of reflections on virtue (taqwa). The principle of nonseparation between religion and politics (din wa siyasa), which for traditional ulamas amounted to casting politics into the realm of the empirical and the contingent, becomes, paradoxically, for the Islamists, a negation of politics itself in favor of an impossible quest for a virtue that can never be attained. The Islamist political model being attainable only in a man, and not in institutions, it alone makes the creation of a *polis,* an Islamist "polity," impossible.

A successful re-Islamization would bring an end to political society. If everyone is virtuous, why should institutions be necessary? Institutions, which are always discredited in Islamist thought, are accorded a simple pedagogical role—that of providing a permanent constraint that, on the one hand, removes any opportunities for sin and, on the other hand, establishes a system of punishment that aims to reestablish the purity of the community, to eliminate sin. The advent of a truly Islamic society would thus cause a withering of the state, because then the only sovereignty would be with God; social relationships would be an outgrowth of individual virtues and would require no institutional mediation. The goal is not the state, but devotion, which is both an individual and a social practice.

"An Islamic form of government exists when its members are Muslims, abide by their own Islamic duties and religious obligations, and do not disobey the Islamic laws."[10] For Islamists, what truly propels the Islamic society is man the believer. To become a true believer, a *homo islamicus,* he must destroy the old society through political action. But once the Islamic state is in place, justice results not so much from state actions as from the convergence of men who are virtuous at last, who spontaneously conform to the *sharia* without any external pressure. Social relationships are reduced to the horizontal relationships among individuals, in which the state intervenes only when there has been a transgression. The state has a purely pedagogical role: to make men virtuous. Its success is its own demise. If everyone is virtuous, then harmony automatically exists among men. The state is not a mediator between individuals and citizens; it does not construct a civil society. The more virtuous the society is, the more the state withers. The society exists in and of itself and results from the interaction of men among themselves: this interaction is very simply the *sharia;* no longer a simple catalogue of prescriptions, as it was considered among traditional jurists, the *sharia* becomes the differentiated expression of this totality that is the creature of God acting with the fear of God as his primary consideration. Because there is no theory of original sin in Islam, man can create God's kingdom on earth.

The issue is not one of a state or of a democracy. The fact that divergent opinions exist is not denied, but consensus remains the ideal. That is why the debating of ideas must be sustained among individuals, and not be embodied in different parties. "While there may be a multiparty system, an Islamic government should function more as a consensus-oriented rather than a minority/majority system with political parties rigidly confronting each other over decisions."[11]

The paradox is that the Islamists, who began by concerning themselves with politics, can at this point reject the autonomous space of politics that the ulamas accepted: specifically, the possibility for the state to elaborate a positive law to legislate in areas not covered by the *sharia* (this type of legislation is called *ta'zir* and *qanun*). Having begun with criticism of the overly legalistic and casuistic spirit of the ulamas as well as their indifference to politics, the Islamists arrive at an even more radical negation of the political sphere: "In a *tawhid* society there is no place for *ta'zir* and *qanun*."[12] The state effaces itself when it has accomplished its historic task: to establish the exclusivity of the *sharia*, the only norm for social relations; "for the people to be just and happy, it is necessary and sufficient for the *sharia* to be implemented."[13] But of course this *sharia*, as we shall see, no longer bears any resemblance to the casuistry and formalism of the ulamas: it is a dynamic *sharia (haraki)*, an active *sharia*, for it is internalized, lived, essentially becoming one's religious practice. The circle is closed: political action leads to religion, but to a religion of a mystical order.

❖   ❖   ❖

Holiness versus Anthropology

The Mystical Dimension

At this point in the return to fundamentalism, the *sharia* is no longer perceived as the finicky casuistics of the ulamas: it expresses a new being, the born-again Muslim. Society cannot be changed without a change in men. This idea of a "spiritual revival" runs throughout the work of al-Banna; Muhammad Qutb, brother of Sayyid, writes: "Islam, in its general and wide sense, means that man should give himself up to God, surrender his soul completely to Him and leave everything, however small, in His hands."[14] This quietist position only appears to contradict the political activism characteristic of the Islamists.

For Islamists, the political detour is not an illusion, resulting in a return to the point of departure: it is the means by which a new conversion of the individual will occur. The political phase is the experience of total commitment, of a militancy inscribed within a psychological agenda. Respect for the *sharia* is not the mechanical application of a formalist legalism; it is the translation of true virtue into human behavior. Thus, on the subject of the Christian and Jewish *dhimmi* living in Islamic territory, Hassan al-Turabi writes: "It is more than a matter of tolerance or legal immunity. Muslims have a moral obligation to be fair and friendly in their person-to-person conduct with non-Muslim citizens, and will be answerable to God for that."[15] In a word, beyond the text of the *sharia* itself lie virtue and fear: the issues of formal law and of institutions could not be more clearly dismissed. The acquisition of this virtue presupposes a true mystical experience.

The ultimate experience is of course jihad, which, for the Islamists, means armed battle: against communists (Afghanistan) or Zionists (Palestine) or, for the radicals, against renegades and the impious. But the literature of jihad places less emphasis on the objective (to create an Islamic state) than on the mystical dimension (to sacrifice one's life); it is the act of supreme devotion. The fact that jihad is not part of the five pillars of the religion disturbs radical

Islamists, one of whom, the Egyptian Farag, made it the sixth, absent obligation.[16]

At the same time, devotion is opposed to organization: martyrdom has more meaning than victory. There is no "obligation to produce a result" in jihad: it is an affair between the believer and God and not between the *mujahid* and his enemy.[17] Jihad does not operate within a territorialized state, but within the *umma*. One can perform one's jihad anywhere and within any institutional framework. We will see later on how this conception led thousands of young Arabs to do battle in Afghanistan, even though they were completely uninterested in the ethnic and political context, with all the perverse results one can imagine.

This concept of jihad, in which the individual act has more value than collective action, also goes against the organizational model borrowed from the Third World liberation wars, based on the encadrement of a mass movement within a single Leninist-type party. As Mohammed Arkoun notes, "The debate with the colonialist West transforms religious language into an ideological language, that is to say, the mythical intention into an immediate historical objective. Nevertheless it never attains the Marxist level of efficiency, for ... the ideological discourse remains ensnared in a subjective imagery of the past and present."[18] Nonetheless, it is not fatalistic, for action, or activism, is valued, but victory is not perceived to be the consequence of a series of human acts: it is a gift from God, which may or may not be granted. One of the most frequently employed slogans in jihad propaganda is *tawfiq min Allah*, "success comes from God."

This mystical dimension naturally became highly visible in the Afghan underground forces and among the Iranian Revolutionary Guards of the first Gulf war. It is always difficult to establish the political sociology of mysticism, because in such instances we are dealing with "the institutionalization of charisma," to quote Weber (again!). One loses the *moment*, the kind of moment that normally occurs only in literature. These periods of exaltation are transitory: the same individuals who were prepared to die on the Iranian or

Afghan front may now be local chiefs demanding their due. But this fall to earth is considered to be corruption by the actors themselves, who dream of the past moment of purity instead of attempting to build institutions capable of handling the weakness of men. Failure brings a setback to square one. Failure is scandalous. Either God has forgotten men, or men have forgotten God. Obviously, it is the latter proposition that is adopted. Far from militants' questioning their religion, political failure pushes them to retreat toward forms of quietism (neofundamentalism) or despair (the martyrdom of Shiite combatants).[19]

No doubt one should see in the individual's transition to terrorism the suicidal quest for an unattainable virtue. It is curious that almost all Western reflection on Islamic terrorism traces it back to the Ismaili "Assassins" *(hashashin)* of the twelfth century, without seeing its continuity with the Western terrorist tradition, which dates back to the Carbonari, the anarchists, and the Russian populists, a terrorism whose ethical and mystical aspects have been amply described by novelists (Camus, Malraux): suicide when faced with the impossibility of perfection, and the eradication of man's split between good and evil through one individual's sacrificial death.

After the mystical moment, Islamist thought undergoes a characteristic turnabout: starting with politics, it returns to a form of neofundamentalism, that is, a negation of politics: "You cannot have an Islamic state except insofar [as] you have an Islamic society," writes the same Hassan al-Turabi who emphasizes: "States come and go; Islamic society can exist and has existed without the structures of a state for centuries."[20]

From Party to Sect

How can one escape the cycle: no Islamic state without virtuous Muslims, no virtuous Muslims without an Islamic state? This is the function of the party: a training site for the pure, a synthesis between a political actor and a moral instructor, the party functions more as a sect than as an instrument for obtaining power. Within the Muslim Brotherhood and the Pakistani Jamaat, it is explicitly stated that the party is reserved for an elite.[21]

The strictly Leninist model of the party never really caught on in Islamism. In Iran, where the revolution was closer to the great revolutionary movements of the Third World, the single party, which could have been incarnated by the Islamic Republican Party (IRP), never really functioned, and the IRP was dissolved by Khomeini himself; politics were overrun by political factions and more informal associations, built around networks of personal relationships. The Arab MBs have remained influence groups and have never converted into true political parties. The most Leninist of all the Islamist parties is unquestionably Hikmatyar's Hizb-i Islami in Afghanistan, which was strongly influenced by the communist organizational model as a result of the long history of interaction between Islamist students and communists and the connections uniting the two groups. But the HI remained very much in the minority in the Afghan resistance.

Nonetheless it is clear, from a straightforward reading of the available statutes of these parties and associations, that their method of functioning anticipates, in the eyes of their founders, the creation of the Islamic society. The institutions (the amir and the *shura*) and the principle for the party's functioning (the *sharia*) are the same as those that would govern the ideal society. The party's hierarchy corresponds to degrees of introduction and purification—basically to an initiation process for militants, who must ultimately incorporate the Islamic principles within themselves. Membership being voluntary, the militant must internalize the party's principles and attain, through participation in the party's actions and the training he acquires in his heart, the state of virtue that is the condition for the advent of any Islamic society.

The militant must be separated from "ignorant" society (*jahili*) and live according to purely Islamic criteria. The party is an island of purity in an ocean of ignorance and corruption. Militants are generally invited to live as much as possible among themselves, as indicated by the Egyptian MB's use of the term *usra* (family) to designate the basic cell. For the most extremist organizations, endogamy is required, accentuating the impression of a sect. The members of this countersociety, this community of the pure, nonetheless live among human society (which is reminiscent of the old Sufi principle: *khalvat dar anjoman,* "solitude in the midst of society").

The degrees of affiliation to the party correspond to stages of personal conversion, of psychological internalization, and not to the simple acquisition of knowledge and techniques. The career of the militant is thus a kind of ladder of virtues, the quintessence of which is embodied in the one who stands at the summit, the amir.[22] The members of the party advance on this scale as a function of their degree of initiation and purification, the criteria for their position in the hierarchy.[23] The same type of organization is found in the Egyptian, Jordanian, and Palestinian Muslim Brotherhoods,[24] as well as in the Afghan Hizb-i Islami, many of whose statutes are simple translations of Egyptian MB texts, such as the *Risalat al-ta'alim,* written by al-Banna.[25]

There are generally four stages to the initiation-membership process; the list for the Afghan Hizb-i Islami is as follows: sympathizers, members, "pillars," and *shura-ye markazi* (the "Central Council"), which elects the amir, assisted by an Executive Committee *(komite-ye ijra'iyya).*[26] The degrees of "initiation" are explicitly likened to a mystical initiation: "From the point of view of morality, this party is an avant-garde founded on spirituality [*ruhaniyya*] and Sufism [*tasawwuf*]."[27] The new member must purify his soul to achieve a "spiritual education" *(tarbiya-ye irfani)* (page 83 of the HI statutes). Initiation includes three degrees, which correspond to the three first stages of membership: *ta'arruf* ("the search for knowledge"), during which the candidate must acquire knowledge of the society, preaching, and the Islamic books; *takwin* ("genesis"), during which the candidate must acquire absolute obedience to the principles of the party, the better to purify himself; and *tanfidh* ("implementation"), during which the candidate can finally put the politics of the party into genuine practice.

More than an instrument for attaining power, the party, or rather the "society," the association, is the place where the individual is transformed. It is a mirror of what the *umma* in general should be. The militant must convince others by the example he offers in his personal actions rather than in his political activity per se. There are two possibilities for attaining power: either through the indefinite extension of the party, conceived of as a countersociety that ends up attracting the majority of the population and gradually incorporating those who have fallen into ignorance *(jahili)*—in this scenario the society becomes Islamized without a violent takeover of state power; or through a putsch that aims to slay the "Pharaoh" (the renegade sovereign), hoping, in the nineteenth-century Russian socialist revolutionary tradition, to awaken the "consciousness" of the masses and bring about a spontaneous uprising.[28] The practices of the Islamist movements oscillate between these two conceptions. In reality there is no precise theory for the seizing of power, aside from the idea that the party, by the influence of its members, will be ushered to rather than take power.

Preaching *(da'wa)* is the instrument of the march to power. The difference between preaching and propaganda is that the first presupposes the immediate creation of an Islamist model: the militant must behave like the Prophet, dress, eat, express himself like the Prophet. By achieving in his person a model that is ethical and no longer political, he can hardly guide true political action, for he demands conversion, and not membership, and replaces political action by the display of his own behavior.

The party thus becomes a sect, a countersociety, as its name often indicates (*jam'iyya, jama'a:* "society, association"), a refuge for pure believers who undergo a kind of internal hegira *(hijra)* to shelter themselves from the impious and from bad Muslims,[29] thereby developing means of avoidance that are clearly inconsistent with political action (endogamy, refusal to associate with nonmembers, and so on).

The Lost Anthropology

There is no true Islamist political thought, because Islamism rejects political philosophy and the human sciences as such. The magical appeal to virtue masks the impossibility of defining the Islamist political program in terms of the social reality.

Because it sees social segmentation as negative, Islamism can envision its return to the political arena only as sin ... or a plot. The ideal Islamic society is defined as *umma,* an egalitarian community of believers. The political concept that expresses *umma* for Islamists is thus *tawhid,* "oneness," the negation both of social classes and of national, ethnic, or tribal divisions. All differentiation is inherently a negation of *umma.* At the very worst, this leads to *fitna,* a rupture, separation, splitting of the community: this, no doubt, is the supreme political sin. Segmentation is perceived as a sin and not as a sociological fact. Which is why Islamist thought denies whatever may result from divisions, first and foremost the division of religious schools (the four traditional Sunni schools—Hanafi, Maliki, Shafii, Hanbali—as well as the division between Shiism and Sunnism), but also the divisions between countries, ethnic groups, tribes, classes, social categories, interest groups, and so on. The interest in Ibn Khaldun—the inventor of the concept of *asabiyya* ("solidarity group")—in the West, where he is considered to be an outstanding sociologist, strikes the Islamists as highly suspect.

Good cannot be analyzed or broken down into elements: for Islamist theoreticians, Islam has no history, *umma* has no divisions, man has no unconscious. As the instrument of political analysis and thus of action, the human sciences are pushed back into the realm of the unthought or the unsaid when it comes to Islamic society.

"[Islam] comprehends every aspect of the human soul because it is revealed for every single person living on this earth irrespective of his race, colour, language, location, environment, historical or geographic circumstances, intellectual or cultural heritage ... It comprehends and fulfills all the requirements of life, past and future

. . . whether these requirements are spiritual, material, political, economic, social, moral, intellectual or aesthetic."[30] The universality of the message compensates for the great poverty of its anthropological object: a universal human nature perceived as an ensemble of needs, desires, and physical capacities, centered on the primordial fact of the biological difference of the sexes, upon which culture and history merely skim the surface. The quest for the "pure Muslim" presupposes that man will tear himself away from social and cultural determinisms, in particular from any of the reference points that define identity (other than Islamic) and that structure the society in the realm of the unsaid (ethnic, tribal, social, national, or other segmentation), in order to return to and spiritualize the initial anthropological model.

The human sciences, which bring to light the objective foundations of differentiation and segmentation and thus consider the attainment of a "universal man" to be an illusion, are seen as instruments of cultural Westernization and the perpetuation of divisions in the *umma*. Beyond criticizing the values and ideology peddled by the human sciences (the idea that the intellectual practices of sociologists carry the prejudices of their own society is not new and has been used by Marxist intellectuals), Islamist intellectuals question the very procedures and methodology of these sciences, which are by definition "reductionist": these sciences deconstruct the totality (the *umma*, for example, finds itself divided into the *madhahib*— legal schools—ethnic, tribal, and other cultural ensembles; the Revelation itself is historicized). They make totalities like Man and God into myths or secondary, peripheral constructions with respect to the structures. They deny the Revelation.

The general criticism of the human sciences, particularly sociology and history, by Islamists who place value on the "hard" sciences and rationality, is problematic, whether this critique entails a complete rejection of these disciplines or the desire to elaborate new human sciences that are Islamic not only in their values but also in their methodology.[31] In this sense, an "Islamic sociology" is not one that would adopt an Islamic perspective and values, but one that would deny itself a methodological deconstruction of its object: it is a contradiction in terms. An Islamist will speak more easily about the concordances between the Quran and nuclear physics than about those between the Quran and structuralism. Exact sciences, not the human sciences, fascinate the Islamist, precisely because the human sciences are a deconstruction of total Man, of Man in general, to which the exact sciences make no pretension.

The paradigm of man is the Prophet; the paradigm of society is the community at the time of Medina or at most during the first four caliphs. Good militants aim to reconstitute the model of the Prophet in their very person, in their bodies, their gestures, their dress, their table manners. Imitation of the Prophet replaces revolution.[32]

Thus there is neither history, since nothing new has happened except a return to the *jahiliyya* of pre-Islamic times, nor anthropology, since man is simply the exercise of virtue (there is no depth psychology in Islam: sin is not an introduction to the other within), nor sociology, since segmentation is *fitna,* splitting of the community, and thus an attack on the divine oneness the community reflects. Anything, in fact, that differentiates is seen as a menace to the unity of the community, and thus as *fitna.*[33]

Differentiation is thus either attributed to nature (man/woman) or denied in favor of the sublimated anthropological model represented by the Prophet and the sociological model of the ideal community of Medina applied to the ensemble of the *umma.* Differentiation is explicitly and willfully rejected: it is even presented as proof of the superiority of Islam. Rationalizing apologetics (Islam is the best religion because it is the best adapted to the nature of man) regularly punctuate today's popular sermons.

The Denial of History

"Secular history is obviously present, especially among the Muslim Brotherhood, whose armed commitment to the political struggle we know; but it is contingent and entirely subordinate to the history of salvation by God," writes Arkoun.[34] For Islamists, the supposed Muslim societies of today have fallen into a state of *jahiliyya,* the state in which they found themselves before the Revelation: there has never been an Islamic state or society except during the time of the Prophet and his four successors. Thus history, far from being the means of the advent of modernity, is just a parenthesis, a perdition, which will be canceled out by the arrival of a new Islamic society. All that has been created during this parenthesis of nearly fourteen centuries, that is to say, Islamic culture (literature, philosophy, mysticism), must also be rejected, since everything that has happened since the death of the last "just" caliph (Ali) has been decline and descent into ignorance, aside from the appeals to this return (the works of Ibn Taymiyya, for example). History is but a repository of paradigms and anecdotes.[35]

At the same time the "fall," or rather the second fall that followed the four caliphs, remains incomprehensible:[36] why did God allow His community to fall into decline?

❖ 5 ❖

Neofundamentalism: From the Muslim Brotherhood to the Algerian FIS

T HE ENCLOSURE OF Islamist thought within its own premises goes hand in hand with the weakening of Islamist specificity in relation to the strictly fundamentalist movement. During the 1980s there was an observable drift of political Islamism toward a "neofundamentalism." Militants who were previously striving for the Islamic revolution are becoming involved in a process of re-Islamization from below; they preach an individual return to the practices of Islam and, with their pro-*sharia* campaign, resemble the traditional fundamentalist mullahs from whom they are now distinguished only by their intellectual origins, professional insertion in modern society, and involvement in politics. I speak of a drift because there is no break between Islamism and neofundamentalism; it is the entire Islamist movement, with the exception of a few small, often Shiite, revolutionary groups, that is changing strategy little by little, rediscovering the puritanical and formalist inspiration that was always present among the founders, such as Hasan al-Banna. Islamism was a moment, a fragile synthesis between Islam and political modernity, which ultimately never took root.

The populist theme of the "return to Islam" is still just as powerful a motivator, but it is taking on a new conservative, polymorphous form, and it is more socioeducational than political; while playing the card of political integration, this neofundamentalism works its way deeply into the society before questioning the state. It turns out to be perhaps even more distant from Western values than political Islamism, fascinated as the latter has been by modernity.

It is true that the goal of taking power has not been abandoned, as is shown by the activities of the Algerian FIS (Islamic Salvation Front) or the Hizb-i Islami in Afghanistan, but the revolutionary project of ideologically transforming the society is being replaced by a plan to implement the *sharia* and to purify mores, while the political, economic, and social realms are challenged only in words. Women are denied participation in political life. The right to individual interpretation *(ijtihad)* has been surrendered. Today's Islamism, from which both political reflection and ascetic elitism have disappeared, focuses all its actions on filling daily life with morality and establishing the *sharia*. It replaces a discourse on the state with a discourse on society. This is the model of the Algerian FIS, which, if it takes power, will alter mores, but not the economy or the functioning of politics.

This evolution was determined by internal and external factors: (1) the subordination, within Islamism itself, of strictly political action in favor of the reformation of morality; (2) the loss of the Iranian model; (3) the failure of terrorist or revolutionary efforts; (4) the adoption by states of Islamic symbols, while conservative countries such as Saudi Arabia have set out to finance and thereby control Islamist networks, attempting to influence their activities and ideology in the direction of a more conservative neofundamentalism.

The "neofundamentalist" movements have maintained the idealism of Islamism, the millenarianism, and the demand for social justice: the idea that the integral application of Islam will guarantee the reign of justice and the advent of a perfect society still bears the imprint of a revolutionary mindset, which cannot be found in the legalism and casuistics of fundamentalist mullahs. When conditions permit, they advance under their own banner onto the political scene, forming parties and running for office, unlike the strictly fundamentalist or quietist movements such as the associations of ulamas or the Tablighi Jamaat.

New Strategies

Three strategies, which are not necessarily mutually exclusive, can be detected: entry into official political life; reinvestment in the social sphere, either on the level of mores and customs, or on the level of the economy; and the formation of small groups—either ultraorthodox religious movements or terrorist groups. Thus we find a series of highly varied practices, many of which hark back to the activities of the Egyptian Muslim Brotherhood during the time of al-Banna, that is, before the political radicalization of the entire Muslim world that we began witnessing in the 1960s.

In the 1980s the Egyptian Muslim Brotherhood entered electoral politics and saw a few of its deputies voted into office; we find Muslim Brothers in circles close to power in Jordan and Kuwait; the team of technocrats that surrounded Turkish president Turgut Özal was composed largely of former Islamist militants from the National Salvation Party (rechristened the Prosperity Party in 1983), an Islamist movement that is involved in parliamentary elections and participates in government. The Algerian FIS ran candidates in the 1990 and 1991 elections. In Tunisia, the Islamic Tendency Movement, which became the Nahda party in 1989, attempted to redeploy itself within the legal political system, despite ferocious opposition in governmental circles. Significantly, these groups are now demanding to head ministries affecting culture and ideology, including that of education: thus in 1990, in the Jordanian cabinet directed by Mudar Badran, the MB held the ministries of education, of higher education, of social development, and of information.

Yet this strategy of insertion into political life underwent a series of reversals in 1991: the repression of the FIS in Algeria and of the Nahda party in Tunisia, the formation of cabinets in Jordan that did not include the MB. This reversal is also a consequence of the Gulf

War, in which the Islamists generally supported Saddam Husayn and condemned the peace process with Israel.

On the other hand, the spread of Islamist and neofundamentalist themes in modern professional circles is striking. The social base of neofundamentalism combines that of Islamism (intellectuals with modern educations who have experienced a loss of social status, the recently urbanized masses) and that of traditional fundamentalism (merchants, the urban lower middle classes). From the Islamists' ideology, the neofundamentalists have retained the idea of addressing all of society; their actions extend to all levels—canvassing preachers, organizers of various associations, union or grassroots organizers. We are talking about militants of every stripe, and not mosque keepers or practitioners of religious rituals. As a group their objective is society and not the state. Their policy is to reconquer society through social action, a little like the old Western leftists who became grassroots militants in the 1970s.

Many former Muslim Brothers are leaving politics to commit themselves to preaching, the transformation of daily mores, the return to strict religious practice, and lobbying for the implementation of the *sharia,* thus also returning, after a period of political activism, to a typically fundamentalist approach. The revival of the *sharia* is becoming the primary theme in neofundamentalist demands.

But in Egypt as in Turkey, the Islamists are also assuming positions in professional associations (lawyers, engineers), even in finance (Islamic banking institutions, which, despite their rejection of interest, turn out to be very profitable).[1] In short, far from being the revolutionary, political avant-garde, the Islamists have branched out into both civil society and the political class. Although the specter of Islamic revolution is fading, Islamic symbols are penetrating the society and the political discourse of the Muslim world more than ever. The retreat of political Islamism has been accompanied by the advancement of Islam as a social phenomenon.

The formation of small groups concerns the most extremist movements. This was latent, as we saw, in the conception of the party as a sect more than as an instrument for attaining power. It is in the most extremist Egyptian group, Takfir wal-Hijra, which takes the Islamist ideas of Sayyid Qutb to their full extension, that the abandonment of politics can be seen in the idea of the hegira, retreat from the world, *hijra* (even though the group didn't give itself this name). The group is openly terrorist and at the same time renounces the notion of taking power; it is as if radical Islamism's underlying pessimism has pushed it to no longer believe in its own actions: without the purification of souls, what's the point of political success?

A Populist, Puritan, and Messianic Islam

The neofundamentalists try to re-Islamize society on a grassroots level, and no longer through state power. This is consistent with what we have noted about Islamism: if the Islamic society is above all based on the virtue of its members, then individuals and practices must be reformed. The spread of this Islamization will necessarily lead to an Islamic society.

Preaching aims to encourage individuals to agree to return to the practice of Islam in daily life (prayer, fasting, but also exclusive consumption of religiously approved food—*halal*—and the wearing of veils for women), while accompanied by local social activities: meeting spaces, clubs, lending libraries, classes for children, as well as cooperatives, the establishment of alternative (segregated) mass transportation, and so on. Re-Islamization thus takes place along two axes: individual reform through preaching *(da'wa)* and the establishment of Islamized spaces, either in purely spatial terms (cities, neighborhoods) or in terms of practical considerations and networks (Islamic banks). One can prepare for the Islamic society through local militancy, associations, cooperatives, and other institutions: in this sense neofundamentalism is to Islamism what social democracy was to Marxism.

The reform of mores centers on the return to individual religious practice. Here neofundamentalism coincides with far older movements, such as the Tablighi Jamaat.[2] The preachers go door to door in city entryways; they "sermonize" and reprimand Muslims who have forgotten their practices, touching on a sense of guilt and respectful nostalgia that the "sociological" Muslim (nonpracticing, but to whom being a Muslim is still important) maintains with respect to Quranic references and the *sharia*. They also touch on the uneasiness of those who see their values and families falling to pieces, tracing a parallel between this demise or loss of status and the misleading seductions of Western society (alcohol, licentious films, permissiveness for girls).

"Puritanism" is characterized by the rejection of all distraction, of music, theater, and all diversion in the Pascalian sense of the word, and the desire to eradicate places of pleasure and leisure (cafés, video and dance clubs, cinemas, certain sports clubs). Preaching focuses on a return to the essentials: religious practice and fear of God. There is a kind of millenarian pessimism, which is actually rather far from traditional Islam, in which pleasure is legitimate as long as it does not transgress either the *sharia* or the superior goals of man.

But beyond individual conversions, this preaching aims to create "Islamized spaces," the equivalent of the "liberated zones" of the liberation movements of yesteryear, that is, spaces already ruled by the ideals of the future society; yet unlike liberated zones, no counterpower is established, no counterstate. Here again, we find a striking parallel with the "alternative" spaces and networks of the post-1968 movements, especially in Germany. Once such a space is established, as much through persuasion as through intimidation, one endeavors to force the state to confirm its existence, with the idea of later spreading the principles on which it is founded to the whole of society. This strategy is illustrated by the Algerian FIS, whose first concern was to win over municipalities (the elections of June 1990) and establish Islamic principles there (the Algerian motto and flag have been replaced with the inscription "Islamic Municipality"). But we find similar efforts in such disparate places as the Muslim areas of Great Britain, certain neighborhoods or cities in Egypt (Asyut), Turkey, Soviet Tadzhikistan, and so on. In Great Britain, for instance, Kalim Siddiqi, president of the Muslim Institute of London, is attempting to obtain from the British government the legalization of a certain number of *sharia* principles, to be applied to the entire Muslim community, conceived of as a kind of "separate society." As in the case of Islamism, the movement is an essentially urban one, except, once again, in Afghanistan, where the liberated zones were like Islamized spaces, usually devoid of true political structures.

In these spaces, women are pushed to wear veils, alcohol is banned, coeducation is condemned, and attempts are made to promote the moralization of the society by fighting (just as fundamentalist Christians or Jews might do) against "pornography," gambling, cafés, and sometimes music, drugs, and delinquency. On another front, there is the demand that daily life be adapted to the practice of Islam (free time for prayers, the consumption of *halal* food, special hours for Ramadan). Finally, one of the highest priorities is the adaptation of the school system to Islam (Arabization, censoring impious materials, banning coeducation). In short, the goal is to create an authentically Muslim microsociety within the society at large, which is no longer in, or has not yet attained, such a state. These methods can be adapted, to varying degrees, to European societies, where Muslims can live as more or less ghettoized minorities: the ghetto is thereby naturally reinforced.

These Islamized spaces thus form their own territories, hence the importance of strategies for winning local elections. At the municipal elections of June 1990 in Algeria, the FIS seized most of the large mayoralties: it immediately banned *rai* (a blend of traditional music and rock), had nightclubs closed, forbade the serving of alcohol, stopped subsidizing athletic activities, organized "Islamic markets" (where back-to-school supplies at the start of the school year and food products during Ramadan were available, in contrast to shortages in the official markets and the high prices on the black markets), and issued a municipal decree making "Islamic attire" (a code of modest dress) obligatory.[3] Thus a neofundamentalist social space serves as heir to Islamism. The strategy for the creation of Islamized spaces has sometimes been attempted in Europe, among immigrants, with limited success (the 1989 "affaire des foulards" in France, in which two Muslim schoolgirls tried in vain to obtain permission to wear a veil in the schoolroom).

But although the question of morals is key, it is not the sole objective. The Islamized spaces are also replete with networks of mutual social and economic aid. The insufficiency of the state is mitigated by the establishment of mutual help networks (in Egypt and Algeria, separate male and female buses for students, lending of photocopies; in Algeria, the municipal social activity described above). The mosque is again becoming central as a social space.[4]

The results vary greatly. In fact, one may observe the establishment of "fundamentalist pockets" much more along the lines of social strata and region than of country. Where the social context and tradition are favorable to neofundamentalists, their demands are imposed without state interference. The bastions are sometimes regional (Upper Egypt, Erzurum in Turkey, the Muslim immigrants in Great Britain), but generally the popular sections of the large metropolises are the most fertile grounds for neofundamentalism.

Rejecting Cultural Compromise

Neofundamentalists are obsessed with the corrupting influence of Western culture. Unlike the Islamists, they are not fascinated by modernity or by Western models in politics or economics. The break they want to effect with the Western model occurs within the very body of the believer and in the very forms of conviviality. It takes on a "cultural" aspect in the anthropological sense of the term. Body language and clothing are recast: while Islamists didn't hesitate to dress in a European manner, so long as they Islamized them (scarves and raincoats for women), neofundamentalists adopt traditional clothing. The contrast is striking between the leader of the Egyptian MB, Umar al-Talmasani, photographed in about 1974 in a suit and tie, and Sheikh Madani, leader of the FIS, who is seen only in a long shirt, baggy trousers, and a white skullcap.[5] The Islamists attempted to create a synthesis, a compromise in fact, between modernity and Islam, which the neofundamentalists reject. Compromise with the West is forbidden: neckties, laughter, the use of Western forms of salutation, handshakes, applause. The difference is marked by avoidance. Non-Muslims are discouraged from participating in rituals or using expressions considered to be exclusively Muslim: the foreigner who risks using the term *salam alaykum* as a salutation is snubbed. Certain social practices are avoided even if they are not expressly condemned, such as participation in sports. The believer is confronted with a sort of obligation to prove he is a true Muslim, which would be absurd in the context of popular religious practice or of the Islam of ulamas, but which makes sense for someone who lives in a society that functions in a profoundly Western manner, whether he be immigrant or city-dweller. Neofundamentalism entails a shrinking of the public space to the family and the mosque.

Women

One of the most striking differences between Islamism and neofundamentalism is the status of women. As we saw, Islamist politicization allowed women access to the public sphere, which the neofundamentalists are now taking away. Whereas there were female Islamist militants, there are no neofundamentalist militant women: the women's organizations of the FIS are singularly silent; only men appear at demonstrations and mosques. The FIS is against women's right to work, a right that Khomeini considered self-evident. Here, the conservatism is apparent. Many foreign women, doctors or journalists, who were accepted by Afghan and Iranian Islamists, have become *personae non gratae*. The neofundamentalists are exerting pressure to limit women's right to vote (they found unexpected allies in Algeria among the chiefs of the FLN during the 1991 electoral debates). It is significant that the 1990 agreements between the Afghan Shiite *mujahidin* backed by Iran and the Sunnis backed by Saudi Arabia failed, among other things, on the question of women: the Shiites demanded women's right to vote; the Sunnis denied it. The question of personal status (wives, family, divorce) is becoming the principal area of neofundamentalist assertions, which brutally reestablish the letter of the *sharia* without the social and educational measures that the Iranian or Egyptian Islamists favored.

"Lumpenization"

As the strategy of Islamizing spaces tends to become the neofundamentalist priority, we are witnessing a profound degradation in the
Islamist political apparatus. The elitist conception of the Islamist
party, as an assembly of the pure, is tending inevitably to become a
mass movement, a danger of which Maududi was well aware, concerned as he was with making the Jamaat-i Islami as well as the
Muslim Brotherhood parties of elites, insisting on the personal formation of the militant. The drift of these elitist parties, of strong
mystical inspiration, toward populist parties of the masses, on the
order of the Algerian FIS, has brought a drastic drop in the formation
of militants. These new parties seek mainly to mobilize the popular
masses for immediate political action; since they are recent creations,
they are not deeply implanted. The rhetoric of virtue is a poor cover
for the purely demagogic and populist nature of such organizations.
The Algerian FIS, for example, is more a "front," a movement, than
a true party: it groups together different tendencies, some of MB
inspiration, others, on the contrary, more nationalistic, the union of
which lies mostly in a fragile consensus (to participate or not to
participate in elections) that will not hold together when faced with
the actual management of power.

How can one combine neofundamentalism and the expression
of popular demands? How can one enter into politics on the basis
of a program that devalues the process? How can one act within a
democracy one disdains? The transformation of Islamist movements
into neofundamentalist, populist, and contestant movements saps
their originality, but also the model of virtue they put forward, in
favor of formalism and appearances, in favor, in other words, of
hypocrisy. The neofundamentalism of today is but a lumpen-
Islamism.

Intellectual research, which was already deficient in the Islamist
movement, is absent from neofundamentalism and has been
replaced by fideism, a reliance on faith: everything Islam says is true
and rational. It is pointless to seek an accommodation or a compromise with modernity. The literature for sale in Islamic libraries is a
collection of defensive brochures, hitting the reader repeatedly over

the head with the simple truths necessary for the believer in a preaching, admonishing tone. The neofundamentalists no longer even demand the right to *ijtihad* or the renewal of thought.

Since Islam has an answer to everything, the troubles from which Muslim society is suffering are due to nonbelievers and to plots, whether Zionist or Christian. Attacks against Jews and Christians appear regularly in neofundamentalist articles. In Egypt, Copts are physically attacked. In Afghanistan, the presence of Western humanitarians, who are associated with Christian missionaries (which makes one smile, given the secular and often leftist backgrounds of most "French doctors"—those serving in the organization Médecins sans Frontières, Doctors without Borders) is denounced. This obsession with the internal enemy and the homogeneity of the Muslim community is more reminiscent of a sect with its concern for purity than of a society confident in its identity. It thus becomes necessary either to convert or to expel, which goes against the traditional vision of the ulamas, who, whatever their ideological position, all recognize the legality of the presence of Christian or Jewish communities on Islamic soil in conformity with the *sharia*. Compare, for instance, the Egyptian neofundamentalists' hostility toward Copts to the tolerance Maududi showed Hindus and Khomeini Armenians.[6]

Another sign of the regression of the neofundamentalists with respect to the Islamists is their critique of the perverse effects of modern technology. The Algerian FIS has declared war on satellite antennas, which facilitate the reception of Western television. The neofundamentalists do not share the Islamist fascination with science and technology. They preach a retreat from modernity and not its adoption.

The New Mullahs

The spread of Islamist themes through a variety of social milieus has diversified the profile of neofundamentalist militants. Two categories play an important role: graduates and what I will call the "lumpen-intelligentsia." Graduates generally play a role in professional associations (engineers, doctors, lawyers) striving for a re-Islamization of society. But some get involved in religious preaching, like Zuhayr Mahmud, an Iraqi with a doctoral degree in electronics who is director of the Institute of Islamic Studies at Saint-Léger du Fougeret in France. Yet most militants active in preaching today come from a lumpenintelligentsia that is poorly educated and quickly cast out of an overpopulated educational system in crisis. It is significant that in the 1980s the recruitment of Islamist "intellectuals" moved from the universities to the secondary schools; thus, in Pakistan, for the first time in 1983 the student branch of the Jamaat, the Jam'iyyat-i Tulaba, counted more militants from secondary schools than from institutions of higher learning.[7]

Aside from this distinctly more mediocre education, what is new about neofundamentalists as compared to Islamist militants is that they try to pass for mullahs. While both share the same disdain for the official ulamas, the same anticlericalism does not obtain. Political militants have given way to a new category of mullahs, imams, and other sheikhs, this time self-proclaimed. They have abandoned the political discourse of the Islamists in favor of a self-authorized form of preaching. The figure of the mullah is taking on positive connotations again, even though the official training centers are repudiated. The new mullah dons "Islamic" attire, white skullcap and robe. The neighborhood mosque, managed by such a mullah, is again becoming a center of activism, a base for the reconquest of the neighborhood, which begins with loudspeakers: the Islamized space is wired for sound. These mosques are becoming disputed territories in a political struggle between neofundamentalists and the state, but also between the different associations themselves. Thus, it was through the conquest of the mosques that the Algerian FIS was able to ensure its local power, which was not the case of the Arab MBs.

Since the 1980s, this new tier of mullahs has been courted for training by Islamic centers that are separate from the *madrasa* and the religious universities, which have been taken over by the state. These Islamic centers and institutes are financed by essentially private organizations close to the Saudis, most often by the intermediary of the World Muslim League, but often also by the Tablighi Jamaat and groups tied to the MB. The students at these institutes are generally Islamist militants or neofundamentalists who have already completed some studies (high school, even university) and have decided to become mullahs. They are syntheses between Islamist militants and traditional mullahs, since, on the one hand, these students come out of Westernized school systems, but on the other, they aspire to become "religious professionals" who will then be in charge of mosques in areas of re-Islamization (suburbs, immigrant communities), sometimes far from their country of origin: hence the Iraqi imams found in France. The Islamic Institute of Saint-Léger de Fougeret was created by the French Union of Islamic Organizations in January 1992 to provide cadres for Muslims living in France.

In Afghanistan, for example, religious schools or centers of Islamic education sponsored by the Saudis take in young educated Afghans who are living as refugees in Pakistan; they sometimes do prolonged internships in Saudi Arabia. Once they are back among the refugees, they little by little supplant the older generation of Islamist militants, such as Masud, who have been present in the area since the beginning of the war, or the generation of ulamas educated in traditional *madrasa* but now becoming extinct.

In the following chapter on the "new intellectuals," we will examine the cognitive matrix of these militants as well as the activities of the institutes.

A New Popular Islam

The degradation of Islamism into neofundamentalism has allowed it to penetrate milieus that were previously unwilling to accept its approach, in particular those of popular Islam and Sufi brotherhoods.[8] The areas of "popular Islam," generally composed of peasants strongly imbued with Sufism, like the Barelvis on the Indian subcontinent, have long been the target of both Islamists and reforming fundamentalists, particularly the Wahhabis, who are virulent opponents of all forms of Sufism. But these "popular Islams" were radicalized by contemporary conflicts (the struggle against communism in Afghanistan, the second Gulf war) and the sociological evolution of the modern world: urbanization and emigration.

The Rushdie affair is a good example of this radicalization of popular Islam: it was launched by Pakistani immigrant milieus in Great Britain, which are generally very conservative, and only later picked up by Iran. In Pakistan there has been an evident penetration of neofundamentalist ideas in more or less conservative and Sufi circles. Islam in Pakistan is divided into three tendencies: the Jamaat, which is the Islamist party and which, although it does not have extensive popular roots, is politically influential; the *deobandi,* administered by fundamentalists and reformist ulamas; and the Barelvi, which recruits from popular and Sufi Islamic circles. These three currents were united in the Rushdie affair, as well as in the criticism of the alliance between Saudi Arabia and the United States during the second Gulf war. Thus we are seeing Sufi milieus, generally fairly lax with respect to the strict application of the *sharia,* move toward neofundamentalism, despite the age-old hostility that sets them against Wahhabism. In fact, we are also witnessing a reconstitution of Sufism: the brotherhoods were either of a marabout variety, implying the adherence of entire segments of the population, which is often clannish and tied to guilds, to a "saint" supposedly gifted with quasi-supernatural powers, or of a *sharia* type, corresponding to "meditation clubs" that united educated people around a master who, among other things, had all the qualities demanded of an ulama. The destruction of old solidarities, induced by the modernization of Middle Eastern societies, has increased the fragility of these traditional brotherhoods. As a result the brotherhoods are becoming less mystical and more fundamentalist. The phenomenon is particularly evident in Turkey, where modern, recently established brotherhoods like the *süleymanci* and *nurçu* are displaying a willingness to reconcile Islam and modern science.[9] In Senegal, Abdou Lahat M'Backé, who assumed leadership of the Murid Brotherhood in 1969, imposed stricter rules, forbidding dancing, games of chance, and the consumption of alcohol.[10] This tendency can also be found in immigrant milieus, such as the Pakistani Barelvis in Great Britain.

❖ 6 ❖

The Islamist New Intellectuals

W E H A V E B R I E F L Y discussed the sociology of the Islamist movement and noted that the militants of political Islam came essentially from the modern educational system, but found themselves in a position of decreased social status.[1] They reject the ulamas, whom they accuse of making compromises with modern society, but do not possess their theological knowledge. They also reject as "Christian" or "colonial" the analysis of their own society in terms of the human sciences. They have thus broken with the ulamas and with the Westernized Muslim intellectuals who, whatever their political positions, accept the idea of modern, universal intellectual knowledge unconnected to religion. We are now going to examine the relationship to knowledge that characterizes contemporary Islamist intellectuals with respect to these two other categories. This undertaking seems useful in order to mark the ways in which the premises of political Islam also correspond to a kind of existential premise, a gap between two cultures and sometimes between two languages, a contradiction between the Islamist's sociological origins and the mythical origins of the society of his dreams, between a body of knowledge he hasn't mastered and the categories in which he conceives of it, between an image of himself as an intellectual and a society that offers no future—in short, the discomfort of the Islamist and neofundamentalist lumpenintelligentsia, those whom I will call here the "new intellectuals." For, as we have seen, the age of thinkers has ended. Now is the era of reassessment or emigration.

The Relationship to Knowledge

It is their relationship to knowledge that allows us to distinguish between clerical scholars (the ulamas), Westernized intellectuals, and "new intellectuals." These three figures do not belong exclusively to the Muslim world (we also find them in Western cultural history), but they coexist today in an original configuration. Four criteria characterize the relationship to intellectual knowledge (as opposed to technical or mythical knowledge): the definition of a corpus of texts; the position of a universal principle that explains the world, which makes sense by unifying the social field through a system of values (religious, ethnic, political, or simply "rational"); a discursive instrument, language as a principle of rational explication; and finally the designation of an "other" (the secular man as opposed to the cleric, the illiterate as opposed to the educated, or common sense as opposed to the philosopher), whether this distinction is institutionalized (by a diploma, membership in a group, or the exercise of a profession) or experienced as a value.

Clerical scholars and Western-style intellectuals distinguish themselves first of all by their respective relationships to the corpus. For the clerical scholar, the corpus is closed, it is a fact that one comments upon; it is anchored in transcendency, and the relationship one maintains with it is a religious, and thus not a critical, one. The corpus is first and foremost a library, and the ulama's curriculum consists in memorizing and commenting on a finite number of books, which are themselves commentaries on *the* Book. The corpus is homogeneous, even though this homogeneity may be a creation after the fact. The discourse is gloss: it aims to make clear and to explain rationally something whose foundation is beyond reason.

For the Western-style intellectual, on the contrary, the text loses its sacredness. It is resituated in its historical actuality and contingency; it is open, for one can at any moment introduce new breaking points and add new elements; it is heterogeneous, in the sense that it juxtaposes elements of different cultural and historical origins. The intellectual assumes the desacralization of the corpus and of the world. Thus historicization brings up the matter of politics, which no doubt most clearly separates clerics and intellectuals of today.

The passage from the clerical scholar to the intellectual does not seem to have been a historical process. Certainly, one can present Western history as a passage *sui generis* from the cleric to the intellectual; but just as the cleric may resurface beneath the intellectual, so the figure of the intellectual was already present in Greek philosophy, which was obsessed with politics, or in the medieval jurist, whose nominalism was a manner of desacralizing the text and bringing forth the law of will, thus of politics, and not of the text, thus the sacred. The disappearance of the cleric in the West has not caused the sacred relationship to the text to disappear: the definition of a closed corpus that is beyond criticism, the historicity of which is denied and which cannot be commented upon, is found in classical mythology, in Marxism, and even in a certain Freudianism: the "returns to . . ." that have occurred in France over the last twenty years are returns to the behavior of the cleric on the part of intellectuals; the teaching of Marxism in socialist countries was also based on a cleric's perception.

The Institutionalization of Clerical Scholars and Intellectuals

Only for the intellectual do politics exist, since for the clerical scholar politics remain contingent as compared to the ethics deduced from the text. For ulamas, the refusal to distinguish religion from politics indicates a devaluation of politics and not their elevation to the rank of the universal. The cleric can express opinions on political questions in the name of the ethics deduced from the corpus, but his conception of politics boils down to an imitation of the founding model or an expression of the leader's virtue. Politics here always lie between the empirical reality and ethics. The cleric who gets involved in politics is either an adviser to the prince or an exile.

In contrast to the cleric, who wonders about the legitimacy of the sovereign (is he fulfilling his role? is he a good Muslim?), the intellectual wonders about the legitimacy of the state. He sees himself as bringing some distance and reflection to the foundations of this legitimacy: legitimacy does not boil down to the state's capacity to put an ethical or religious model into practice, but has to do with its very origin. The intellectual thus appears at a moment when the image of the state exists as separate and distinct from the person of the sovereign and as a historical process: History replaces the ruler. History is the intellectual's universal principle.

Western-style intellectuals and clerical scholars have one point in common: their social status is guaranteed by processes of investiture and authorization that distinguish them from the masses. The clerical scholar is a former student of the religious schools and is inducted by a master or a chapter. The intellectual has a university diploma, whose curriculum has in many cases been completed in the West. Both have a vocation to exist as a "profession," the intellectual mostly within the university, the ulamas within a judicial system. The contemporary breadth of the state apparatus turns them primarily into functionaries and occasional competitors—both for certain posts and for control of the dominant ideology—but in solidarity as representatives of a state establishment.[2]

In the Muslim world, the permanence of the clerical scholar is striking: the ulamas maintain legitimacy if not power. Unlike the procedure within the Catholic church, they exist as a corporation and not as a clergy; that is, they derive their status not from an institution in which they are members, but from a relationship to knowledge acquired according to procedures that are defined and controlled by the corporation—at least until the recent efforts by various states, from Morocco to the former Soviet Union, to create a bureaucratized clergy, on which the state would henceforth bestow investiture. The corporation of the Muslim cleric has its own network of self-perpetuation (the *madrasa*), but it is currently experiencing a problem of social and economic insertion: what do ulamas do, and who pays them? The ulamas are becoming "modern" rather than marginal. At the very top, the great *madrasa* increasingly resemble universities, and the ulamas are now functionaries, all of which brings their status closer to that of Westernized intellectuals. On the bottom, there is an increasing "lumpenization" of smalltime mullahs, who must find a second profession, as immigrant workers or peddlers, in the manner of the "new intellectuals," whose journey in the reverse direction leads them to become mullahs.

The New Intellectual: Reduced Social Status, Lack of a State

What permits us to speak of "new intellectuals"? First a sociological change, as observed in Chapter 2: the appearance, in a period of population explosion, of a new category of educated individuals produced by the recent expansion in state-funded education established along Western lines. These young people are hard pressed to find positions or professions that correspond to their expectations or visions of themselves, either in the state apparatus (the administrations are saturated), in industry (national capitalism is weak), or, for that matter, in the traditional network (devaluation of religious schools) or modern universities (where Westernized intellectuals feel a loss of social status themselves). Whereas Western societies were able to integrate the new lower middle classes graduating from the mass educational system with a differentiated "trade" or "professional" status, the newly "educated" of the Muslim world find no social ratification, either real or symbolic, for what they perceive as their new status. Note the persistence of the term "educated" (*muta'allim* in the Arab world, *ta'lim kardi* in Afghanistan, or simply "educated" in Pakistan), designating a category that is no longer distinguished in the West, where the terms "high school student," "college student," and so on tend to designate states, not results. The boundaries that mark the differences between "people of the pen" (ulamas, scribes, university professors) and the *vulgum pecus* are growing blurry through the combined effects of mass literacy, the democratization of the means of transmitting knowledge (television, offset-printed brochures, cassettes) which facilitate access to a popularized discourse, and the impoverishment of the middle classes. The corpus is no longer defined by a place and a specific process of acquisition: anything printed or even "said" (cassettes) is the corpus. This lack of definition of the field of knowledge results in a lack of definition of the status of the "educated." The new intellectuals live in permanent tension: they repeatedly demand the right to manipulate, even to monopolize symbols (especially since they disqualify Westernized intellectuals for their lack of authenticity, and ulamas for excessive traditionalism and compromise with illegitimate powers), while their weak separation from the other, the "uneducated," is patent in terms of social and professional status. The educated also live from small trades, also work as cab drivers or night watchmen. Education bestows neither knowledge nor power nor status.

It is thus all the more important to distinguish oneself as "educated" because there is no outward sign of this condition: neither social status, nor operational knowledge (like that of the technician), nor income, nor institution, like the mosque. The new intellectual identifies himself by his dress (the Islamic "look" combines an often anachronistic return to traditionalism with marks of modernity, like pens and parkas), by his language (use of a language and not a dialect, with an abundance of neologisms and borrowed terms), as well as, and particularly, through political contestation or, as a last resort, withdrawal to a sect. The creation of a distinction, the marking of a difference with respect to the other, is based on the way one presents oneself, since neither the state nor the society furnishes institutional criteria for recognizing the category.

The New Intellectual as Autodidact: Tinkering and Mysticism

Behind the sociological mutation, a new mode of acquisition of knowledge is being sketched out, which in turn is creating a new field of knowledge. In this mode of acquisition, we find both a quasi-mystical and ontological perception of knowledge—which acts in a sense by proxy, outside of any normed and discursive acquisition—a true autodidactic practice.

For the new intellectuals, neither the transmission of knowledge nor the place of this transmission is institutionalized. Everyone is "authorized." The modes of authorization of the cleric and of the Westernized intellectual (investiture by a master or an exam) are rejected, for they occur within the framework of the institution. Instead the new intellectuals approach knowledge with the attitude that the state, the institution, and even the society have lost their legitimacy; they are perceived as steeped in ignorance and sin *(jahiliyya)*. There is no "body" of new intellectuals. Although the Western-style intellectual has always claimed the individualization of thought as his prerogative (as well as freedom of thought and independence with respect to the state), he is every bit as defined by membership in the body to which he belongs as the ulamas, a body with its own procedures of acceptance and legitimation. The Western-style intellectual insists that the state itself organize a free zone within the institution (university charters, autonomous hiring and promotion procedures, freedom of expression).

The state has no means by which it can control the new Islamist intellectual in his social function. His thought does not correspond to his social position, he does not live from his profession, the networks of his activities are on the fringe of institutions, when they are not entirely clandestine. He operates in remote places (meeting houses, sites of worship, educational centers) and in spaces outside of the traditional society that the state has not resocialized (the new suburbs). For the state, better a Marxist university professor than a sermonizing, vagabond new intellectual. The problem for the police has always been to create a setting, whether it be mafia or criminal, red-light or university: they wish to place, limit, anchor, the better to control.[3] There is a very distinct relationship between the configuration of the new intellectual's knowledge and the form he assumes socially. The new intellectual is voluntarily outside the norms, although he may dream of a new society.

❖   ❖   ❖

Of what does the new intellectual's corpus consist? It is splintered off and borrowed from different matrices (Western-style curricula, the religious corpus, educational manuals assembled by the state as a function of its ideological imperatives of legitimation . . .); this corpus is accessible in a popularized, fragmented form. The new intellectual juxtaposes the educational programs of the "modern" establishments he attended and the religious tradition, to which he has had indirect access (through a religious school he may have attended in his childhood or through a member of his family while waiting for the preacher to come knocking at the door). In both cases, the corpus is disparate and fragmented, never grasped as a whole. In both areas, the techniques of apprenticeship are identical, based on memorization and repetition: the student learns snatches of information by heart.[4] Yet this apparent symmetry does not produce the same effects. These modern schools lack a progressive pedagogical approach, as well as the unifying figure of the professor (who is overworked, poorly remunerated, and who therefore must be paid to make himself available). The *madrasa,* on the contrary, constitutes a social, intellectual, affective "milieu"; the master is accessible, and there attaches to him the image of a unified body of knowledge, which the student has yet to master. The cleric, finally, is certain of the corpus and of its closure, even if the content is infinite; the excerpt refers back to the original. This corpus is guaranteed by the Tradition and History; it is sealed by an act of faith, by belief in a Revelation developed in its commentaries. But how can the new intellectual recreate the universal from a corpus that has been broken to pieces?

The new intellectual has an autodidactic relationship to knowledge. Knowledge is acquired in a fragmented (manuals, excerpts, popular brochures), encyclopedic, and immediate manner: everything is discussed without the mediation of an apprenticeship, a method, or a professor. Popularization implies direct access to material that has become dogmatic through the obfuscation of the procedures by which it emerged. The new media, such as radio, television, cassettes, and inexpensive offset brochures, make snatches of this content available. The new intellectual is a tinkerer; he creates a montage, as his personal itinerary guides him, of segments of knowledge, using methods that come from a different conceptual universe than the segments he recombines, creating a totality that is more imaginary than theoretical.[5] The absence of a genuine, fully mastered corpus is compensated for by reference to an emblematic knowledge, which one may display but may not study, for the detour would imply becoming a scientist or a clergyman, which the "modern" educational network that produces the new intellectual would not allow. It is understandable that Science with a capital "S" (the type that allows us to say: "modern Science has shown that . . ."), the Quran (with which they are not very familiar, but which they know has an answer to everything) or historical materialism (in the past . . .) would serve as frames of reference and not as objects of knowledge, for the more infinite and transcendent the domain is considered to be, the less one has to answer to its content.

The field of knowledge evoked in this way is immense, with neither closure nor norm: one can speak with equal authority of sociology, nuclear physics, economics, or theology. It is true that such a configuration is reminiscent of a French high school senior-year philosophy textbook, for example, but the methodology is lacking, or rather the idea of methodology and the unifying figure (the "professeur," in the case of French secondary schools). What is gone is the ritual of transmission, which is as important for clerics as it is for intellectuals: the corpus seems immediately accessible, available. Thus, one of the leitmotifs of the new Islamist intellectuals is: "everything is in the Quran," followed by an immediate offer of demonstration regarding any theme proposed.

For want of mediators, the reconstitution of this knowledge as totality and truth occurs on the basis of a religious position: this point (along with the weakness of social insertion) distinguishes the new Islamist intellectual from his European counterpart, who is also a product of the mass educational system, who appropriates a corpus in an autodidactic and ideological fashion, and who has furnished the mass of post-1968 "leftist" militants. The new Islamist intellectual borrows from religion the unifying figure that is lacking in the knowledge proposed by the school. Fragmentary modern knowledge, acquired autodidactically, is integrated within a Quranic intellectual framework, developing, on the one hand, the image of a transcendent totality, the *tawhid* (the oneness of God, which extends to His Creation), in which all knowledge comes together, and, on the other hand, a terminology drawn from the Tradition, supported by the citation of verses, but often positioned as the equivalent of concepts issued from modern ideologies. The two bodies of knowledge (modern through brochures and manuals, Quranic by citation) in fact cover a "do-it-yourself" creation, the juxtaposition of segments of knowledge into a whole whose logic cannot be reduced to the sum of its parts. Yet the new intellectual's fragments of knowledge also include ready-made ideological schemas, such as Marxism. The synthesis takes different forms depending on whether one is talking about a politicized Islamist or a neofundamentalist. The former gives priority to the conceptual space of the borrowed ideology, with the Quran furnishing only the language to enable the rewriting of Marxism: this was the case of the Iranian Islamists (with the term *mustadafin,* for example, "damned of the earth"), who retain the unifying figure of the *tawhid,* the mythical site of the montage's unity. The approach is reminiscent of Christian "liberation theology." The neofundamentalist, on the other hand, will simply insert popularized scientific information within the strands of a religious sermon: less politicized, less preoccupied with the matter of the state and the revolution, he conceives of the establishment of a truly Islamic society more through the re-Islamization of Muslims in contact with the Western world than through an Islamic revolution. In this he agrees with the traditionalist clergy.

Rejecting Methodology, Rejecting the Modern University

Let's return to a seemingly innocuous point, but one in which the conception of knowledge and its position with respect to the state and institutions come together: the general protest against school and university exams, and not only among Islamists.[6] The rejection of examinations implies the rejection of access to knowledge as a compelled, normalized reading process. The exam simultaneously denies self-proclamation, the figure of the master, and the image of knowledge as truth founded in transcendency. On an exam, the relationship to knowledge is analytic and presupposes a graduated progression that can be measured in years. The rejection of examinations is a challenge not to the notion of the progressive acquisition of knowledge (nothing is more gradual than a Sufi initiation), but rather to the idea that knowledge can be decomposed, classified—in short, that it is a process of reduction not grasped all at once as a whole. The image of knowledge that is resurfacing beneath this challenge is on the one hand that of the traditional *madrasa,* where acquisition occurs at the student's own pace, and on the other hand that of Sufism, in which access to total knowledge (to the state of total man) retrospectively devalues the path of access. As in the Platonic myth of the cave, there is a qualitative leap between apprenticeship and knowledge, while according to the Western, Cartesian conception of knowledge, science *is* the ensemble of its methods of acquisition. In the human sciences, the methods of learning about reality are ultimately richer than the reality, and in any case are never meant to disappear before the result. Herein lies the major difference: the methods of access to knowledge are valid in and of themselves in modern Western science, whereas they nullify themselves in access to the One. The university exam shows that access to knowledge depends on the manner in which an institution has decided to break up the knowledge (especially since exams are made up of questions and answers that must be learned by heart), not on the essence of the knowledge: it is the negation of knowledge as oneness. And this oneness is the assumption of all autodidacticism, but also of all religion.

The rejection of institutional validation accentuates the process of delegitimation of the state, which is always latent in Muslim countries, and again raises the problem of authority: who is the master? For, to return to our previous criteria, one's differentiation from the "other," those who don't know (whether the ignorance is that of the "illiterate" or of the *jahiliyya*), can be established only through a decisive, even violent act, for want of set procedures recognized by the new intellectuals. This is the violence of the new intellectual faced with the violence of the state.

Perfect Man

If we take it that all knowledge can be unified in the figure of the divine *tawhid,* how can this unity occur in man? Here we find that the new intellectuals readopt, more or less explicitly, one of the Muslim mystic's old figures, that of Perfect Man *(insan kamil),* which is the place where all knowledge merges, not because Perfect Man has methodically acquired it, but because he himself is the image of God. Knowledge, seen as a transcendent totality, cannot be acquired by a quantifiable, normative accumulation, but only by the transformation of the individual being, by a conversion. It is in the myth of the complete and Perfect Man, and not in a corpus or in History, that one can read the universal, that all knowledge adds up and that the return to the golden age—the time of the Prophet—is foreshadowed. It is with this mystical conception of knowledge that the new intellectual completes his homemade construction. We have here the primary ethical and mystical concept that in fact conditions all Islamist thought.

Access to truth means a break with *jahiliyya,* ignorance composed more of false knowledge than of emptiness, or rather, belief that this false knowledge is enough to fill the world. Just as *jahiliyya* is as much false scientific position as it is "sin," so true knowledge is first and foremost a matter of ethics and faith. The constant citation from and recitation of the Quran regarding every topic—using the *bismillah* to introduce all discourse, for instance—whether it has to do with politics or with nuclear physics, is the magical act that subsumes partial knowledge into the divine unity and makes whoever pronounces it more than just a scientist, who may say the same thing, but without situating it within the absolute.

According to the myth of Perfect Man, *insan kamil,* it is the ethical disposition of one's soul that gives unity to one's knowledge and practices.[7] The underlying assumption is that one can have access to knowledge beyond the methods of acquisition, which are challenged on the levels both of methodology and of the institution. The first is seen as an importation of Western thought and ideology, which boils down to denying the transcendency and the fundamental totality of the sacred; the second is seen as an instrument of an integrationist and *jahili* state, which denies the ultimate goals in favor of self-perpetuation. These two points mark the break with the Westernized intellectual: the latter accepted the validity of the methodology and organization of Western knowledge (but not the underlying values and philosophy),[8] and sought to ensure the autonomy of the university with respect to the state, without denying the validity of associating the goals of knowledge and the goals of the state (the problem was thus that of the "good state"). The new intellectual questions the university in and of itself, in its methods as in its ties to the state.

This insistence on "oneness" devalues partial knowledge as such (research is not highly regarded), but does place value on its use for defensive purposes or for winning over society; both the cultured preacher and the Islamist engineer find meaning here in the autodidactic method of acquisition: in their eyes, tinkering with pieces of knowledge is not a sign of ignorance, but indicates the fundamental relationship between partial bits of knowledge and truth, God's transcendency. Knowledge is not the result of analytic reasoning, but a mystical object, which is refracted and fragmented into the many facets of the world.

Although Sufism is generally devalued by the new intellectuals, the image of Perfect Man that conditions their relationship to knowledge, action, and leadership is of mystical origin. But this mysticism harks back to militant, conquering Sufism, defender of the *sharia*, more than to popular maraboutism. Islamist vocabulary is often derived from the Sufi world: *da'wa* ("call"), *muballigh* ("preacher"), and so on.[9] The objective is to create a total, wise, fighting man, and especially one who has undergone a kind of "mental conversion": beyond education, this conversion consists in a new vision of the world. Ideological formation is more important than acquiring knowledge.

The myth of Perfect Man implies a rejection of differences (except between the sexes). There are neither ethnic groups, tribes, classes, nor *madhahib* (schools of jurisprudence), and History is but a parenthesis, a moment of initiation before the return of the golden age. Hence the difficulty in conceptualizing fragmentation, differences, distances, as well as failure. All differentiation not founded on a moral or metaphysical essence (*batil* versus *haqiqa*, "false" versus "true": this is how Iran presented the war against Iraq) becomes the product of a plot, an external intervention against what is *one*. The theme of the oneness of the political party is expressed in this way: *la hizb illa hizb Allah,* "no other party than the party of God."

The Praise of Science

Should we see this "tinkering" as an effect of the cultural and social crises or as a desire to restructure the field of knowledge, to recreate an order? Both Islamists and neofundamentalists praise "science" *(ilm),* which is first religious knowledge, but also general knowledge, a sign of the absence of borders between the areas of knowledge. We have seen (Chapter 4) Islamism's profound rejection of the human sciences, which are always accused of deconstructing All—the world, society, the human psyche, reality itself—and thus of negating divine oneness. Ethical, religious, or anthropological knowledge can only be commented upon, since they are given by the Revelation. For all the Islamic reformers of our century, the exact sciences pose fewer theological problems than the human sciences: God gave man the physical world for man "to discover" ("seek science all the way to China," says a famous *hadith*); as for the basic principles of modern science, they are already present in the Quran in metaphorical form. While men at the time of the Revelation could not understand this knowledge,[10] the study of these basic principles can only lead back to unity: the unity of creation.

The pure or applied sciences are presented as the illustration of the coherence of All, of divine will, of the rationality of the One. Popularization plays a major role here. The new intellectual's reinvesting of technical knowledge with broader significance (a process disdained by Westernized intellectuals) is characteristic of this perception of oneness, which though disparaged by the human sciences is on the contrary reaffirmed, in paradigmatic and defensive fashion, by the "exact sciences": one seeks in the Big Bang theories, for instance, proof of God's instantaneous creation of the world. The engineer is more a preacher than a militant: his profession gives him a wealth of paradigms and illustrations of God's greatness. Scientism and religion work hand in hand.[11]

In seeking a status, it is fitting to distance oneself from the "people." Since this distance is not sufficiently clear, the new intellectual recreates one by critiquing popular religious practice, adopting the *salafiyya*'s rationalist discourse against the marabout,[12] against the cult of saints and superstitions. The recourse to reason and science finds new meaning here: rationalism, or ratiocination, is the common ground between the cleric, the Westernized intellectual, and the new intellectual.

The Illusory Exercise of Interpretation

The new Islamist intellectual thus demands the right to manipulate a discursive and rational instrument. Resolutely rationalist (herein lies his rupture with Sufism), he demands the renunciation of *taqlid* (the tradition of exegesis) and a return to *ijtihad,* the only way to get around the body of ulamas. In effect, the return to *ijtihad* devalues the corpus, insofar as its commentary is no longer the essential task of the learned,[13] and especially insofar as the corpus becomes a mere point of departure, even just a reference, ever susceptible to being transformed into rhetoric, proverbs, epigraphs, and interpolations—in short, into a reservoir of quotes. For the new Islamist intellectual, it is a matter of reclaiming religious legitimacy, in opposition to Westernized intellectuals, while also claiming rationality and science. A political speech will begin with a Quranic hook, a few verses meant not to explain, but to anchor the speech in transcendency, even if what is said is purely secular, even Marxist. The two worlds, that of the Tradition (the Quran) and of modernity (political discourse) mirror each other, reciprocally illustrating each other in a rhetoric that may be hair-splitting but is never inventive. The call to reopening *ijtihad* does not bring innovation, but tinkering. Since the corpus (whether borrowed from the religious world or from the library of the Westernized intellectual) is above criticism, political discourse remains on the level of defensive preaching. One aims to demonstrate what is true prior to the demonstration, so that the new intellectual is always seeking some form of mediation toward this knowledge: hence the importance of the party, the leader, or the guide. The leader can speak about everything, he has enlightenment on every subject and it is only because he is called to higher tasks that he doesn't have time to produce particular knowledge.[14] It is in the spirit of *taqlid,* imitation, that one demands *ijtihad,* critical innovation.

The Institutionalization of the New Intellectuals

Although the new intellectual is the result of a process of marginalization from and maladjustment to the state, institutions and models of knowledge, he is nonetheless being granted institutional status today thanks to petrodollars. During the 1980s a movement to create a new kind of Islamic school or institute (between a *madrasa* and a university) began taking shape in the Muslim world: in Nigeria,[15] in Iran and Shiite Lebanon, in Saudi Arabia and in France. These new institutions, both state-run and private, endeavor to return to the corpus and the projects of the new intellectuals, to turn out "militants" or preachers, even bureaucrats. It is noteworthy that in places where the state has taken charge of this institutionalization, it is occurring in the form of institutes or centers of militant training, never as a reorganization of the educational system, which continues to function according to the dichotomy between Westernized systems and Quranic schools (whether in Nigeria or in Iran).

The project is most coherent and developed in Iran. The goal is to train *homo islamicus,* a modern technocrat who thinks according to Islamic ideology, absorbing modern science without being corrupted by Western values. Perfect Man is a polyvalent, ideologized man. It is because knowledge is grasped within the framework of a globalizing ideology (explicitly called "Islamic ideology") that it is assumed to be total by association. The concrete expression of this perfection depends in fact on breadth of education, which extends from theology to living languages, from weapons handling to the study of Islamic "psychology." An example of this training is found at the Rizayi University of the Astan-i Quds (a pious foundation that manages the sanctuary) in Mashhad, established by the Islamic Republic of Iran. Here one finds both the religious structures of the *madrasa* and the pedagogical structures of the modern university: the curriculum is counted in years and not in books read; subjects taught include more modern disciplines than traditional ones; the rooms are laid out in amphitheaters, even though the students prefer to sit in circles, crosslegged, at the foot of the tiers; the equipment is modern, with audiovisual courses and libraries managed by computers. It is a university created both for mullahs and for the secular, where specialization begins only after a common core of study; at which point one chooses to become either a mullah or a multipurpose technocrat (an Islamist higher civil servant).

These institutes are still in operation, but they furnish few high-level executives, and their impact remains marginal.

Other educational networks exist in a clearly neofundamentalist context: they are financed directly or indirectly by the Saudis, often within the framework of the World Muslim League. These institutes have the benefit of up-to-date technology (in computer science, for example), but the content of the teaching is based entirely on the reformist fundamentalism specific to the Salafists and Wahhabis. Many of the students are "new intellectuals" who are thus transformed into preachers and mullahs. Their approach to the modern world is akin to that of the old-time Christian missionaries: "learn the other's culture the better to fight against it." Language and science are taught to apologetic ends: to show the excellence of Islam and its aptitude to respond to the challenges of modernity, not by adapting, but rather by returning to its true foundations.

These institutes and research centers have become bustling sites of intense activity, with publications, conferences, colloquia and seminars. The production of the network differs from the Islamist message in that it evades the question of state legitimacy, out of consideration for the Saudi financial backers, but deals with the whole of society; the message is thus typically neofundamentalist. The issues of both the Islamic bank and the relationship between the Quran and modern science are discussed. This network allows the new intellectual elite to find easy funding for any discourse that bolsters Islam, any program of Islamization, any rereading of science or of history in Islamic terms; plagiarism and pirating of other texts are frequent. An autodidactic literature, turned academic in one fell swoop, thus circulates within a modern system of production and distribution.

This intellectually weak production aims for a broad public, circulating among the "new intellectuals" as well as representing a legitimate area of knowledge for segments of the population that have received little education, who are cut off from quality teaching in their own language yet nostalgic for "culture": this is frequently the case among Muslim emigrants in Europe, who are literate yet not integrated into the culture of the host country, and who work in manual or commercial jobs (the Pakistanis in England). Thus a lumpenintelligentsia perpetuates itself.

7

The Geostrategy of Islamism: States and Networks

THE EVOLUTION OF Islamism is not based solely on ideo-logical factors, but is also in keeping with the geostrategic con-text of the Muslim world. It is clear today that Islamism has not deeply modified this context, which is dominated by state strat-egies and not by ideological, transnational movements.

The failure of the Islamist model is primarily the failure of the Iranian revolution. The war with Iraq identified the Iranian revo-lution with Shiism and Iranian nationalism: the Arab masses turned away from this model. The exportation of revolution has occurred only, and in a partial manner at that, within the Shiite ghettos of Lebanon, Iraq, and Afghanistan.

The Iranian revolution was perceived as a threat by the con-servative Arab states, which tried to develop a Sunni fundamentalist pole of attraction outside their own borders in order to break the momentum of the Islamic revolution: this effort accentuated the gulf between Shiites and Sunnis and contributed to Islamism's drift toward a more conservative neofundamentalism.

But the Sunni Islamist movements were even less successful than the Iranian revolution in establishing a new political order. In

Afghanistan, the 1989 Soviet retreat was followed not by the establishment of an Islamic state, but by an increase in conflicts among Afghan *mujahidin,* based on issues that were more ethnic and tribal than ideological. The Arab regimes, whatever their ideological stripe, have succeeded almost everywhere in dominating their Islamist opposition, while ratifying a form of re-Islamization that affects only mores and symbols.

Finally, the second Gulf war spread confusion in the Arab world by organizing a conservative Arab and Western coalition against Iraq. Arab nationalists identified with Saddam Husayn, who is anything but an Islamist, while the principal backers of Islamists (Saudi Arabia and Kuwait) found themselves in the Western camp. Thus Islam failed to play a unifying role in Arab public opinion.

It is the strategy of states, and not the existence of a mythical Islamist International, that explains the placement and movements of Islamists on the Middle East checkerboard. With the exception of the Muslim Brotherhood, every attempt to create an international union (the Bureau of Islamic Propaganda in Qum, the World Muslim League of Jedda, and the Arab-Islamic People's Conference, founded in 1991 in Khartoum) was primarily the product of a particular state whose main objective was to weaken rivals in the Muslim world itself, and the means to this end was the manipulation of ideological debates (Shiism, Wahhabism, an so on). The ideological struggle set Iran and Saudi Arabia against each other, and both attempted to manipulate Islamist groups to suit their foreign policies: the first played on revolutionary Islamism, the second on neofundamentalism. In the case of Iran, when the Muslim masses did not rise up in favor of the Islamic revolution, it supported and employed the terrorism of extremist Shiite Islamist factions to combat the Western presence in the Middle East. By dint of petrodollars, Saudi Arabia tried to establish itself as the godfather of all Sunni Islamist movements, even of the radical movements like the Afghan Hizb-i Islami, so long as they were hostile to Iran. This bidding war gave a margin of autonomy to Islamist movements, whatever their camp and internal direction.

Syria, Iraq, and Libya have always made use of terrorist groups without regard to their ideological color (from the secular Palestinian Abu Nidal to smaller groups sporting Islamist labels). More recently, Algeria supported the Nahda party in Tunisia while repressing the FIS (Islamic Salvation Front) in its own territory; Tunisia undoubtedly did the reverse.

Upon becoming mere instruments in the hands of existing state powers (Syria and Iran), the most extremist groups were marginalized, leaving the way clear for mass movements such as the Algerian FIS, which lacked the ideological and organizational rigor of earlier Islamist parties. The Islamist movement split into two camps: a radical and isolated avant-garde that did not stop at terrorism, and a cluster of parties and movements that drifted toward a more or less depoliticized neofundamentalism.

Finally, it is appropriate to achieve a certain amount of distance from the vision of the 1980s as a decade of continuous confrontation between Islamism and the West: one mustn't forget the ambiguous actions of the United States, which, like the Saudis, attempted to use the Sunni Islamists as an instrument against the Soviet Union and Iran.

The Islamist Family

We are concerned here with organizations and movements that claim kinship with the founding fathers of Islamism, Hasan al-Banna and Abul-Ala Maududi. Another Islamist center is revolutionary Iran, which we will study later. As we have seen, these movements have always oscillated between a reformist tendency, aiming to re-Islamize the society, and a revolutionary tendency, aiming to achieve state power. With the exception of the Iranians, these organizations are not easily classified into one or the other tendency, since the leaders themselves have varied in their political positions as circumstances have changed.

The Sunni Islamist community is characterized by the circulation of the themes and concepts analyzed in Chapter 1, based in the two centers: the Egyptian MB and the Pakistani Jamaat. These two centers have a very close and egalitarian relationship. In the rest of the Muslim world, the most politicized organizations have borrowed the themes, symbols, and organizational model of the MB. The more conservative groups have generally drawn their influence more from texts published under the auspices of the Pakistani Jamaat.

The networks are arranged around cultural groupings: the Jamaat-i Islami for the Indian subcontinent and its diaspora (from Mauritius to the suburbs of London to South Africa), the MB for the Arab countries. Yet among Muslim immigrants to Western countries and in the countries of the periphery (Afghanistan), influences frequently overlap. Finally, as we shall see, by creating the World Muslim League, the Saudis have tried to sponsor, unify, and manipulate the MB and Jamaat networks in their favor. The Turkish networks are autonomous, and Iran has real influence only over the Shiites.

The Muslim Brotherhood

The center with the greatest political weight today is that of the Arab Muslim Brotherhood, all of whose local branches are theoretically subordinate to the Egyptian leader. Back in the 1940s, the Egyptian MB had organized a "Section for Liaison with the Islamic World," endowed with nine committees.[1] This section dealt not only with propaganda but also with organizing communication among other Islamic movements of the Muslim world. MB branches were soon established in Jordan, Syria, Palestine, Kuwait, Sudan, and Yemen. The MB branch in Sudan, established in 1946, was transformed into the Islamic National Front in 1985 under the direction of Hassan al-Turabi and participates actively in the military regime. The MB branch in Syria was founded in 1945 by Mustafa al-Siba'i, who took the title "general supervisor" *(muraqib amm)*, thereby recognizing the authority of the Egyptian leader. After the Islamist uprising was crushed in 1982, the Syrian MB split: the most radical group, that of Adnan Sa'ad al-Din, took refuge in Iraq, while his rival Ibrahim Abu Ghudda went to Saudi Arabia. The Jordanian MB includes numerous Palestinians in exile and is directed by Abd al-Rahman Khalifa; it maintains good relations with a segment of the entourage of King Husayn. The Palestinian MB, active mostly in the Gaza strip, founded the organization Hamas in 1987, directed by Sheikh Yasin; it immediately contested the legitimacy of the PLO, whose secular and nationalist ideology (there are many Palestinian Christians) is considered anti-Islamic.[2] In Kuwait, on the other hand, the MB is close to the leadership. The MB has never attempted to create a branch in Saudi Arabia or among Shiites.

Outside its own branches, based solely in the Levant and in Yemen, the MB Society sponsors national organizations such as the Islamic Tendency Movement, led by the Tunisian Ghannouchi (which became the Nahda party in 1989), and Abd al-Salam Yasin's Moroccan group "Justice and Charity" *(al-adl wal-ihsan)*. The Algerian FIS was supported by the Saudis; the MB favored the organization of Sheikh Mahfud Nahna (who today leads a party called Hamas, separate from the FIS). Although the Islamic Renaissance Party, created in the Soviet Union in 1990, is not part of the MB either, it shares its ideology. The MB has also had significant influence outside the Arab world proper. The founders of the Afghan Islamist movement (Niazi and Rabbani) adopted the ideas of the MB during their studies at Al-Azhar University in the 1950s. Rabbani undertook the translation into Persian of Sayyid Qutb's *In the Shadow of the Quran*. The organizational charts of the Afghan groups and of the Arab MBs are similar, as are the seals and emblems, which generally depict the Quran between two swords. MB literature translated into Russian was distributed in the Soviet Union from the Afghan *mujahidin* centers in Peshawar (including books such as Muhammad Qutb's *Razvie bolsh'ie niet nieobkhodimosti v religii?* (Do we really no longer need religion?).[3] Finally, in Malaysia, the Movement of Islamic Youth, created in 1971 and close to both the MB and the Jamaat, furnished Islamist cadres such as Anwar Ibrahim, who in 1983 rejoined the governmental coalition and was named minister of culture while maintaining his connections with the MB and the Afghan Hizb-i Islami.

The MBs properly speaking thus exist only in the Arab countries of the Middle East and are theoretically subordinate to the Egyptian leader, who since 1986 has been Muhammad Hamid Abu al-Nasr. As a general rule, the Egyptian center is more moderate than the other Arab MBs or their sister organizations; these are influenced more by the radical theses of Sayyid Qutb, which have been condemned by the guide Hudaybi.[4] Today an international agency assures the cooperation of the ensemble of MBs. Its composition is not well known, but the Egyptians maintain a dominant position.

An Islamic International?

The Islamic International is in no way a Muslim Comintern, with local branches that follow a centrally defined strategy. First of all, there are several centers: the Egyptian MB, the Pakistani Jamaat, and the World Muslim League, based in Saudi Arabia. From there connections and collaborations are established around a network of personal relationships, riddled with disagreements and divisions; their common denominator is not the MB ideology, but the simple desire to re-Islamize the society, a neofundamentalist desire. These networks are periodically torn apart by conflicts that set the states of the Middle East against one another, as in the second Gulf war: MBs, Wahhabis, and Pakistanis side with their respective countries. The national framework still dominates everywhere: local organizations define themselves above all in relation to domestic politics. The supranational authorities serve as networks of financing and distribution rather than of command or organization.

Cultural influence is facilitated by international networks more than by political action. Saudi money has created numerous institutes and publication centers that finance and distribute works by many Islamist intellectuals, whose print-runs in their countries of origin are limited for political or simply financial reasons. This eclectic production generally contains apologies of Islam: they aim to show the good deeds of Islam or to present Islamization projects in intellectual or scientific domains, so as not to leave the West the monopoly on modernity.[5] Seminars, colloquia, and conferences, at which MBs and Wahhabis, mullahs and university professors rub elbows, are held all over the world. The organizers include the World Muslim League and its subsidiaries, such as the Islamic Council of Europe (based in Great Britain) or the International Islamic Federation of Student Organizations (based in Kuwait).

A considerable role is played by the distribution of tracts, half-preaching, half-propaganda, destined for a very large and not very intellectual public, one that is therefore unable to distinguish among

Islamist, fundamentalist, and traditionalist themes. Though distinct at the outset, the Islamist message grows hazy in the course of its diffusion, especially since there is no pyramidal organization to ensure its transformation into a coherent political practice from below, as was the case for Marxist movements. The Muslim Brotherhood, the Jamaat, Turkish organizations, and Shiite networks remain primarily headquarters and dispensaries for propaganda, and not structured, hierarchical militant networks suitable for reiterating a political line and transforming it into a mass movement.

The Small Extremist Groups

Operating at the periphery of the current MB are more radical organizations, many of whose members were and sometimes still are members of the MB or related groups. These are either parties close to the Leninist model, established back in the 1940s and 1950s, such as al-Nabahani's Hizb al-Tahrir al-Islami (Islamic Liberation Party) in Syria, Jordan, Lebanon, and Palestine; or small radical Islamist groups inspired by the thought of Sayyid Qutb, such as the Egyptian groups Takfir wal-Hijra and Jihad. It was in Afghanistan that the "Islamo-Leninist" model found its most perfect incarnation in Gulbadin Hikmatyar's Hizb-i Islami (to the point of aligning itself with the most radical faction of the Communist Party, which had the same ethnic and tribal base). These two types of extremist organizations have often maintained ties to MB networks. Thus Hikmatyar's Hizb-i Islami has an excellent relationship with the Jordanian MBs, while its moderate rival, the Jamaat-i Islami, is closer to the Egyptians.

The other small radical groups were created by former MBs, close to the theses of Sayyid Qutb and disappointed by the moderation of the mother organization, as for example the Palestinian Islamic Jihad, directed by Sheikh Abd al-Aziz Uda and the physician Fathi Shqaqi, or the "Army of Muhammad" created in Jordan in 1990. These small groups share the same ideology (that of Sayyid Qutb), are partisans of violent action, frequently use the same name (Islamic Jihad), but have not created a "radical union": they surface and disappear, rebuild themselves, sometimes transforming themselves into simple signatures, a front for the actions of various secret services or of established political parties not wishing to openly claim affiliation with a violent act. There is a constant back and forth between the "centrist" organizations, which constitute the bulk of the MBs, and these small radical groups, sometimes raising doubt about the moderate nature of the MBs. Nonetheless, it seems that it is the MB's very structure as an "association," and not a party, that allows this uncontrolled circulation of members and sympathizers.

In addition, certain extremist Sunni groups seem to have sprung up locally around charismatic personalities, such as the Saudi group of Juhayman al-Utaybi, responsible for seizing the Mosque in Mecca in November 1979, or the followers of Muhammad Marwa whose uprisings in December 1980 in the city of Kano, in northern Nigeria, left at least four thousand dead. These groups come out of the old millenarian tradition, which was violent and mystical, closer to a sect than to a political party.

The extremist sphere of the early 1980s was weakened and discredited by the shift toward terrorism against state leaders and dignitaries in Sunni countries (Egypt) and by its transformation into an armed branch of secret services and factions in Syria, Iran, Lebanon, and elsewhere. Thus the group of the Tunisian Fuad Ali Salih, responsible for the 1986 attacks in Paris, is not a political organization, but an operational network put together by the Iranian secret services. The ideological heritage of someone like Sayyid Qutb's radicalism would find expression in a new radical cluster beginning in 1990, formed by young "former combatants" of the war in Afghanistan. These youths, from every Arab country (but also including Turks, Iraqi Kurds, Sudanese, and . . . African-Americans), had gone under the auspices of Saudi-financed MB networks to fight the Soviets alongside the *mujahidin*.[6] They also wanted to lend an exclusively Muslim color to the outside support for the Afghan resistance, which until 1985 had been essentially Western. Once back in their native countries, they often ended up disappointed by the moderation of the large Islamist organizations under whose auspices they had gone to war, such as the Algerian FIS. Today they constitute the activist and militarist wing of these movements. Some formed combat groups to move toward insurrection, like the Takfir wal-Hijra (no connection to its Egyptian homonym) of Tayyib "al-Afghani," an Algerian who organized a November 29, 1991, attack against the post of Guemar, on the Algerian-Tunisian border.[7]

Terrorist Manipulation

Islamist terrorism until 1981 (the assassination of Sadat) was essentially an internal political affair. But beginning in 1981, these groups found "sponsors" in states, such as Iran, Syria, Libya, and Iraq. They were then used to further the strategy of destabilizing the conservative states and combating Western influence.

Iran and Syria used small terrorist groups issued most often from the Lebanese Shiite sphere. But it would be overly simplistic to reduce the foreign policy of these states to the simple manipulation of Islamic terrorism. Syria also brought perfectly secular terrorist groups into the action, such as the Palestinian group Abu Nidal, while Iran supported non-terrorist political movements (such as Al-Da'wa in Iraq and the Hizb-i Wahda in Afghanistan). Other countries didn't hesitate to fish from the pool of terrorist groups, which turned mercenary for the purpose of specific attacks (Libya, Iraq). As for Islamist groups, the minority that moved toward terrorism did so either on the basis of an internal radicalization during the 1970s (Egypt and Syria) and then no longer played a role on the international scene, or on the basis of support for Iran after 1981. The latter fell rapidly under the influence of secret services and of Iranian and Syrian factions; nonetheless, the rivalries within the sponsoring countries gave them relative autonomy, which made them difficult to control, especially when Iran and Syria decided to renounce terrorism and the taking of hostages as a method of foreign policy (domestic policy being another story). This manipulation also contributed to cutting these groups off from their popular roots, to transforming them into simple mercenaries and as a result depoliticizing their partisans: only the Lebanese Hizbullah was able to continue both mass political action (under the direction of Sheikh Fadlallah) and terrorist activity (the Islamic Jihad group).

Saudi Arabia Enters the Game

Confident in the legitimacy afforded by its control of the sacred sites, but handicapped by its connection to Wahhabism, a doctrine rejected by a large portion of Sunni ulamas, Saudi Arabia, thanks to petrodollars, has attempted to develop a propaganda of strict religious fundamentalism that avoids the issue of political power. This was the purpose of the creation, in 1962, of the Rabita, the World Muslim League, which prints Qurans and devotional books and subsidizes mosques and Islamic institutes throughout the world, paying the salaries of imams at many mosques in Europe, for example. Certainly the Rabita is not openly Wahhabi, but the type of Islam it encourages is very clearly conservative fundamentalist, based on a return to the Quran and the Sunna. Saudi Arabia also attempts, through publishing, grants, and the organization of colloquia and seminars, to influence Islamist production in a conservative direction. The Iranian revolution of 1979 immediately contested the very legitimacy of the Saudi dynasty ("There is no king in Islam" said the slogans). So as not to leave Iran the monopoly on fundamentalist contestation, Saudi Arabia extended its activities beginning in 1980, encouraging in a more or less direct fashion the formation of Sunni fundamentalist networks essentially directed toward non-Arab countries or toward European emigrant communities. In 1986 King Fahd adopted the title "Custodian of the Two Holy Sites" (Mecca and Medina) to highlight a religious legitimacy that the Islamists denied him. Iran became the main adversary, but this antagonism was translated in religious terms: true Islam versus Shiite heresy.[8] The lines between MB reformism, which is very close to the Salafists, and Wahhabism tended to blur. Thus the journal *Al-Jihad,* produced by Arab MBs supporting the Afghan *mujahidin,* denounces the "Wahhabi" qualifier applied to Arabs who support the resistance, seeing it as a plot by "the Western press, Radio Kaboul, the Sufi Marabouts, the Voice of America and Radio Free Iran."[9]

For want of officers, but also because Wahhabi doctrine often encounters strong opposition among traditionalist Sunni mullahs, the Saudis relied on Sunni networks, which they financed on the basis of personal or even patronage relationships, rather than on a well thought-out strategy. Saudi Arabia thus found itself financing either fundamentalist networks that were indeed conservative, but also violently anti-Western, or far more radical Islamist groups which demanded political power, but seemed more apt to prevent Iran from gaining ground (this is the case, for example, of the Hizb-i Islami in Afghanistan).

In the 1980s a kind of joint venture was established between the Saudis and Arab Muslim Brothers. The Muslim Brothers agreed not to operate in Saudi Arabia itself, but served as a relay for contacts with foreign Islamist movements. Kuwait often served as a revolving stage. The MBs also used as a relay in South Asia movements long established on an indigenous basis (Jamaat-i Islami). Thus the MB played an essential role in the choice of organizations and individuals likely to receive Saudi subsidies. On a doctrinal level, the differences are certainly significant between the MBs and the Wahhabis, but their common references to Hanbalism (the strictest of the four legal schools of the Sunni world), their rejection of the division into jurid-ical schools, and their virulent opposition to Shiism and popular religious practices (the cult of "saints") furnished them with the common themes of a reformist and puritanical preaching. This alli-ance carried in its wake older fundamentalist movements, non-Wah-habi but with strong local roots, such as the Pakistani Ahl-i Hadith or the Ikhwan of continental China.

The War in Afghanistan and MB-Wahhabi Cooperation

The war in Afghanistan furnishes the best example of this collabo-ration: the MBs organized "Islamic" humanitarian aid for the Afghan resistance and established an "Islamic legion," made up of Arab volunteers who would head off to perform jihad in Afghani-stan. The MB bureau in Peshawar was directed by Abdullah Azzam (a Jordanian Palestinian, assassinated in November 1989), who rec-ognized Muhammad Abu al-Nasr, leader of the Egyptian MB, as his spiritual guide; a large portion of the Saudi funds passed through him. In Saudi Arabia, the key man in the operation was Prince Turki, head of information services. The third partner in this joint venture was the secret service of the Pakistani army, ISI (Inter Services Intelligence). The MB and the Saudis did everything they could to rally the Islamist sphere first around Sayyaf, then around Hikmatyar. The training camps of the Afghan *mujahidin* (including the Jaji camp in the Afghan province of Paktya, controlled by the Hizb-i Islami) also trained Islamist groups from Kashmir (including the Kashmiri Hizb-i Islami) and the Philippine Moros, as well, no doubt, as Palestinian Islamists. For the picture to be complete, it should also be mentioned that Yasser Arafat, who was an MB in his youth, attempted to act as liaison between Hikmatyar and the communist regime in Kabul, from a base in . . . Bagdad (in 1989 and 1990).

Thus American and Saudi financing helped to arm radical Islamist networks that in 1990 would find themselves wholeheartedly allied with Saddam Husayn. Moderate Islamists, such as B. Rabbani, director of the Jamaat-i Islami, with personal ties to Sheikh al-Talmasani, the Egyptian MB guide prior to Abu al-Nasr, found themselves marginalized by the decision of the Jordanian MB and the Pakistani ISI to support Hikmatyar; Rabbani chose the Saudi camp in 1990.

This did not prevent other Saudi movements or personalities, such as Sheikh Ibn Baz, the highest authority of Wahhabism, from having their own networks. In Pakistan, the Saudi clergy directly supported certain fundamentalist organizations, such as Ahl-i Hadith, a movement founded in the nineteenth century and classified as "Wahhabi" by the British, wrongly so at the time.[10] They developed theological differences with the Hanafi school, in particular with respect to the manner of praying,[11] which scandalized the Afghans, who are generally very orthodox Sunni Hanafis. In Pakistan, they transformed themselves into a political party. Curiously, they opposed the *sharia* bill (the law that would make the *sharia* state law), because they felt it was not for the state to legislate on the *sharia*. Their leader, Ihsan Illahi Zahir, was assassinated in 1987. The Ahl-i Hadith have been active since the nineteenth century on the border between Pakistan and Afghanistan; they have *madrasa* in

Attock, Akora, and in the Kunar (in the village of Panjpir). From the 1950s on, they trained many Afghan mullahs, especially in the provinces of Kunar and Badakhshan: though designated as Wahhabis by their adversaries, they prefer to call themselves "Salafis." In the course of the war in Afghanistan, they founded small principalities (under Mawlawi Afzal in Nuristan, Mawlawi Shariqi in Badakhshan, Mawlawi Jamil al-Rahman in the Kunar).

The Wahhabis and Ahl-i Hadith, unlike the MB, have always favored religious preaching over political action, and in particular the fight against Sufism (destruction of "saints' " tombs) and Shiism. Their activities in Afghanistan, where Sufism and Hanafism are well rooted, led to religious conflicts among the population, which the MBs would have been happy to avoid.[12] The tensions between specifically MB networks and Wahhabi networks brought about conflicts that were all the more difficult to understand as they were also related to tribal and ethnic differences. Thus, in the Afghan province of Kunar, the Wahhabi "principality," established in 1985 and directed by Jamil al-Rahman, recruited from the Safi tribe of the Pech Valley and enjoyed direct Saudi and Ahl-i Hadith support. This group formed an alliance with the local Hizb-i Islami, which was more established among the Meshwani and Shinwari tribes, until the second Gulf war and control of poppy fields pitted them against one another. The Saudis gave money to the Salafis to chase away the Hizb, supported by the MB (May 1991). Jamil al-Rahman was assassinated by an Egyptian (named "Rumi" . . . the "Christian.") None of which prevented Prince Turki from coming in person to reopen the dialogue with Hikmatyar in November 1991. Internal intrigues, corruption, personal accounts to settle, and tactical blows ended up, as always with the Saudis, supplanting a long-term strategic vision.

The combination of competition and collaboration between the MB and the Saudis that preceded the Gulf war can be observed in other countries: Saudi Arabia financed movements without organizational ties to the MB, such as the Algerian FIS, while the MB tended to support the movement of Sheikh Nahna. For purely strategic reasons, Saudi Arabia also financed a fundamentalist movement in Yemen, mainly rooted in the northern tribes and out of keeping with the Islamist sociological model in that they are essentially tribalized peasants (Sheikh Abdallah al-Ahmar's "Alliance for Reform"). In addition, the Saudis financed networks of mosques in the countries of emigration, without bothering to learn more about the imams preaching there.

The Conjunction between Islamism and Conservative Fundamentalism

The consequences of this rapprochement between Islamists (MB) and conservative fundamentalists (Wahhabis) were twofold: on the one hand, it helped confine Iran to the Shiite ghetto and to involve Sunni Islamists in the politics of their respective countries and in international alliances (including with the United States in the case of Afghanistan). But the blurring of the borders between conservative fundamentalism and political Islamism also helped to create neofundamentalism. Opposition to the West is increasingly expressed in religious terms: criticism of Christianity and Zionism, but also marked anti-Semitism. The neofundamentalists are leading a crusade for a return to a pure, Hanbal-style Islam, one ridded of all syncretism as well as of all external values and influences, whether mystical or arising from Western "materialism." They oppose the assimilation of immigrants, favor the creation of "Islamized spaces" in Western countries, and are waging a relentless war against "renegades" like Salman Rushdie. It was neofundamentalist themes that radicalized circles that had previously rejected political action (in particular the Muslims of the Indian subcontinent), as is shown by the Rushdie affair.

Launched in the autumn of 1988 by Indian Muslims and Pakistani emigrants to Great Britain, all relatively close to Saudi Arabia, the condemnation of Salman Rushdie's novel *The Satanic Verses* became an international event on February 14, 1989, when Imam Khomeini issued a *fatwa* condemning the writer to death. While the crime with which Rushdie is charged, blasphemy and apostasy, comes out of a narrow and apolitical vision of the *sharia*, Khomeini's *fatwa* automatically lends it a political dimension by calling for nothing short of terrorism.

The Gulf War Rift

Meanwhile, during the autumn of 1990, the Islamist and neofundamentalist networks abandoned Saudi Arabia en masse, accusing it of having allowed an infidel army to protect the sacred sites. The quickest to condemn the Saudis' appeal to the Americans were the Sudanese under Hassan al-Turabi, the Tunisians under Ghannouchi, the Jordanian MB, and the Islamic Jihad for the Liberation of Palestine (a Jordanian group led by Sheikh Asad al-Tamimi), all of whom followed the leads of their respective governments in the process. In Egypt, Sheikh Umar Abd al-Rahman's Islamic Jihad and the MB faction led by Ma'mun al-Hudaybi also condemned the Saudis. The Egyptian MB and the leader of the FIS, Abbasi Madani, attempted for a while to balance themselves between the Saudis and the Iraqis before choosing, under grassroots pressure, to support Saddam Husayn; while Hamas, dependent on Saudi money and opposed to a PLO tied to Bagdad, chose Riyadh. The anti-Saudi line was also adopted by the Sa'ad al-Din group, part of the Syrian MB, the Muslim Students' Association (a U.S.-based MB organization financed by the Saudis), and the most radical of the Afghan Islamists (Hikmatyar, Sayyaf); the moderates (Rabbani) took a clear position in favor of Riyadh. Faced with this massive movement of the brotherhood into opposition to Saudi Arabia, the Kuwaiti MB, reorganized into the Islamic Constitutional Movement (Islah, directed by Ismail Shatti), quit the brotherhood's international agency in protest, followed by all MBs in the Gulf states, while the Saudis naturally cut off funds to the Islamist movements that had condemned them, bringing about certain splits, such as the one in Tunisia that divided the Nahda party into moderates closer to Saudi Arabia (Abd al-Fatah Murro) and radicals (Ghannouchi). But in the settling of accounts, the majority of Islamists passed into opposition to Saudi Arabia. All these opponents gathered at the Islamic Popular Conference, called by Saddam Husayn in Bagdad on January 11, 1991; among the participants were the Jordanian minister of religious affairs, Ibrahim Zayd al-Kilani, an MB who had received his appointment a few months earlier; and the vice president of the Algerian FIS, Benazzuz Zubda.

On the whole, then, the MB sphere opposed Saudi Arabia, even though it remained under the contradictory influences of the moderates (still the Egyptians), who had been isolated by the departure of the MBs from the Gulf, and of the radicals, led by Turabi and Ghannouchi. But the break between the MBs and Saudi Arabia left the MBs without sponsorship, especially since the pro-Iraqi regimes (Jordan and Tunisia), wishing their blunder to be forgotten, began marginalizing or repressing the Islamists (in Jordan and Tunisia, respectively). Most Arab countries accepted, or at least paid lip service to accepting, the beginning of the peace process, which the MB violently rejected.

An opposition front extending from the Islamists to the communists and united solely by its rejection of the West and of the regimes in power then attempted to gain support throughout the Middle East. Iran came forward as a sponsor, thanks in particular to the work of Ghannouchi and Turabi.[13] In 1991, Sudan provided refuge and passports to Tunisian Islamists.

The Solidarity Conference with the Muslim peoples of Palestine, held in Tehran on October 19, 1991, and organized by the president of the Assembly, Karrubi, aimed to condemn the peace process and the PLO and to provide support for Palestinian Islamist movements. Iran cast a wide net for this conference, involving groups from Muslim Brothers to Ba'thists and communists (it achieved a rapprochement of all extremists, despite ideological differences: Georges Habache reached an accord with Hamas; Ahmad Jibril grew closer to the Lebanese Hizbullah; and so on). For many, this new combat is only one chapter in the anti-imperialist struggle, which is occurring today under the green banner instead of the red. Essentially, it is the Third World, anticolonialist sensibility, always present in the history of Islamism, that is reemerging today in what is an undoubtedly temporary alliance with secular currents of the same sensibility.

The first reason for the about-face in Iran, which until then had been very prudent with respect to the American presence in the Gulf, was strategic: the only niche Iran could occupy in the Middle East was that of mustering opponents to the peace process, even if it meant that it later had to negotiate this role with the Americans. The acceptance of the peace process by all the large Sunni states (except Sudan) allows Iran to hope to succeed in its goal of the past ten years: to make headway in the Sunni Arab milieu. Previously it had to thwart Iraq, by developing its presence in Lebanon and Syria; now it has to get around Saudi Arabia, by establishing itself in Yemen and Sudan.

To break out of the Shiite ghetto, Iran needs Sunni relays. While it is still possible for Iran to use specific relay points, such as Turabi, it is unlikely that the MBs, which tend to be anti-Shiite and securely anchored in the Arab world, would make a strategic and durable alliance with Iran. As is often the case, geostrategic alliances do not jibe with local alliances. Turabi, who is now allied with Iran with regard to the Middle East, is close to Gulbadin Hikmatyar in Afghanistan, who himself condemns the peace process and is close to the Jordanian MB, but is also violently opposed to Afghan Shiites and to Iran's potential role in that country. Deep antagonisms prevail over tactical alliances, even if the latter would be highly advantageous.

Shiites and Sunnis: Opposition or Alliance?

Islamism, both Sunni and Shiite, denies the opposition between the two schools of Islam. It is characteristic of Islamism in general to put aside specifically theological questions in favor of political discourse. On a doctrinal level, Sunni Islamism even drew closer to Shiite thought by accepting the right to interpretation and by placing emphasis on the charismatic leader, the amir. The year of the Iranian revolution was one of great ecumenical discourse. Yet ten years of Iranian Islamic revolution have shown that, despite Tehran's effort to make headway in Sunni milieus, the opposition between Shiites and Sunnis remains a key aspect of the contemporary Islamic world.

The drift of Islamism toward neofundamentalism has brought a resurgence of Sunni fundamentalism's visceral anti-Shiism. In Afghanistan, for example, the Wahhabis circulated an anti-Shiite pamphlet titled *Tuhfa-i ithna ashariyya* (The gift of the twelve Shiites), republished in Turkey in 1988 and widely distributed in Peshawar; this book was written at the beginning of the nineteenth century by the son of Shah Wali Allah, who was also the religious mentor of Sayyid Barelvi, founder of the Ahl-i Hadith movement. At the same time, some Iranian circles see the Wahhabis as a sect inspired by British imperialism.[14]

Iran has succeeded only in rallying (or facilitating the creation of) small Sunni groups who appear as token Sunnis at conferences but have little influence in their countries of origin. These include Sheikh Sha'ban's Movement of Islamic Unification (Tawhid) in Tripoli, Lebanon; the small Afghan groups led by Mawlawi Mansur and Qazi Amin; and the Jam'iyyat faction called Afzali in and around the city of Herat. Here and there we also find Sunni Hizbullahs (on the Afghan-Iranian border). In sponsoring Islamist groups rejected by Riyadh after the Gulf war (the FIS, Nahda), Iran will undoubtedly come up against the fact that these groups are in no way small and will not accept having their strategies dictated to them.

The opposition between Shiites and Sunnis remains a decisive factor in the foreign relations and domestic policies of the Muslim states, where it corresponds to political, social, and (in Afghanistan) ethnic cleavages. In Lebanon and Iraq, the Shiite community, though in the majority in terms of population, has generally been kept at a distance from national politics. In Iran, loyalty to the state is measured by one's religious, and not ethnic, affiliation: Shiite Azeris and Arab-speakers feel more Iranian than do Sunni Kurds and Baluchis, who are nonetheless closer culturally to the Shiite, Persian majority. In all the petromonarchies, the Shiites are generally considered to be foreign agents.[15]

The great ethnic, religious, and national divisions of the Muslim world are turning out to be stronger than all the calls to Islamic solidarity. Although this imaginary solidarity still has the power to mobilize popular support, it cannot provide the basis for an Islamist international union.

State Concessions to Islamization

During the 1980s the Muslim states showed ambivalence toward domestic Islamist and fundamentalist movements. On the one hand, they repressed radical Islamist groups that contested their legitimacy:

the recapture of the Great Mosque in Mecca in 1979, the execution of the great Shiite Iraqi Ayatollah Baqir al-Sadr and his entire family in 1980, the execution of Sadat's assassins in Egypt in 1982, the bloody repression of the uprising in the city of Hama in Syria in 1982 and of the Shiites in southern Iraq in 1991, the repression of the Algerian FIS and the Tunisian Nahda in 1991 and 1992, and so on. In the countries that tend toward Sunnism but have strong Shiite minorities, the repression often takes an openly anti-Shiite turn (Iraq, Kuwait, Pakistan). But at the same time, almost all the regimes use for their own ends a form of re-Islamization from the top both to take the sting out of Islamist contestation and to give themselves religious legitimacy. They thereby attempt to create a division between small radical groups and centrist groups susceptible to being integrated into the political scene.

The collaboration between states and Islamist milieus has hardly anything to do with the nature of the regime. The same governments who used to refer to Arab socialism, nationalism, or secularism now lay claim to Islam. Islamization from the top is not at all tied in with state clericalization or the emergence of revolutionary regimes. Today, of the four countries that claim to have made the *sharia* the exclusive source of law, three are governed by nonclergy, who are very conservative besides: Pakistan, Sudan, Saudi Arabia, the exception, as always, being Iran. In fact, in the Sudan and in Pakistan during the time of General Zia (1977–1988), the policy of Islamization resulted from an alliance between a putschist military and an Islamist-inspired minority party (the Pakistani Jamaat, the Sudanese Islamic National Front, whose cadres are secular) in opposition to large "Muslim" parties (the Umma party in the Sudan, the two Jam'iyyat al-Ulama parties in Pakistan).

The specific state strategies vary: either moderate Islamist parties are integrated into the political scene without any particular concessions being made to them (Jordan, Kuwait, Turkey), or integration is accompanied by a state-ordered re-Islamization (Pakistan, Sudan, Egypt), or else ideological concessions are made toward re-Islamization while Islamist political participation is blocked (the Maghreb), or, finally, no concessions are made, the contradiction being too great between the founding values of the state and

Islamism (secularism for Iraq and Syria, Qaddafi's philosophy for Libya).

In every case, the objective is to control and claim Islam. To control it, the states attempt to set up an official clergy to whom they guarantee a monopoly on religious activities: they put Islam under state control by turning the mullahs into functionaries and creating centralized institutions. The state creates Islamic universities and state *madrasa*. In Afghanistan, the Faculty of Religious Sciences was created in 1951. In Tunisia the Zaytuna, a famous Islamic *madrasa*, was attached to the university in 1958, and a Grand Mufti of the Republic named; in April 1987 a Higher Islamic Council was created. In Morocco the Qarawin, the equivalent of the Zaytuna, became a state university in 1960, and in 1980 King Hasan II created a High Council of Ulamas. In Algeria in February 1966 a Higher Islamic Council was created and granted the monopoly on *fatwa;*[16] in 1984 the Islamic University Amir Abd al-Qadir was created and directed by Muhammad Ghazali, an Egyptian MB who was replaced in 1990 by another Egyptian. Occasionally the state attempts to outlaw neighborhood mosques in favor of large cathedral mosques, which are easier to control (Morocco).[17]

We are witnessing a process of clericalization of Islam by the states, which are aiming to counter Islamism, and the proliferation of new, uncontrolled, self-authorizing clerics and mullahs. But in order to proceed with this clericalization, they are striking a neofundamentalist chord (the reform of mores, the status of women, *sharia*, and so on) and offering important positions to the reputedly moderate MBs, such as the Egyptian Ghazali in Algeria and Zayd al-Kilani in Jordan.

The reclaiming of Islam also takes the form of a return to Islamic discourse in the official media and the re-Islamization of law, even in "progressive" states such as Algeria, where Friday became an official holy day in 1976. The official radio stations and journals are being opened up to neofundamentalist preaching: *Al-Liwa al-islami,* an official Islamic journal in Egypt, has a higher circulation than the famous *Al-Ahram.*[18] In December 1991 the Egyptian Security Court condemned the writer Ala'a Hamid to eight years in prison for blasphemy. Religious programs are becoming more numerous on television everywhere, including in communist Afghanistan beginning in 1986. In 1972 secular Turkey joined the Organization of the Islamic Conference, and in 1982 it introduced mandatory religious instruction in primary and secondary schools. In Tunisia, President Ben Ali, who took power in 1987, made a point of promoting the country's Arab-Muslim identity while severely repressing the Islamists: this translated into an increase in the number of religious programs on television, the appointment of a minister of religious affairs, the restoration of the Islamic University of Zaytuna, and so on.

In the realm of law, re-Islamization is evident everywhere. It affects constitutions, personal status (the question of women), and penal law. Even the two secular dictatorships, Syria and Iraq, have been forced to make concessions. Religious references are reintroduced into constitutions: article 2 of the Egyptian constitution of 1971 specifies that the *sharia* is "the main source of legislation"; the Syrian constitutions of 1971 and 1973 reintroduce the requirement that the president be a Muslim. The Afghan constitution of 1987 specifies that Islam is the state religion.

States that had previously legislated without taking the *sharia* into account (even if they mentioned it in their texts) began in 1979 explicitly to claim it as their own. The law on personal status was promulgated by presidential decree in Egypt in 1979, although it was still criticized by the most ardent fundamentalists. In 1983 Sudan proclaimed the shariatic penal code. In Pakistan General Zia introduced a system of shariatic tribunals to function parallel to the ordinary tribunals; new laws were put into effect (in 1979, shariatic penalties and authorized collection of the *zakat,* "the Islamic tax," on bank accounts; in 1984, the law of testimony); but the *Sharia* Bill, presented in 1985 to definitively replace Anglo-Saxon law, was in fact never passed. The Algerian Family Code of 1984 reintroduced into divorce and child custody the Quranic dissymmetry between men and women.[19] A new Family Code was promulgated in 1992 in reunified Yemen: polygamy was thus made legal in South Yemen. In 1986 even the secular Indian parliament made the Islamic Code obligatory with respect to the personal status of Muslims.[20] Turkey is a separate case, since secularity is in its constitution, but without openly saying so the state made concessions to local forces: the veil is authorized in certain universities, forbidden in others; the obligatory teaching manuals for religion give only the Muslim point of view.

The reclaiming of Islamism by states also occurred through politics, in which Islamist participation grew during the 1980s, even though this participation came to an abrupt (and temporary?) halt in 1991.

In Malaysia in 1982 the leader of the restless Islamic Youth Movement, Anwar Ibrahim, joined the centrist coalition that governs the country, the United Malays National Organization, and became successively minister of culture, of agriculture, and of education (in 1987). In 1984 and 1987 the Egyptian MBs, within the framework of an electoral coalition, obtained first twelve, then thirty-two seats in parliament, but boycotted the 1990 elections. In Jordan in 1989 parliamentary elections were held for the first time in twenty-two years; Islamist candidates (MBs and independents) took thirty-four of forty-two seats (twenty-two of these thirty-four being MB). A Muslim Brother, Abd al-Latif Arabiyya, was elected president of the National Assembly, and the cabinet formed in January 1991 included several MBs. The MBs disappeared from the Jordanian cabinet during a ministerial shakeup in September 1991, but Arabiyya was reelected president of the National Assembly with the support of partisans of the king. In Morocco, while repressing the Al-Adl wal-Ihsan party, the monarchy supported a neofundamentalist group, Abdellilah Benkirane's Jama'at al-Islamiyya. In Tunisia, the Islamic Tendency Movement, rebaptized Hizb al-Nahda, gained 14.5 percent of the votes in the elections of April 1989, but found itself outlawed in 1991. An identical sequence of events occurred in Algeria, where the FIS, after winning 54 percent of the vote in municipal elections in June 1990, attempted a coup and saw its leaders arrested by the army a year later; it again carried the legislative elections in December 1991, and found itself outlawed in the weeks that followed.

The last chapter in the states' reclaiming of Islam concerns diplomacy. Since independence, Algeria has controlled the Grand Mosque in Paris, whose rector, Sheikh Tijani Haddam, became a member of the Algerian High Committee in January 1992. The delegations from Al-Azhar University sent both to central Asia and to Africa are resuming the general lines of Egyptian diplomacy: to thwart Iran, Libya, Sudan, and the radical MBs.

Islamist themes were thus mixed together, reclaimed, watered down, but also distributed more widely. The enfeeblement of Islamism into neofundamentalism brought an end to the revolutionary dynamic but contributed to the popularization and legalization of re-Islamization.

The Vitality of the Nation-States

The supranational networks (the MB, the World Muslim League) play a definite role in the distribution of Islamist propaganda, but, as we have seen, they have never been able to shape an international policy that amounts to anything more than a reflection of the conflicts of interest among regional states. They therefore find themselves reduced to agreement on their smallest common denominator: pure neofundamentalist propaganda, isolated from its political dimension. It is true that this propaganda in favor of the re-Islamization of society can have geostrategic consequences, relating essentially to the question of the integration of Muslim immigrants in Western society. For the rest, the place of the *sharia* in Saudi law bears no relationship to the question of Saudi Arabia's strategic alliances, as we saw during the Gulf war. One could almost say the same for Iran, which is primarily following a policy of regional power. Thus the nation-state framework continues to be the determining one.

When Islamists participate in politics, it is on a national level and based on local stakes. The positions taken by the MB have always been tied extremely closely to the situations in their respective countries—collaborationist in Kuwait and Jordan, pacific opposition in Egypt, armed opposition in Libya and Syria: it is the domestic situation and not the ideology of each branch that determines the positions adopted. Although the MB maintains a supranational agency, the same cannot be said for the Maghrebis, Afghans, former Soviet Muslims, and Turks, whose organizations are always adapted to the national framework. Despite its references to the Muslim *umma*, the FIS is an Algerian nationalist movement as much as an Islamist movement. It is appropriate to speak henceforth of Islamo-nationalism.

A significant case is that of the former Soviet Union: the decomposition of the empire prompted Islamist groups to organize on the basis of the new states and not to establish a supranational authority. Stalin had organized Soviet Islam into four geographic *muftiyya* (spiritual directorates) in 1941: Europe and Siberia, Northern Caucasus, Azerbaijan, Central Asia, and Kazakhstan. These four *muftiyya* are now breaking apart with the creation of new national borders: the Turkmans, Tadzhikis, and Kazakhs have split off from the *muftiyya* of Central Asia, which is considered exclusively Uzbeki. The *muftiyya* of the Northern Caucasus splintered in 1991 into five entities, corresponding to administrative and political divisions (four autonomous republics and one autonomous region, all included in the Russian Republic). The only active Islamist party in the entire former Soviet territory, the Islamic Renaissance Party, created in 1990, proved incapable of maintaining the *umma* of Soviet Muslims and splintered into national branches, the "Russian" section under Tartar and Northern Caucasian direction, while the Tadzhiki branch is autonomous.

The de-ideologization of international relations is confirmed by the American attitude toward Islamism. The notion of a radical opposition between fundamentalism and the West is typically French, as is the association between Islamism and terrorism. The American attitude has been more ambiguous: Americans have never seen Islamism as an ideological enemy. They have favored conservative fundamentalism (Saudi Arabia, Pakistan, General Numayri's Sudan), in order to take the wind out of the radicals' sails. They accepted as a lesser evil the cultural anti-Westernism of the MBs and of all the conservative fundamentalists, since it seemed primarily an obstacle to Iranian and Soviet expansion. But they supported large sectors of radical Islamism until the Gulf war (the Afghan Hizb-i Islami, which also had contacts with the FIS in Algeria and Ghannouchi in Tunisia, was armed by the Americans until 1989). The Americans have subcontracted to their Muslim allies (Pakistan and Saudi Arabia) the management of certain Islamist groups: since 1982 the Saudi embassy in Washington has housed a "Department of Islamic Affairs," directed by Prince Muhammad ibn Faysal ibn Abd al-Rahman, who is active in Islamization programs for black Americans and who maintains contact with American Islamic organizations (such as the Muslim Students' Association, founded in 1963, one of whose leaders during the 1970s was Muhammad Abu Sayyid, an Egyptian MB now established in Saudi Arabia.)

Thus the impact of Islamism, aside from the parentheses of the Iranian revolution and the war in Afghanistan, is essentially sociocultural: it marks the streets and customs but has no power relationship in the Middle East. It does not influence either state borders or interests. It has not created a "third force" in the world. It has not even been able to offer the Muslim masses a concrete political expression for their anticolonialism. Can it offer an economic alternative or deeply transform a society? The answer seems to be no.

The Islamic Economy: Between Illusions and Rhetoric

T HE CONCEPT OF an Islamic economy seems to be a twentieth-century creation. In the earlier Islamic tradition, the economy was not considered an autonomous agent: the economic act (buying, selling, owning . . .) was merely one aspect of human activity in general, and as such was regulated by the *sharia*. The *sharia* sets forth a certain number of concepts with an economic impact:[1] the *zakat* (taxing of certain goods, such as harvests, with an eye to allocating these taxes to expenditures that are also explicitly defined, such as aid to the needy); the interdiction of chance *(gharar)*, that is, of the presence of any element of uncertainty, in a contract (which excludes not only insurance but also the lending of money without participation in the risks); and, finally, the prohibition of what is referred to as usury *(riba)*;[2] all of this defines the permissible use of money to buy goods. The *sharia* also pronounces on inheritance, property, usufruct, booty, community rights, and so on. As always in Muslim law, these concepts are constructed on the basis of isolated prescriptions, anecdotes, examples, words of the Prophet, all gathered together and systematized by commentators according to an inductive, casuistic method.

132

For traditionalist ulamas, these prescriptions are elements of Muslim law among others: in no way do they carve out an autonomous space that could be called "commercial law" or an economic theory, even if they have consequences on economic activity. A good example of this process can be found, curiously, in the writings of Imam Khomeini: in his work *Tawzih al-masa'il* (The explanation of problems) he approaches the economy as the classical ulamas do; the term "economy" does not appear; the chapter on selling and buying *(kharid o forush)* comes after the one on pilgrimage and presents economic questions as individual acts open to moral analysis: "To lend [*without interest,* on a note from the lender] is among the good works that are particularly recommended in the verses of the Quran and in the Tradition."[3]

As we have seen, the Salafist reformers were fairly uninterested in socioeconomic questions. Reflection on the Islamic economy is thus an Islamist novelty despite the recent appearance of a conservative technocratic trend (especially in Saudi and Pakistani milieus) that endeavors to adapt modern banking practices to Quranic norms.

The Islamic Economy: An Ideological Construct

As in the case of politics, the Islamists took a category, the "economy," that had been isolated and defined by Western modernity: the "economy" *(iqtisad)* is becoming the object of specific research, as indicated by the large number of books or articles devoted exclusively to it in the past half-century, instead of being integrated into generalized treatises on law.[4] The Islamists have undertaken the systematization and conceptualization of basic shariatic prescriptions in order to construct a coherent and functional ensemble that would offer a middle ground between the two systems of the twentieth century, Marxism and capitalism.[5] Capitalism never having been an economic ideology, it is Marxism that is the mirror and foil of the Islamist effort. Whatever the synthesis created in the name of an Islamic economy, it is above all an ideological construct.

The point of departure for the economy according to the Islamists lies not in the concepts of the *sharia* (usury, and so on), as it does for the ulamas, but in an anthropology like the one we have already encountered in Chapter 3: a "theological anthropology" in which man is defined as a creature of God, gifted with reason, evolving in the realms both of need and of salvation—in short, as a goal-oriented, teleological "nature" (with its physical needs), oriented toward the goal of its salvation. The economy exists because man is a creature of needs; it therefore aims to satisfy these needs. But because man's superior aim is salvation, his economic activity must be exercised within the ethical framework defined by the Quran. The economy is a means, not an end. Islamist theoreticians do not praise asceticism: respecting values allows the believer not only to enjoy the goods of the earth, but necessarily brings about the prosperity of the community as well as economic development.

Evil is a logic that causes man to forget his goal in the satisfaction of his needs: it is excess, bloating *(tavarrum)*. It is therefore necessary to strike a balance between consumption on the one hand, and redistribution to the poor on the other.

Sometimes more radical Islamists draw the philosophical and anthropological definition of the economy (such as the extension of man conceived of as a creature of needs) from the analysis of Western classics (mostly Rousseau and Marx), and illustrate it with Quranic citations; they position Islam as the solution to the aporias of Western thought, but within a conceptual framework established by Western philosophy.[6] Thus Abdul Hasan Bani Sadr adopted a Marxist-leaning anthropology ("work and only work is the basis of the relationship between man and God, between man and others, between man and things"), but based it on a quotation from the Quran: "Man will possess only what he acquires through his own efforts" (sura 53 [The Star], verse 39), concluding with the assertion that the right to property depends above all on work.[7]

The Islamist Economy: A Social-Democratic Vision

Even among the most radical Islamists, there is no communist interpretation of the Islamic economy. The concept of "social justice," even of "Islamic socialism," however, does appear among the MBs and the Iranians;[8] this socialist current tends to highlight areas of Islamic law that allow for the limitation of property, whereas the conservative current makes the right to property the cornerstone of the Islamic economy. Generally the radicals develop a "social-democratic" vision of the economy: they recognize private property, but want the State to ensure social justice through limiting the accumulation of wealth and through its redistribution, systematizing the scattered economic principles in the *sharia* (*zakat,* and so on). In keeping with the logic of legitimating innovation by returning to the sources, they hark back to the first Islamic society, at the time of the Prophet, whose companion, Abu Dharr, is considered a harbinger of Islamic socialism.

The limitation on accumulation is implemented by condemning whatever goes beyond the satisfaction of needs: luxury, amassing wealth, certain types of income—in short, any income that is not earned through work or running a risk, basically, hoarding (*ihtikar*).[9] Thus it is necessary to begin by placing limits on the thirst for possessing; the first limit is the ethical model of a good Muslim, the paradigm of the Prophet, who offers an image of self-control and moderation. But radical Islamists do not consider this ethical exhortation to be sufficient; they interpret the Quran's prescriptions as a system that authorizes the State to organize the redistribution of wealth. The first limitation is on ownership, even if it is lawful in principle. This limitation has a theological basis: man has only usufruct of the earth and its goods, the highest ownership of which is God's alone.[10] This highest level of ownership can successively devolve to the *umma,* then to the Islamic state, embodied for Shiites in the imam.[11] Thus a policy of nationalization and state ownership is justified, reinforced by the Quranic interdiction of the appropriation of certain "primary goods": water, mines, pasturage and combustibles.[12]

Next one must ensure redistribution, first because it averts accumulation, second because it allows one to fulfill the legal obligations of the religion (*sadaqa* and *zakat*). *Zakat* meets both requirements: it deals with capital and serves to limit accumulation, but must benefit specific categories of the population, including the needy, as well as defend the religion and the community.[13] The laws of inheritance, by favoring the breaking up of patrimony, also work against accumulation, for in Islamic law there is no privileged heir: parents, descendants, and relatives inherit equally as a function of their proximity to the defunct and of their sex (a half-share for women).

This delegation from God to the *umma*, and from the *umma* to the Islamic state allows radical Islamists to consider the state an engine of economic planning, justifying a policy of bank nationalization and of centralized economic development, which would turn out in particular to be the credo of Iranian governments under the authority of Prime Minister M. H. Musavi (1981–1989).

But many Islamists reject this socialist-leaning reading of Islam; they emphasize instead all that is compatible with capitalism in Islam (the right to ownership and a market economy) while assigning the state a relatively important role in planning, fighting monopolies, and acting as an engine for industrialization and social action; this is the line of thought of the Turkish Prosperity Party, the Iranian Hujjatiyya group, and the Algerian FIS. The latter two examples indicate that there is no systematic link between radicalism in politics, ideology, and economics.

One point is generally absent from Islamist economic thought, whether moderate or radical, except in the writings of Sayyid Qutb: it is the question of agrarian reform. On the one hand, such reform would imply a reexamination of the concept of ownership, but most of all it would throw into question the *waqf*, endowments whose revenue ensures the functioning of religious institutions. Thus in the Iranian province of Khorasan, 50 percent of the cultivated lands belong to the religious foundation Astan-i Quds, which oversees the mausoleum of the Imam Reza in Mashhad. Questioning *waqf* property, therefore, would mean questioning the foundation of the financial autonomy of the mullahs and mosques. Even during the most Third World period of the Islamic revolution in Iran, there was no agrarian reform. Opposition to agrarian reform has even played a role in Islamist uprisings (Iran, 1963; Afghanistan, 1978).

The Primacy of Ethics

In the Islamist conception of the economy, the ethical model is central. Even if the Quranic prescriptions must be implemented by institutions like the state, they also rest on an anthropology in which man, a creature of needs, must organize his activities according to a moral model, which is that of the Prophet. According to Bani Sadr, the ideal in an Islamic society is "to produce according to one's capacities, to consume according to virtue [*taqwa*]," for only this limitation of consumption can ensure a surplus and its redistribution—voluntary and automatic for those who follow the path of virtue, forced for those who do not.[14] Virtue is self-limitation. Redistribution ensures that everyone's needs will be met, since God could not have put his creature into a world of scarcity: scarcity is a consequence of hoarding, thus an absence of virtue. The satisfaction of needs enables one to devote oneself to the essentials: "Material self-sufficiency is an opportunity to advance toward virtue."[15] Institutions exist only to lead man to the ethical model. If each man followed the Prophet's ethical model on his own, there would be no need to legislate it from without. Even in as political an author as Bani Sadr, state authority disappears in favor of the figure of the imam, defined as someone who does not govern, but who symbolizes and unifies a society that has finally become "one" *(tawhidi)*; his mere presence at the highest point of the system prevents the constitution of a separate seat of power, capable of appropriating the surplus to maintain its power. The imam is the "symbol of consensus" and "the mirror that reflects the image of *towhid*."[16]

Respect for ethics is seen as a way to enjoy the goods of the earth, unlike in Christian asceticism. A leitmotif of the "Islamic economy" is the combination of the respect for ethics and prosperity. The world is not a "vale of tears," but was entrusted with a sense of pleasure, for lifelong enjoyment, to man. In every case, the basic economic actor remains the individual, who behaves in conformity with the norms of the *sharia,* which are implemented by the state.

❖   ❖   ❖

The image of the "left-wing Islamist," incarnated in the Iranian revolution, was little by little supplanted by a less state-oriented and more liberal image, at least with respect to the economy, in Iran as in the rest of the Muslim world. This evolution goes hand in hand both with Islamism's shift toward neofundamentalism and with the diffusion of the Islamist message to a wider audience (businessmen, students of economics, and others). In any case, the Islamist program has never been collectivist, unlike Christian liberation theology, which attempts at times to make the base communities the economic actors. Although one can find a certain associative or cooperative spirit among the Islamist left (for example, the militants of the "reconstruction crusade" in Iran), the general attitude of the Islamists, and even more so of the neofundamentalists, is favorable to individual free enterprise, balanced by a moral discourse regarding the preferred practices of the economic actors. Both the Algerian FIS and the Turkish Prosperity Party (the reference to earthly pleasure is no accident) support individual initiative and privatization: here political radicalism (for the FIS) or technocratism has no fascination with a socialist model (which is, besides, rapidly losing viability).

Khomeini's Iran: A Variation on Third World State Socialism

In Iran, the slogan "Islamize the economy" had two different meanings, depending on who said it. For the Islamists, it meant above all introducing state control and redistributing wealth toward the people; this vision, which was that of all Third World models of state socialism, prevailed in Iran until Khomeini's death. For the conservatives (the high clergy, the market), it was a matter mostly of protecting private property and furnishing a legal religious framework for seeking profit. This permanent conflict resulted in the blockage of all important decisions: those in favor of state control sat in the parliament, which has considerable power over economic matters (voting on laws, but also the censure of ministers), while the "liberals" occupied the Supervisory Council, controlled by the high clergy and responsible for verifying the conformity with Islam of the laws passed by parliament. The supporters of each school Islamize their arguments in order to legitimate them. There is no automatic correspondence between political radicalism and state socialism: economic liberals, such as the group constituted by Ayatollah Azari Qumi around the newspaper *Risalat* or the association Hujjatiyya, are highly dogmatic on a theological level.

For the most part the Supervisory Council has opposed laws that would have had an economic impact (like agrarian reform) but has never tried to define positively what an Islamic economy would look like. In fact, under the pretext of conformity with Islam, the Council constantly defended a liberal vision of the economy, in opposition to the state-controlled Islamo-socialist vision of the parliament, which translated into a series of measures that had nothing Islamic about them in and of themselves, but were in keeping with a Third World socialist vision: control of imports through licensing, setting of foreign exchange rates, a state monopoly on some activities, impediments to the development of national capitalism in favor of the state sector, and so on.

On balance, the Islamization of the Iranian economy is superficial. The *waqf*, which the Shah had attempted to control without totally eliminating, have been fully reestablished but are often managed in a perfectly technocratic fashion: the Astan-i Quds, which oversees considerable *waqf* connected with the mausoleum of the Imam Reza, is closer to a modern financial holding company than to a pious foundation, except insofar as it maintains a role of philanthropic sponsorship. Similarly, the revolutionary foundations ("Foundation of the Disinherited," "Foundation of Martyrs") are patronage-oriented holding companies that ensure the channeling of revenues to groups and milieus supporting the regime (but not to specific classes or sectors of the population). The diversion of revenues (the impoverishment of salaried employees, the enrichment of those who are in an intermediary position between the state and the market) is common to all regimes of the Third World, where a centralized state dominates the market economy in a system short on currency.[17] This has nothing to do with a redistribution based on the quest for social justice.

More surprisingly, the financial system has barely been Islamized; Christians, for example, are not subject to a poll tax and pay according to the common scheme. Insurance is maintained (even though chance, the very basis for insurance, should theoretically be excluded from all contracts). The contracts signed with foreigners all accept the matter of interest. The basic mechanisms of the economy oscillate between capitalist liberalism and state-controlled socialism.

As for the financial and banking system, it functions essentially on speculation. In Iran, 1,300 Islamic credit unions "became usurers' dens";[18] under the influence of the market, they were regrouped into an "Organization of the Islamic Economy" and pay annual interest rates of from 25 to 50 percent that are designated as "participation in the profits of enterprise"; they thereby pull into the speculative sector savings that the state banks, more concerned with investment, can remunerate at only 9 percent. In any case, the principles governing the Iranian banks are the same as those of the Sunni Islamic financial institutions that sprang up in the 1980s.

The Conservative and Technocratic Version of the Islamic Economy: The Islamic Bank

Today there are two versions of an Islamic economy. The Islamist, socialist, and state-run version existed in Iran only during the Khomeini era (1979–1989). The technocratic, conservative version was put partially into practice in Pakistan and in some Islamic banks or financial institutions in the Middle East. The two endeavors occurred during the same period, starting in 1980. If we look closely, we see that in all cases the establishment of an "Islamic economy" concerns the banking system exclusively, and that on this point there is essentially no difference between the two visions. Curiously, despite their penchant for productivity, the Islamists seem quite uninterested in developing an Islamic system of production. The Egyptian MBs under Hasan al-Banna created a "Company for Islamic Transactions" (sharikat al-mu'amalat al-islamiyya) in 1938,[19] an investment company based on Islamic principles (the distribution of profits), as well as small industrial enterprises; but these institutions did not survive the political crisis of 1948. In fact the Islamists have contented themselves with preaching the Islamization of the financial and banking systems on a far from revolutionary basis.

The idea of an "Islamic bank" rests on a technocratic and non-ideological conception of the Islamic economy, one that does not extend beyond the financial and, occasionally, fiscal domain.[20] The mechanism aims, in countries such as Pakistan and Saudi Arabia, to Islamize the current practices of the modern economy in the fiscal and banking areas, without calling into question the social and political order: we are dealing here with a "technocratic" extension of traditionalist fundamentalism, which aims to enable a good Muslim to participate in a modern economy.[21] The end result of economic activity, not to mention its social impact, is ignored: this is a far cry from political Islamism. Yet this technocratic vision governs both the Iranian banking system and the Islamic financial institutions associated with MB circles.

The objective of the Islamic bank is to make depositors' money bear fruit according to a system that complies with the *sharia;* the notion is far from the moral conception of the loan, according to which it is a pious act to refuse any growth in the sum.[22] Lawful profit is profit in which the borrower takes part in the financial operation and thus shares the risks, losses, and profits. The two main types of contracts provided for are: the joint venture (*mudaraba,* or *muzarebe* in Persian pronunciation), in which the bank furnishes the capital, receives its share of the profits, and bears its share of the losses; and the partnership (*musharaka*), in which the bank cannot invest more than its private partner and owns shares that can be resold.

It is interesting that there is no divergence between Shiites and Sunnis on this matter of the Islamic bank. Iran developed a banking system on the same bases as the one created by Pakistani or Saudi theoreticians. The "Islamic banking system," the object of a 1983 decree, is in fact a reconciliation of capitalistic practices and the Islamic prohibition against interest. There are joint venture (*muzarebe)* and partnership (*musharaka)* contracts in Iran, as well as the concept of the "anticipated sale" (*salaf),* a legal form of loan.[23] Banks are required to make interest-free loans, but fees are deducted. Banks can also invest directly according to complex terms and conditions that are tightly controlled by the state. There are two types of deposits: *qard hasan,* a bank deposit made by individuals that bears no interest, but on which the bank is authorized to offer bonuses or various incentives to depositors; and the term investment, in which the bank and the depositor share the risks and profits.

As for the matter of taxation, Pakistan introduced the *zakat,* the Islamic tax, in the form of an automatic and obligatory tax on bank accounts; the sums collected are given to a special committee responsible for distributing them among the beneficiaries provided for in the *sharia* (including the collectors themselves).

Manifestations of the Islamic Economy outside Iran

The Islamization of the economy consists solely in installing "Islamic" windows that open onto a reality that is far less Islamic, but are based on the model one could call "conservative techno-cratic": the goal is to offer the believer a means of making his money grow without violating the *sharia.* These enterprises are always private. The large Islamic banks (Dubai Islamic Bank, founded in 1975, Faysal Islamic Bank, Kuwait Finance, Al-Taqwa Islamic Bank) are completely separate from the Islamic states: they serve essentially to make the capital of high-level shareholders bear fruit and to attract popular savings. The creation of an Islamic bank is not proof of an Islamist state. Saudi Arabia has never Islamized its official banking system. Private Islamic banks do not aim to change the society, but to capture a specific new clientele.

The theory behind Islamic banks is that they avoid sin while yielding more than ordinary banks.[24] Established in countries with unstable, high-inflation economies (Iran, Pakistan), the banks cannot draw their profits from industrial production, yet they must pay yields higher than inflation. The necessity of producing profits to appear more attractive than ordinary banks implies a certain economic adventurism, thus speculation. The concept of sharing risks and profits, even when applied honestly, encourages the banks to get involved in only short-term operations. No matter where Islamic banks have been created, or where "normal" banks have created an

"Islamic division" (such as the BCCI, with Pakistani management and Dubai capital, the resounding crash of which shook the Muslim world in 1991), they have functioned essentially on speculation and short-term investment.

Sooner or later, speculation entails a crash. The examples of crashes of "Islamic" financial institutions are legion. In Egypt, the Al-Rayan Bank, founded in the early 1980s on the concept of sharing profits (which introduces the concept of sharing risks, which is essential in order to distinguish legitimate profit from interest), boasted profits between 24 and 30 percent, while the state banks were offering 13 percent.[25] It soon came to light that such revenues were drawn from speculation on international markets: the ephemeral success of the Islamic banks was founded on playing the most unstable elements of Western markets (the gold market in New York in the case of Al-Rayan); when circumstances changed (the Wall Street crash of October 1987), bankruptcy loomed.

The economies of the Middle East are quite often economies of speculation, because of the fact that the state is the primary agent of economic impetus (nationalism, protectionism, control of import and export licenses as well as of currency); the state turns out, generally, to be hostile to national capitalism (Iran, Syria, Algeria), but it maintains a relationship of patronage between bureaucrats and speculators. It is the state machine that allows the appropriation of surplus; hence the image of the "functionary-prebendary," in Michel Seurat's apt term.[26] Money is invested in speculation and not in production: despite its boastful discourse, the "Islamic economy" is no different from the economies of speculation that support social groups who have attached themselves to a particular state apparatus. Islamization often merely provides more ample, "whiter" garb for these speculation- and patronage-oriented relationships.

The lack of real impact of an Islamization policy on the economy and the society can be seen in Pakistan, where the establishment of *zakat* has had no serious effect on the redistribution of income, if one assumes that the *zakat* is being honestly divided up.[27]

Thus Islamic banks are not institutions used to finance Islamist movements. Behind these banks, we are likely to find Saudis,

Kuwaitis, and Pakistanis. It is true that a certain number of Islamic bank founders, such as the Saudi Salih Kamil who directs the Baraka group, are devout Muslims, personally concerned with offering an Islamic alternative to the existing banks. Many have ties to the MB, including Kamil himself, or the Saudi Tijani Abu Jederi, a member of Hassan al-Turabi's Islamic Front who in 1983 was named to the board of directors of the Islamic Banking System, a subsidiary of Al-Baraka, based in Copenhagen. But the Islamic banks have taken care not to become identified with Islamist movements.[28]

The goal is to tap into a type of savings among "Islamic" depositors and not to finance Islamic movements or even to contribute to the creation of Islamized spaces. The "Islamic bank" is a marketing tool and not a scheme for a new economic order. That Islam is an inviting product is confirmed by the fact that several banks, without changing their commercial practices, have opened an "Islamic" branch, or even just a window, or provide "Islamic" interpretations of their practices. The following example, which is quite typical, appeared in a bilingual French-Arab monthly:

> The Winterthur Company . . . is offering very favorable conditions for the insurance of your possessions; and we are doing even more. For moral reasons connected to religion, it is not desirable to speak of life insurance. Winterthur has established a savings account to be withdrawn by specified parties. The name of this contract is *Cap Retraite.* The idea is this: by signing this contract, you open a savings account that is remunerated, for several years, at an annual rate of 12.5 percent. As you will see, Winterthur pays its clients a share of 95 percent of the profits . . .[29]

In short, it is a matter of translating into Islamic terms (no speculation on death, share in the profits) a financial product defined by the French minister of finance and unrelated to a Quranic exegesis. The financial facts don't change; the presentation does.

The Impossible Islamic Economy

The Islamization of the economy is thus largely rhetorical. The failure of the Iranian revolution to transform the society chips away at the dream of a purely Islamic economy. All a devout Muslim can do is bring his activities into conformity with the *sharia:* to do so, he can either withdraw from the modern world or utilize the instruments for the purification of profits, the Islamic banks and windows. But as far as the economy goes, these institutions function between two models, neither of which is specifically Islamic: the declining model of the centralized, socialist-leaning state, or the triumphant model of liberalism and capitalism.

The "Islamization" of the economy is, to borrow a term from computer terminology, an interface between two systems: one ethical and legal (the *sharia*), the other the reality of the universal economy. The conversion works in only one direction; it is a simply transference, with hardly any influence on the reality. This interface can function not only in terms of rhetoric, but also through the "ruse" *(hile)* that enables one to get around interdictions, particularly the one regarding interest: the ruse can be considered legal if appearances are sound.[30]

The economic institution is never considered as such: everything rests on individual virtue.[31] But the economies of modern societies assume that whatever the motivation and the goals of each individual, mechanisms are in place that meld the heterogeneity of the actors and their actions into a whole, the market, independent of their individual wills, but more or less regulated by institutions (states, stock exchanges). The idea of building a modern economy that would function only through the virtue of the economic actors is an illusion, a sweet one to be sure in terms of collectivist utopias, but for this reason totally nonfunctional, as various attempts have shown. And, in economics as in politics, when virtue doesn't function, its opposite emerges: the abuse of power, speculation, and corruption, the banes of "Islamized" economic systems.

Here again the social sciences are unregarded.[32] Islamism is distinguished by a total absence of socioeconomic analyses (causes of inflation, definition of economic agents, and so on) except in the rare instances in which a recent university graduate sets himself the task of translating his final honors paper into vaguely religious terms.

The object of the reflection is never the society, but man and the revealed text. We are thus still within the framework of the meeting of anthropology and ethics: if the economic agent acted justly and with the *sharia* in mind, then the society (and he himself) would be just and prosperous. Disorder comes from transgressing the rules set forth by God, which aim to keep man at a happy medium between the satisfaction of his needs and his ethical goal. Like politics, the Islamic economy is the filling in of a matrix borrowed from the West with legal terminology based on an ethical anthropology.

❖ 9 ❖

Afghanistan: Jihad and Traditional Society

T HE WAR IN Afghanistan allowed Islamist militants to put
into effect their conceptions of the organization, since the main
resistance parties (the Jamaat-i Islami, the two Hizb-i Islami,
but also the Shiite parties) are Islamist. It is true that the case of
Afghanistan is particular in the sense that we are dealing mostly with
rural guerrillas in a very traditional society. But the weight of Islam
is such that no other ideology, nationalist or secular, could have
established itself in the resistance. Without attempting to tally up
ten years of Islamist practice, we will focus exclusively on the models
of war in operation in the Afghan resistance, and examine the extent
to which the ideological model of jihad allowed new forms of organization to be imposed.

A war, especially a guerrilla war, does not occur in the abstract space
of a chessboard. It presupposes first of all the existence of a society
with its own cultural relationship to violence and conflict. It implies
social mobilization and is related to the political structure of the
society. It brings into action individuals who think in terms of a
strategy—defining objectives and the means of attaining them. In a

guerrilla war, the objectives are primarily political: What should be seized? What is a victory? The goal is to determine where the seat of power lies, which, when taken, will ensure victory. Is it with the state? We will see that during the uprisings of 1978–1980 few Afghan *muja-hidin* perceived the state as the ultimate goal of their movement. The exercise of war is structured by ideological models of collective violence (tribal war and jihad); these models presuppose a geographic space, a temporality, and an end result that are not those of modern guerrilla warfare as it was conceptualized by Mao Tse-tung, in which the goal is the seizing of state power through the organization of "liberated zones" as countersocieties.

The relationship to the state traditionally maintained by the various Afghan communities is one of externality and compromise, not of exclusion.[1] That is, the violence that regularly characterizes these relationships aims to reestablish an equilibrium, after measuring the balance of strength on which the necessary compromises will be based. Violence in general, whether it opposes the state and communities, or individuals or even family members, is not an attempt to break off relations or to destroy the adversary; rather, it aims to establish a complex system of priority, which can be expressed through other symbolic relationships (one gives or takes a wife according to the rules).[2] Tribal violence or even political violence (coups d'état, fights for succession, and so on) takes place in an essentially private space, according to rules that are more anthropological than political.[3] Ethnic conflicts, family vendettas, the arrogance of a ruler or notable combine at the moment of crisis to define alliance networks, to which the state will be both judge and party. But everyone needs for the state to exist, for it ensures functions that no one wants to take over, not out of deference, but out of disdain for these functions. Pillaging depends on the existence of some wealth; obtaining subsidies and arms depends on the existence and operation of a state that can implement strategies to receive them. For contraband to exist, there must be borders. To be chief of one's village, it is useful for a minister or a general (and, later, a humanitarian organization or an information service) to give the nod of approval that marks the definitive distancing of the rival (this input can range from arresting the rival, to subsidizing the official candidate, to transferring administrative duties to the loyal chief). Hence there ultimately develops a certain codification of violence within a determined space and temporality, according to tactical rules that are without a strategy: this codification makes coups d'état closer to vendettas, tribal conflicts, or ethnic rivalries than to the imposition of a new political model (the communist coup d'état was perceived, in the days that followed, as the triumph of the Ghilzay Pakhtuns over the Durani Pakhtuns, although the ideological dimension was quickly felt). This ambivalent relationship between the state and groups is reconstituted regularly after each crisis. It was always a factor throughout the war, both in the resistance and in the regime.

Yet this war introduced profoundly new elements without eliminating certain permanent situations. The first novelty was the notion of total war, that is, of a war that threatens the society at its roots instead of being one of its modes of operation (and no doubt regulation): modern war has no closed space unto itself, either geographic or social. There is no longer a battlefield, a separation between public and private, a specific time for combat. Aviation, air-transported artillery and troops, brings combat everywhere, at any moment, and without distinguishing among people. One leaves the closed space, the compartmentalization inherent in Afghanistan, to enter an open space; since the old solidarities that defined the closed spaces had a hard time standing up to modern war, this open space was either empty (the population having fled en masse) or anarchic, or, finally, structured by previously unknown political institutions: the political parties of the resistance. The second novel element is thus the politicization of the Afghan resistance, perceptible in the establishment of political parties, which were formed according to three noncontradictory parameters: (1) the ideologization of political life (faced with Marxism, Islam is thought of as a political ideology and not simply as a religion); (2) the necessity of adhering to a party in order to obtain arms (which entails new patronage relationships between chiefs of foreign-based parties and local commanders); and (3) the persistence of traditional solidarities (brotherhoods, ethnicities, clans, families, patronage networks, and so on) beneath modern political forms (parties).

Behind the politicization of the society, we therefore find networks of infrapolitical solidarities, as well as tribal and ethnic fragmentation. Very quickly, in fact, the communist state began to play the traditional tribal game. The more the Afghan resistance endowed itself with political structures, the more the communist state went about ridding itself of all that qualified it as *communist* (abandoning the term "democratic" in the country's name in 1987, recognizing Islam as the official religion, establishing a multiparty system).

This de-ideologization of the state brought about the quasi-disappearance of ideological Islamist references in the Afghan resistance, especially after the departure of Soviet troops in 1989: on the one hand, the parties functioned openly as simple networks of patronage and of ethnic or tribal solidarity; on the other hand, the program of the *mujahidin* became limited to neofundamentalist-type demands.

Does this mean that Afghanistan is back to square one, that the traditional society has again come to the fore now that the superficial modernities have been exhausted? It is true that the explicit discourse of political modernity is weak in both camps: ethnic nationalism and neofundamentalism are the only ideologies that remain after the collapse of Marxism and the crises in Islamism.[4] But the war profoundly changed the society. The intermixing and displacement of segments of the population, as well as the rise in power of a new elite, changed the sociology of the country and led highly insular populations to assume new identities (ethnic, linguistic) beyond their connection to local solidarity groups. But rather than a return to the traditional society, it is more apt to speak of a transference of the solidarity networks and power of a traditional society into a modern and international context. The logic of modern war forced a restructuring of power relationships and of loyalty upon people who had previously only two models of war, which were also traditional: tribal war and jihad.

Regardless of their political tendencies, all the military commanders of the resistance began by borrowing their tactics as well as their strategies from a traditional model of war, that is, from a model that presupposed a defined space and an externalized state. Thus there was a contradiction between the emergence of parties and of modern political ideologies and an abiding traditional vision of war, a nonideological vision—even in jihad—in which one does not aim to destroy the state. In fact, it seems that the true shift toward politics occurred through militarization, and not through the implantation of parties or of modern ideological discourse. It was the necessity of maneuvering one's troops in a strategic space that was no longer defined by solidarity groups, but by a desire to paralyze and thereby destroy the state apparatus, that in certain cases brought about the establishment of political structures that could rise above the fragmentation of solidarity groups, while on the other hand the absence of strategic imperatives, or more exactly of a strategic vision, brought about an appropriation of political structures by preexisting networks, even among the Islamist militants. Militarization and a shift toward political involvement go hand in hand.

We will therefore examine the traditional forms of combat, the relationship to politics that they imply, their persistence in the Afghan resistance, and, finally, the type of societal structure that exists today: a new society, the old tradition maintained, or the transference of the traditional structure into a new sociological reality and discourse.

In the field, there is a wide variety of cases: we go from the state-organized type of front (like Masud's) to the resurgence of medieval military traditions (the *ribat*, a fortress held by a fighting religious brotherhood that transcends tribal cleavages),[5] by way of the implosion of resistance fronts, in which the old cleavages have reemerged in a climate of overarmament and exacerbation that renders ineffectual the traditional modes of mediation and arbitration.

The Traditional Models of War

The Muslim insurgents who first opposed the communist regime, established by a coup d'état on April 27, 1978, and then opposed the Soviet invasion in December 1979 have two models of war: tribal war and jihad; each implies a defined space, strategy, and values and accords priority to formal staging over any real strategy.

Tribal War

Whether or not it is a matter of tribal zones in the strict sense, we find throughout Afghan society solidarity groups called *qawm*, the sociological definition of which can vary (tribal clans, of course, but also endogamous professional groups, people from the same village or valley, an ethnic subgroup, an extended family, caste, or simply any network of patronage formed around an eminent citizen, the *khan*).[6] These groups determine one's allegiance network and constitute the primary identity of every Afghan. The tribal system *stricto sensu* rests on a far narrower definition of these groups, through genealogy, a group legend, a tribal code (in every sense of the word: definition of the ideal warrior, common law, value systems), and an ensemble of institutions peculiar to the tribal world (the *jirga*, or council). The tribal system remains dominant within the Pakhtun ethnic group, particularly in the eastern part of the country. It is there that anthropologists studied the model of tribal war, which will serve in a broad fashion to define traditional war—one that does not integrate politics—and which may serve as a paradigm for the spontaneous mode of waging war in operation within the Afghan resistance.[7]

Tribal war is not a war; that is to say, the framework for violence remains that of ordinary society: the warrior is any adult man, the warlord is the civil chief, the "army" is the mass levy of warriors belonging to the group in question, which is generally struggling against the symmetrically equivalent group in the segmentary structure of tribal society. Tribal war is never total war and takes place in a specific space and at a specific time: fighting occurs among adult men, outside the village—except in the case of vendetta raids—and not during the harvest. The battles are more symbolic than real. The goal is plunder as an end in itself or as a punishment inflicted on the adversary, not the conquest of territory or the destruction of a group. The adversary's very existence is not at stake. What is at stake is preeminence, made manifest in an economic advantage over the other (land or booty). The notions of equilibrium and of the status quo are regular features of the tribal vision of violence and war.

Tribal war is in fact not very mobile; it occurs within the "solidarity space" as designated by the network of a solidarity group (except in tribal zones, it is rare for a *qawm* to occupy a defined space exclusively). Tribal war occurs "in private." The stranger is safer than the native; the inferior is safer than the equal.

Precisely because it takes place at a private level, tribal war is neither ideological nor political: the state being outside the tribal space, a group does not hesitate to form an alliance with it against a rival. The state's existence is not denied, but instrumentalized, on the condition, of course, that it not appear to desire a change in the rules of the game (by constructing a road or a military post, for example). But even in this case, the combat techniques against the state will be the same as in the war among clans, only more demonstrative: one mimics an assault against the post in order to improve one's negotiating position.

Jihad

Jihad, a concept peculiar to the political imagination of Islam, is meant to introduce a radical break: it goes beyond tribal segmentation by appealing to the *umma* and transcends the values and the tribal code by calling on Islam and the *sharia*. It is declared by a religious leader, who is generally outside the tribal world; it does not occur at a private level, but opposes interior and exterior, Islam versus the infidel. It addresses each Muslim as an individual and not his group, his clan, or his ethnicity. By breaking up the *asabiyya* in favor of the *umma*, it therefore effects a rupture with the world of tribal warfare. The tribal obsession with symmetry and balance no longer applies.

Yet in the history of Afghanistan over the past two centuries, the tactics of jihad have been those of tribal war: temporal discontinuity, relative respect of civilians (although women can be booty), demonstration being more important than annihilation, taste for plunder, and rivalry among *qawm* chiefs (the *khan*), which resurfaces the instant victory is in sight and is generally enough to prevent it. Victories are never exploited, and the ulamas have been able to impose *sharia* and discipline only fleetingly. Jihad ignores the ABCs of war according to Clausewitz. Although the scale is larger than that of the vendetta or the revolt, jihad brings no innovation in tactics or in strategy, but only in the references of legitimation. Jihad in fact knows no political space, no state. Its space is that of the *umma*, of the community of Muslims; it is a symbolic space that one traces in an ascending direction, toward conquest, or in a descending one, from the *hijra*. Jihad knows no borders; thus it too has only an instrumental vision of the state, which ends up being devalued. The state *(dawla)* is the provisional incarnation of the Muslim nation *(milla)*; in reality, it exists only in crises and is not institutionalized. The ethical model that is at the heart of the notion of jihad prohibits political structures.

Modern War and Traditional Society

For the first time with the Soviet invasion of 1979, the Afghans were confronted with *total war,* that is, a war that knows no boundary between war and peace, either in space, in time, or between categories of the population. Aerial bombardment can occur anywhere and at any moment of the day or year. More "civilians" are killed than combatants. The Soviet army waged a conventional war, which beginning in 1984 would just barely adapt to the realities of counterguerrilla warfare. The goal of the Soviets was to transform Afghan society into one centered on the state. The Soviets' profoundly state-managed vision contrasted with the Afghans' indifference to the idea of the state.

The Space of War: Center and Closure

The 1978–79 anticommunist insurrection occurred along the lines of the model of jihad described above. Yet from the start, the insurrection space was not a national space. One fights to liberate one's solidarity space, that is, the territory of a *qawm* or of an ensemble of interdependent *qawm*. It is true that the solidarity space is not necessarily a homogeneous territory, enclosed by borders: it is above all an ensemble of networks (*qawm*, brotherhoods, ethnicities); but in any case this space produces its own borders (always in relation to the other *qawm* or other ethnic group). The destruction of the state apparatus is closer to a purification and a symbolic reappropriation of the solidarity space than to a strategic desire for isolation and destruction of the state. One of the primary characteristics of the Afghan resistance is its strategic immobility.

The first level of politicization is the establishment of political parties.[8] Beginning in 1980, most of the Sunni fronts belonged to the so-called Peshawar parties. This membership should not be seen as merely a means of obtaining arms. Political affiliations remained relatively stable over ten years of war. The best-armed parties (Hikmatyar's Hizb, Sayyaf's Ittihad, and Khali's Hizb) remained in the minority in relation to the Jamaat (moderate Islamist) and the Haraka (traditionalist fundamentalist), which would not have been the case if the commanders had joined only to stock up on weapons. The map of political affiliations in Afghanistan would be just as complex as a Western electoral map. Thus, several political parties may be juxtaposed within a single space, with each one's front interwoven among those of its competitors, including duplicate administrations and headquarters. In a large part of the territory, the resistance groups constitute not a mosaic, but an interlinking of identical and competitive networks, each one founded on solidarities that are ultimately expressed by affiliation to a political party.

Modern guerrilla warfare should take place within a geographic space defined in terms of military strategy, with ethnic questions becoming secondary (the typical example of this being Mao Tse-tung's Long March). Guerrilla warfare therefore needs an "open" space. But in Afghanistan, the primary space has remained that of the *qawm*. For an armed group to leave this space, a psychological transformation must occur not only among the combatants, but also among the populations of the other spaces.

Tactics and Strategy as the Insertion of Politics into the Waging of War

The definition of the objective (the Soviet-Afghan post situated on the border of the solidarity space) and the conception of the attack (demonstrating force without aiming to conquer or destroy the objective) are inherited from tribal war; this type of war is essentially defensive and not offensive, since it places little value on capturing the only place whose conquest would end the aggression—the capital, thus the state—and since it rejects the only effective military strategy—the destruction of the adversary's momentum. The warrior doesn't take power; he amasses it.[9] The state in and of itself is not an objective: what is empty attracts the warrior, not what is occupied; you sack the bazaar when the king has left the palace. Similarly, the ideal tactic for most *mujahidin* is that of the surrender of the governmental post after negotiations or betrayal. Which explains a phenomenon that has generally gone unnoticed: during this entire war, the *mujahidin,* with the exception of Commander Masud, almost never attacked a government post, *a fortiori* a Soviet one, of a level higher than that of the company.

It is as if there were a desire (unconscious?) inherent in the *mujahidin* behavior to preserve an equilibrium between war and civil society, an equilibrium that would be thrown into question by the Vietnamese model of systematic assault. Hence no doubt the apparent immobility of many *mujahidin,* who defend themselves like lions but, when it comes to going on the offensive, are content to call a vague de facto cease-fire that will preserve the autonomy of the local community and the permanence of its way of life.

The way in which most of the *mujahidin* fronts have managed the Afghan campaign displays their rejection of the establishment of a counterstate and the desire to maintain an equilibrium, in opposition to the notion of total war. There is none of the fiercely ideological aspect of our wars in Spain or Ireland, in which a man could have his brother shot. The networks not only survive the war, but become an integral part of it. The Soviet reprisals that inevitably followed a successful attack were thus perceived as particularly destabilizing, resulting as they did in the flight of civilian populations and dishonor for the *mujahidin,* who had failed to protect the sacred family domain. The space and temporality of traditional war that they have attempted to preserve has thereby been destroyed. Avoiding reprisals is a priority for the traditional fronts. The resistance of the civilian populations is tied to the maintenance of this equilibrium: in order to resist, it is more important for the society to survive in its structures and values than in its demography.

Yet jihad, which presupposes the absolute externality of the enemy, should have enabled the politicization of tribal war by giving it the taking of the state as an objective. Two things should be mentioned here.

- Jihad really aimed only at Russia and left intact the interplay of hierarchies and competition within the "Muslim" camp, even if this favored the introduction of Islamist parties. Within the government one found the same tribal game, that is, permanent negotiations. It is as if the Soviet invasion had displaced the notion of the infidel, from the local communist to the foreign soldier. This tendency was reinforced by the fact that beginning in 1980 the regime developed a "tribal policy" that obliterated any Marxist, or even revolutionary, references and reactivated a tribal mode of operation.

- Jihad, as is well illustrated by Jean-Paul Charnay,[10] is an affair between the believer and God and not between the believer and his enemy. There is no obligation to obtain a result. Hence the demonstrative, even exhibitionist, aspect of the attacks. It is an act of faith, the passion of penitents, who are satisfied with nocturnal fireworks *ad maiorem Dei gloriam.* Jihad is not political.

What is needed to create a strategy is precisely a perception of the state as an objective of military strategy. Tribal strategy does not aim to take power, but to prevent its expansion. It is only with the goal of taking control of the state that it is worth destroying the adversary or even simply taking over a post. One sometimes has the impression that this reluctance to proceed with the "definitive" assault comes from the perception of the irreversible nature of this act: it would be the end of the closed and symmetrical world, the end of balance.

The Refusal to Insert the State into the Resistance

A true strategy of rupture with respect to the central government would have meant a perception of the society in terms of a state, and thus the creation of a counterstate in liberated zones. Similarly, a move toward truly effective combat tactics would have meant a militarization of the resistance (professionalization, centralization, mobility), which would also imply the introduction of a state-run model in the resistance. But this militarization would not occur automatically, for it presupposes a relationship with the society extremely different from the traditional one.

Spontaneously, the majority of local resistance commanders endeavored to avoid any professionalization and militarization that would call into question the structures of the traditional society. Rather, they attempted to translate into traditional terms the new state of affairs brought about by modern war. Not only combat tactics, as we have seen, but also the distribution of arms, the collection of taxes, the maintenance of justice, and the organization of logistics were managed in accordance with traditional models. There was little or no organization of a passive defense, enrollment of civilians, creation of an administration. Here are two typical examples: women and the economy. There were no women fighters. The respect of the *haram* and of *purda* (confining women to the private space) was part of what the Afghans were defending against the Soviets. Integrating women into combat would have negated the reason for the combat. War's influence on the modernization of the society reached its limits here: women are part of the private sphere. The private economy functioned without much interference on the part of the *mujahidin,* who relied on it both for logistics and for provisions. There was no "*mujahidin* economy."

In the resistance we encounter a regular feature of Islamic wars: the professional soldier *(asker)* is devalued not only with respect to the *mujahidin,* who is a volunteer and a believer, but also with respect to the warrior and the merchant and artisan.[11] The *asker* is perceived as a simple mercenary (*mazdur,* the salaried odd-job man), as a victim of forced enrollment, or as too stupid to have plied any other trade. From the Iranian Revolutionary Guard to the Lebanese

Hizbullah militiamen, disdain for the professional military man goes hand in hand with the spirit of jihad.

The strategic and cultural immobility of jihad is illustrated by the role of the "military base" *(markaz)*, a *mujahidin* camp protected by antiaircraft and antimissile defense and heavy weaponry. Families never live there, and the *mujahidin* are set up for daily life, with bakeries, gardeners, stablemen, service boys, and so on. The *markaz* didn't exist in traditional tribal war, since the warrior lived at home between campaigns. Mobile groups leave from the *markaz* to scour the solidarity space (considered to be identical with the "front," *jabha*) and mark out any governmental presence: the adversary's post will be passively besieged for years, and the roads occasionally ambushed.

We find two antecedents for the *markaz* in Muslim history: the refuge of the honorable bandit and the *ribat* of the fighting brotherhoods on the frontiers of the Muslim world.[12] In Afghanistan we find some *markaz* that come close to banditry, such as Amir Rasul's, in the Baghlan, whose control of a mountain pass serves mainly for the collection of a tax. But even for the authentic *mujahidin*, the "base" is less an element of military strategy than the sociopolitical restructuring of the space: it is a matter of reconstituting a solidarity group (*qawm* or *asabiyya*) around a chief who comes from the new elite yet behaves like a traditional *khan*, even if he is of modest origins: he keeps open board and distributes munitions, money, and small gifts. The social reshuffling brought about by the war in no way implies the renunciation of the traditional conception of the exercise of authority: the newly risen adopt the way of life and behavior of the former notables (significantly, the title *khan* is attached to the names of commanders, formerly students without prestige but now at the head of important fronts: Basir Khan, Ismail Khan, Bashir Khan . . .). The sociology of the chief has changed with respect to the past,[13] but not the behavior of those who are perceived as the new *khans*. The chief is first and foremost the one who gives; arms and munitions have replaced money and food.

This analysis explains the unexpected turn taken by the war in Afghanistan after the Soviets' departure in February 1989. The *muja-*

hidin failed to shift from a guerrilla war to a conventional war, less because they lacked arms than because such a shift would have presupposed the abandonment of traditional models of war, as well as the acceptance of the state by the guerrillas, and in particular the establishment of a single command and the circulation of combat units in a homogeneous space. The Pakistani armed forces who pushed the guerrillas to launch a conventional war in 1989 saw Afghanistan as a military map, about which one could move little blue, red, and green flags: the units were interchangeable, the objectives quantifiable. But the space as the Afghans see it is sociocultural: it is one of tribes, ethnic groups, or influence zones of a particular chief.

The failure of the assaults against the cities of Jalalabad in March 1989 and Gardez in the autumn of 1991 illustrates the permanence of the models of traditional war. With Masud's seizure of Kabul in April 1992, however, the question arises whether he has brought a new model of war to Afghanistan.

Masud's Example: A Compromise between Jihad and Modern Warfare

Of the few hundred Afghan *mujahidin* "commanders" active within the country, all employ a model of traditional war. Only one has attempted not only to launch an army but to employ a modern strategy.

In the beginning, Masud's front, situated in the northeast of Afghanistan, maintained a typical *qawm* structure. Masud, an Islamist militant and former student in engineering, took over the lower valley of Panjshir, of which he is a native, and which he conquered with a handful of members of the Jamaat-i Islami party who came from Peshawar during the winter of 1979–80. The population joined the Jamaat because its chief, Rabbani, was a fellow Sunni Persian-speaker, because it was the first party to bring in arms, and because the valley has an old tradition of fundamentalist opposition, transmitted by a network of traditionalist ulamas. The adjacent valleys (Shotol, Hazara) and upper valley (Paryan) immediately entered into the disposition, even though their inhabitants did not consider themselves Panjshiris. From the start, then, there was an enlargement of the solidarity space. There are many reasons for this. The base of Masud's operation is composed of Panjshiris either educated or working in Kabul, who are therefore less subject to the *qawm*'s resolutions. Although it is true that inhabitants of the Panjshir are peasants, they have been in the habit of emigrating to Kabul for some time, where they furnish a good number of the drivers, mechanics, and cooks for foreigners. Among these "emigrant" Panjshiris a regional "Panjshiri" identity has developed that transcends one's village *qawm* association. For these people, the *qawm* is simply "Panjshiri" and no longer, for example, Nuruzkhayl (the name of the Masud family *qawm,* reputed to have come from central Asia), Sayyid, or other denominations. Masud's two assets are thus that he controls a homogeneous solidarity space (without tribal or other subdivisions) and that, while remaining anchored to the traditional society, he has at his disposition urbanized, technically trained cadres. Very quickly, after having eliminated a few "Maoists" and Hizb-i Islami pockets and following his first victory over the Soviet-governmental forces in the spring of 1980, Masud reigned in the name of the Jamaat over all Panjshiris. Up to this point, there is nothing new.

The personal Masud factor came into play from this moment on, in the establishment of an original military model, well before the matter of moving beyond the solidarity space arose. The Masud model consisted in militarizing and specializing the troops. The military apparatus is no longer an armed duplication of civilian society, at least the farther one goes up the organizational chart. In fact it is the Vietnamese General Giap model. First we have the base *(qar-arga),* where an unspecialized *(grup-e mahali),* locally recruited group ensures order and self-defense for several villages at a time, while continuing to attend by rotation to productive tasks. Then, on the district level, a "strike force" *(grup-e zarbati)* assembles local but permanent combatants, who are given uniforms and more sophisticated arms (antitank devices, machine guns); this group participates only in the operations that occur within the framework of the district and furnishes the first level of defense in case of a surprise enemy attack. Up to this point, we are still within the traditional solidarity space. Next comes the "mobile group" *(mutaharrik)*, which recruits locally and is stationed at a base, but circulates beyond the limits of the solidarity space, as military imperatives require. This is the first example of a unit that goes beyond the bounds of the solidarity space. Beginning in 1985 "central units" *(qatiha-ye mar-kazi)* were created, recruitment for which was totally independent of the *qawm* network. These elite units served as training centers for officers in a future army. All military operations against a post involved the participation of central units, mobile groups and local groups. Beginning in the autumn of 1986, Masud launched a series of assaults against government bases held by battalion-level troops: the garrisons of Nahrin, Fakhar, Kalafgan, Kashm, Koranomunjan; finally, in August 1988, the first provincial capital, Taloqan, fell into Masud's hands. These operations took place in four different provinces.

The essential problem was thus to leave the Panjshiri solidarity space and to integrate others in order to move into a "national" space conceived of in strategic terms. Masud's method consisted in bringing in local non-Panjshiri groups and leaders, generally on bad terms with the traditional leaders, training them and convincing them of the superiority of his model, then sending them back to their zones of origin with a few Panjshiri advisers to develop his system there. These new commanders, who generally belonged to this same educated and urbanized generation, found a form of social promotion in entering the Masud movement, which allowed them to get around local hierarchies that had become oppressive. It was by playing on a sociological mutation (the rise of an "educated" class outside the powerful network of family relations) that Masud could hope to impose a military, and thus a political, mutation. The peasant population followed along insofar as this system generally enabled it to escape petty warlords. Beginning in 1982, groups who considered themselves ethnically different from the Panjshiris declared themselves of the Panjshiri *qawm:* these included the Sunni Hazaras of the Hazara valley, and the people of Shotol, who, more-over, speak a different language (Parachi).

On the village level, Masud does not tamper at all with traditional structures. His system is imposed from above and through
the military. To provide a political arm for his system, he created
the "Northern Supervisory Council" *(shura-ye nazar)* in 1985, a collective structure meant to transcend solidarity space segmentation;
it used the political framework of the Jamaat (although some party
commanders remained reluctant to adopt a structure that once again
deprived them of the status of *khan,* the traditional status acquired
through war). The district leaders were named by the Council and,
as far as possible, were recruited from outside the local *qawm.* Com-
missions (culture, health, finance, legal) formed the embryo of future
ministries. Behind the military organization, a model of state organization was taking shape, even though it superposed, without eliminating, the traditional notables and the *qawm* system: any attempt
to eliminate the traditional system would have thrown a part of the
population into the arms of rival parties or the government. The
traditional *qawm* and solidarity space rules have not disappeared.
The local chief's prerogatives are respected. At the same time, Masud
does not touch either the economy or the society (except to build
schools): this is where the base of the "civilian" identity resides. State
control, in fact, touches only one very limited sector of the society:
the political-military sector. Elsewhere the civil society has complete
autonomy, in particular with regard to logistics, which is surprising
for such a militarized system: arms are carried by lapis lazuli drivers,
who ride with empty saddle packs one way and are therefore happy
to carry arms, but have no qualms about striking for a rate increase.
Ethnicity is the limit of the process of modernization, and might
even be a consequence of this process. But Masud's army, at the
peak of its efficiency, remained a Tadzhik ethnic army, with few
Pakhtuns.

New Segmentations

The Masud model is unique in Afghanistan. Even an Islamo-
Leninist-type party like the Hizb-i Islami was unable to establish an
instrument of modern war: the "professional armies" put together
with Afghan refugees in Pakistan, then trained and equipped by the

Pakistani army, turned out to be incapable of waging modern battles and found themselves rejected by the local populations, despite the fact that these populations had generally been won over by the *mujahidin*. This predicament brings to light the problems of the process of modernization brought on by war.

This war brought about the decline of the traditional elite (the Pakhtun aristocracy of tribal origin) and the rise of a new elite: Islamist intellectuals, mullahs, small warlords inside Afghanistan on the one hand, neofundamentalist "new intellectuals" among the emigrants to Pakistan on the other—all people who owe their emergence to the war and who, in some instances, have become "war entrepreneurs," living from and by the war. We have seen that the "new notable" status acquired by the resistance leaders is due solely to their redistribution activity. But in order to distribute, one has to be plugged into the network of goods circulation; these goods cannot be the products of peasants, because then the leader would be perceived as exploitative and rejected. The goods that circulate—arms, subsidies, humanitarian aid—come from abroad or from the government and are allocated for political reasons. Thus this network originates with a state: either the local capital or foreign powers. The new powers are made more secure by the internationalization of the war and of the distribution networks.

The protagonists, without always being conscious of it and without ever gaining control of the process, have seen their activities inserted into a global geostrategy: between East and West, between fundamentalist and secular, between Shiite and Sunni, between the MB and the Wahhabis, between producers and consumers of drugs, and so on. This internationalization brought with it an influx of international support (arms, money, humanitarian aid), which has profoundly modified and monetarized a rural and more or less autarkic economy. But the network for the circulation of goods and money became autonomous with respect to the state sponsors. Today, many chiefs make their living through the production of drugs, which necessarily circulate through an international network, since they are not consumed in the country. Gun-running, drug production, and the corruption that ensues free these new economic circuits from dependence on the decisions of foreign powers (the United States, Russia, or Saudi Arabia) to aid or not to aid their allies in Afghanistan. The many power centers that manage this flow of goods were created by the war and are in direct contact with international networks: the domestic state and foreign states are short-circuited by the growing autonomy of these networks for the circulation of "goods."

These new power centers are proving to be the nuclei of a new segmentation. The Islamists have used a modern political structure, that of parties, to insert themselves into and attempt to transcend the traditional segmentation into *qawm,* clans, tribes, and ethnic groups, in which the traditional power of notables was rooted. The result is not so much the imposition of political modernity as a transferring of traditional forms of segmentation and power into a new system.

In a first phase, the Afghan resistance, although it did often supplant the usual notables, developed around the society's traditional structure of segmentation into *qawm:* a growing number of "local commanders," who were at times in charge of only a few dozen combatants, preserved their independence with respect to the more important commanders by adhering to a rival party from which they drew sufficient subsidies to maintain their status. We have noted the link between the military immobility of the *mujahidin* and the fact that the protagonists perceived the geography of the networks and territories as natural: a "commander" rarely seeks to eliminate or chase away a *qawm* that has given itself a political identity by adhering to a party opposed to his own.

In a second phase, the new chiefs that emerged from the war assumed the same manner of exercising power as the notables: they established a patronage network, this time made possible because they could redistribute goods by plugging into an international network (of input: arms, subsidies; of output: drugs and . . . arms). By acting as distributors, they could avoid leeching off their own society. Political factions tend to structure themselves on the operational model of the *qawm,* through matrimonial alliances, exchange of benefits, nepotism, and so on. Thus we see new *qawm* appearing, created around a pole of power and the distribution of goods, and no longer representative of the old *qawm*. The former segmentation, including that of ethnic identity, tends to be reorganized around new poles of power.[14] But these new poles are perpetuated only through the internationalization of the conflict. Essentially, the attainment of any power within a political party gives access to a new commodity—weapons—at times accompanied, for the most powerful commanders or those most gifted at public relations, by the arrival of humanitarian and financial aid from abroad. Often a right-hand man jealous of his chief will open a front the way one opens a shop; to attract a clientele, one has to give something (guns, but also humanitarian aid: "French doctors," for example, became political money); one must pledge to take the civilian population under one's wing. It is like a true smalltime electoral campaign in which the "constituent" is king.

Islamism and the Transfer of Traditional Segmentations

Thus the politicization of traditional society in Afghanistan both by war and by Islamism has produced only one form of relatively modern politico-military organization: the Masud system. Should the Afghan case be interpreted as a concrete illustration of Islamism's inability to produce an effective political model? It would be premature to generalize and to conclude that Islamist discourse generally is a mere cover not for the permanence, but for the rewriting in modern terms of traditional modes of segmentation, patronage, and the exercise of power. A more probing study remains to be done. But other field inquiries tend in this direction. The restructuring of politics in the form of a new segmentation is not unique to the Afghan Islamists; the same case is found in the ex-Soviet Tadzhikistan.

It is striking that the militia war in Lebanon from 1975 to 1991 offered an urban version of the Afghan model. There is, first of all, a surprising correlation between the two guerrilla wars: according to Michel Seurat, the armed groups did not encroach on enemy territory or seek to destroy the enemy. It was primarily a matter of marking a territory in order to exploit this advantage later in terms of profits and redistribution to one's group. This guerrilla warfare is also demonstrative and symbolic; hence the role played by the taking of hostages.[15] We have here a transference of traditional war to an urban model.

The Lebanese militia, like the Afghan guerrillas, also perpetuated themselves by plugging into a globalized system for the circulation of goods: arms, drugs, subsidies, and then, in peacetime, real estate speculation (the reconstruction of Beirut with Saudi capital).

But what about jihad? In Lebanon, the Islamist militia's forms of combat did not seem fundamentally different from those of the other militias, whether Christian, Druze, or "progressive." Lebanon offers an excellent field for comparative studies, since it presents the entire spectrum of ideological motivations: communalist, jihad, mercenary, mafia, and so on. The "progressive" groups were the first to lose their ideological color and transform themselves into purely communal groups, but the Islamists did not follow suit.

Jihad furnishes a discourse of legitimation for the new elite, but neither an organizational model nor a new political structure for the combatant society. It remains to be seen what will happen to the model created by Masud, particularly since it will be called on to play a role in the void created by the disappearance of the Soviet Union, provided that it doesn't fall into this void itself.

10

Iran: Shiism and Revolution

IRAN IS THE only country in which Shiism is the state religion, and the only one in which a true Islamic revolution took place. The Iranian revolution is tightly linked to Shiism, conceived of not as a corpus, but as a history. The identification of Shiism with Iran reflects a historical process that occurred in two phases: first, Iran's conversion to Shiism under the Safavids during our sixteenth century, then the unfinished Iranianization of foreign Shiite minorities through the progressive establishment of a predominantly Iranian, hierarchized, and centralized clergy, a considerable innovation with respect to Sunnism.

Nothing in Shiite thought, however, predisposes the clergy to play a contestant political role.[1] Shiism even developed a remarkable quietist and Sufi current (first made known to the West by Henry Corbin). It was the historical process of the Shiite clergy's evolution into a self-perpetuating hierarchical body that is autonomous both financially (followers pay dues directly) and politically (the hierarchy is established in a territory that eludes control by the Iranian state), that in the twentieth century enabled it to become an instrument for taking power. On the fringes of the Shiite corpus, a synthesis of

168

traditionalist fundamentalism and Marxist-leaning ideology was developed.

The Iranian revolution is the only Islamist movement in which the clergy played a decisive role, but it was also the most overtly ideological one: a Third World revolutionary movement generated by an unprecedented alliance between a radical intelligentsia and a fundamentalist clergy. The Islamization that followed victory therefore did not take on the conservative cast which marked the process of state Islamization in Pakistan, Saudi Arabia, or Sudan, and which we may still see in Algeria. Nevertheless, there was an anticlerical tendency in Iranian Islamism that contested the clergy's religious monopoly; this tendency was embodied in the thinker Ali Shariati and in extremist groups such as the People's Mujahidin (Mujahidin-e Khalq), but was rejected by the opposition as soon as revolutionary institutions were established.

Iran's Conversion to Shiism

Shiism is historically an Arab phenomenon: it is based on belief in the legitimacy of the Prophet's family, which is Arab par excellence; the language of the imams, direct descendants of Ali, as well as of the theological literature, is Arabic; most of the holy sites of Shiism are on Arab soil; most of the great ayatollahs have been *sayyid,* a title bestowed on descendants of the Prophet; many are of Arab ancestry, and all are perfectly fluent in the Arabic language.

In the early sixteenth century, the spiritual guide of a sect combining Shiism with shamanism that had become established among Turkoman tribes (the Qizilbash) took control of the territory that is now Iran and founded the Safavid dynasty. The new sovereigns, who spoke Turkish, had to rid themselves of their purely tribal and sectarian origins in order to build a stable state. They chose as their state religion "Twelver" Shiism (which awaits the return of the twelfth imam, a direct descendant of Muhammad who is absent but not dead, who may at any moment reappear and establish justice on earth), which was closer to Sunnism than the faith of their troops.

Shiism was so foreign to Iran at that time that in order to create a state clergy the Safavids had to call on Arab theologians from what is now south Lebanon (the region of Jabal Amil) and from the Persian Gulf (Bahrain). The Shiitization of Iran was part of the process of constructing a territorialized state apparatus.[2] The religious leader of the Iranian clergy (the *sadr*) was a functionary at the court. In its structure, the Shiite clergy of that era differed little from its Sunni counterpart: on the one hand were the court ulamas; on the other, the village mullahs. The formation of an autonomous clergy was made all the less likely by the fact that the Safavid dynasty itself was invested with religious legitimacy.

Iran's conversion to Shiism did not occur without the resistance and massacre of Sunni clerics, as witnessed in Herat; Shiism did not become fully established until the reign of King Abbas (1587–1629). The current borders between Iran, on the one hand, and Afghanistan and Turkey on the other, date from this time and are not ethnic but religious, opposing Shiites and Sunnis.

The Creation of a Structured, Transnational Shiite Clergy

The eighteenth century brought a series of fundamental changes. First, the Zand and later the Qajar dynasties (the latter also Turkish-speaking) no longer held religious legitimacy and were perceived as purely secular. Then the Persian ulamas, feeling threatened in Iran (following the Afghan invasion of 1722, Nadir Shah attempted to restore Sunnism), developed a pattern of settling in Najaf and Karbala, holy Shiite sites in Iraq. These two cities had been under Ottoman jurisdiction since 1638. The move posed no obstacle to the freedom of the Shiite clergy; on the contrary: since the Ottoman empire was not a "nation," it was far more receptive than Iran to according extraterritoriality to exogenous religious groups; the Shiites were persecuted only insofar as they appeared to challenge the central power (in south Lebanon), and not as a religion. The first Iranian spiritual leader to settle permanently at Najaf was Muhammad Baqir Akmal Vahid Bahbahani (1705–1791).[3] This extraterritoriality would last until 1978, when Ayatollah Khomeini fled to Neauphle-le-Château, in France.

This movement was concomitant with a theological debate that rocked through the Shiite clergy; it had to do with the reopening of the right to interpretation *(ijtihad)*. The *akhbari* ("traditionalists") believed that this right had been closed since the disappearance of the twelfth imam; their position was close to that of the Sunnis. The *usuli* ("fundamentalists") believed that this right resided with the high ulamas.[4] The victory of the second group (generally Iranians) marked a fundamental rift with Sunnism and paved the way for the creation of the modern Shiite clergy. The right to *ijtihad* is recognized only for high ulamas, who form a collegial body and who are referred to as *mujtahid* or ayatollah ("sign of God"). As a result, each believer must follow the interpretation of an ulama, whom he chooses from among the college of grand ayatollahs, in general by intermediary of the local mullahs, who have received their investiture either directly or indirectly from a grand ayatollah. Clericalization (the formation of an autonomous body of clerics separate from the state) is a consequence of the victory of the *usuli*.

This evolution also consecrated the financial autonomy of the clergy, which is still in effect, with followers paying the Islamic tax directly to their *mujtahid*'s representative rather than to the state. The money is gathered by the clergy, then redistributed into pious works, many of which have a social component. Since the eighteenth century, then, the Shiite clergy has played a social and educational role with no parallel among the Sunni clergy.

The nineteenth century saw the establishment of an internal hierarchy within the clergy, ratified by co-optation, as a function of the level and prestige of one's diploma: *hujjat al-islam* ("proof of Islam"), *ayat allah* ("sign of God"), *ayat allah al-'uzma* ("grand ayatollah" or *mujtahid*); only the last can be sources of imitation *(marja'al-taqlid)*. Financial and geographic independence (Najaf and Karbala were outside the borders of the Iranian empire); the right to interpretation, even to innovation, on all questions; delegitimation of the state (this was new since the time of the Safavids); strong hierarchy and structures: all operated to make the clergy a political force. The Shiite clergy first turned political at the end of the nineteenth century, when the weakness of the Qajar dynasty in the face of British and Russian encroachment made it the only protest force.

From this period on, the defense of the Iranian nation has been intertwined with that of Islam and Shiism. The clergy's entry into politics began with Ayatollah Shirazi's *fatwa*, which in 1891 forbade the use of tobacco so long as the monopoly that had been granted to a British company the previous year was not rescinded. In 1906 the majority of the high clergy supported the Iranian constitutionalist movement. In 1920 the Shiite clergy was the soul of the resistance against the English in southern Iraq.[5] Even though the clergy made demands of a traditionalist-fundamentalist nature (that the state apply the *sharia*), it would regularly serve as a pole of contestation, especially during crises in power (1890–1921, 1950–1953, 1978).

The concept of *vilayat-i faqih,* elaborated by Imam Khomeini, was the culmination of this politicization and would serve to mobilize Shiite communities beyond nationalist references and state apparatuses.

The Alliance of Clerics and Intellectuals

We find in Iran the same factors that feed Islamism throughout the Muslim world (Islamist intellectuals, urban masses who have experienced a loss of social status). The originality of the Iranian revolution lies in the alliance between the Islamist intelligentsia and a part of the clergy, which was able to bring with it the entire corporation, out of esprit de corps as much as conviction.

The Shiite clergy is incontestably more open to the non-Islamic corpus than the Sunni ulamas. The ayatollahs are great readers (including of Marx and Feuerbach): there is something of the Jesuit or Dominican in them. Hence they combine clear philosophical syncretism with an exacting casuistic legalism. The opening of the Shiite *madrasa* to a non-Islamic corpus dates from far earlier than that of the Sunni *madrasa.*[6] The twofold culture of the Shiite clergy is striking: highly traditionalist (one need only read the Imam Khomeini's *Tawzih al-masa'il*) and yet very open to the modern world; behind the legalism lies philosophical thought.

Nonetheless, it was not until Khomeini that the logic of the clergy's politicization, pushed to the extreme, came to require that clerics exercise power. During his courses in Najaf in the 1960s, Ayatollah Khomeini developed the concept of *vilayat-i faqih* (government of the doctor of law). This concept is the Shiite version of the Islamist idea that there cannot be an Islamic society without an Islamic state: it is not enough that the laws promulgated be in conformity with the *sharia;* the state must be Islamic in its essence. But while Sunni theoreticians have had trouble defining the form of such a state, as we have seen, Khomeini had an answer, for unlike the Sunnis, the Shiites have an institution that can determine who is the most learned, the best Muslim, the guide. Since there is a supreme religious authority in Shiism, this authority should hold supreme state power. Thus the exercise of power should fall to the supreme clerical authority. This does not mean that the clergy governs directly as a body: although the guide is a cleric, he does not represent the clergy; he is above all institutions, for he is nothing less than the representative of the hidden twelfth imam. Khomeini never favored the clergy as an institution: on the contrary, he sought the support of the Islamists and the *hujjat al-islam,* younger clergy of lower rank, rather than that of the high clergy, guardians of the century-old tradition of clerical "corporatism."

It is therefore not surprising that the *vilayat-i faqih* thesis was rejected by almost the entire dozen grand ayatollahs living in 1981: they either openly opposed Khomeini, as did Abu al-Qasim al-Khu'i and Shariat Madari (who died in 1986), or they maintained a discreet distance, refusing official posts, as did Gulpaygani, al-Qummi, al-Shirazi and al-Najafi al-Mar'ashi. In fact, the high clergy kept its distance from the revolution. Only one grand ayatollah, Muntazari, a former student and the designated successor of Khomeini before being rejected in 1989, approved the concept. Moreover, Khomeini was not the most influential ayatollah at the moment of the Islamic revolution. The one who had the most developed network of disciples and former students was the very old Ayatollah al-Khu'i (born in 1899), an Iranian Azeri whose great influence reached from Lebanon (the spiritual leader of the Hizbullah, Sheikh Fadlallah, is one of his disciples) to Afghanistan, by way of the Iran's Khorasan province and the former Soviet Azerbaijan (where the current religious chief, Sheikh al-Islam Pashazada, is his disciple). Al-Khu'i did not leave Najaf during the war between Iran and Iraq and always rejected the concept of *vilayat-i faqih;* certain religious chiefs, such as Fadlallah, would follow him in this theological opposition while politically supporting the Islamic revolution. There is still no direct link between dogma and political action.

Thus the Iranian revolution was not a revolution of ayatollahs, but of the *hujjat al-islam,* many of them former students of Khomeini, who preferred political activism to studies in the press of movements against the Shah in 1963. Imam Khomeini relied on this network of former students, backed up by young Islamists of secular origin, who saw in him the synthesis they were seeking between political radicalism and religious conviction, and which they obviously were unable to find either among the more prestigious ayatollahs, such as al-Khu'i, or among the groups of the extreme left, which though very active were also highly dogmatic.

These two networks, clerical and Islamist, became interpenetrated because there was an environment of cultural mobility in Iran; clerical families did not hesitate to give certain of their children perfectly Western educations, while many of the youth educated in the West followed courses part-time at religious establishments for the "secular" (the *husayniyya*). The distinction between mullahs and intellectuals was not as sharp in Iran as in the Sunni world.

Ideologization

Even though one can read Shiism both as a quietist and mystical religion and as a political one, as did Ali Shariati, there is unquestionably a thematic in the "Shiite imagination" that is more easily adaptable to the idea of revolution: a sense of history, millenarianism, the idea of social justice, the devaluation of temporal power, martyrdom.[7] These themes are illustrated by the founding paradigms: the martyrdom of the "just" Husayn, son of Ali, and

of his companions in Karbala at the sword of an illegitimate tyrant; the figure of the politicized woman (Zaynab, Husayn's sister),
and so on.[8]

For the Sunnis the Islamic revolution is a negation of History,
while on the contrary for the Shiites it is an advent, a Parousia, the
realization of a promise that is made possible only by the process of
occultation of the hidden Imam, the one who will return to earth to
ensure the reign of justice.[9]

Contemporary Iran has also had a more extensive development
of syncretist ideologies (Hegelian-Islamic, Islamo-Marxist) than the
Sunni world, as illustrated by an author like Ali Shariati and by the
organization, half sect, half political party, of the People's Mujahidin.[10] Even though the clergy may have endeavored to reject this
syncretism, it has rubbed off on the secular Islamists. One of the
reasons for this syncretism is undoubtedly the influence of Marxism
in Iran, an influence that is unparalleled in the Arab countries: Iran
has one of the oldest communist parties in the world, the Tudeh,
whose membership includes respected intellectuals.

Sympathy for the Third World was a constant of the Islamic
revolution. The Iranian press, during the ten years when revolution
was the keynote (until the death of Khomeini in 1989), devoted
extensive coverage to non-Muslim revolutionary movements (from
the Sandinistas to the African National Congress and the Irish
Republican Army) and downplayed the role of the Islamic movements considered conservative, such as the Afghan *mujahidin*.
During this period Third World solidarity took precedence over
Muslim fraternity, in an utter departure from all other Islamist
movements.

Yet a schism appeared when ideologization found itself in contradiction with the *sharia*. For most of the members of the clergy,
Islamization had to take precedence over revolutionary logic, which
meant, for instance, that private property took precedence over state
control, respect of the private home over police investigations, repudiation over divorce proceedings, and so on. For the radicals, on the
contrary, revolutionary logic was more important than legalism,

even the legalism imposed by the *sharia*. In Iran during his lifetime Imam Khomeini always imposed revolutionary logic, represented in the guide's will, if need be over the *sharia*.

The State and the Institutionalization of the Islamic Revolution

The Iranian revolution had a national, state-controlled, and institutional framework. It endowed itself with institutions and never had a true single party (the Islamic Republican Party was dissolved in 1986 at Khomeini's request). The Iranian nation-state, despite a pan-Islamist rhetoric, was never called into question by the Islamic revolution. True, the constitution does specify that the guide need not be Iranian, but the nationality code is extremely strict: it is as difficult for a Persian-speaking Shiite from Afghanistan to marry an Iranian as it is for a Frenchman to do so. One of Khomeini's close collaborators, Jalal al-Din Farsi, could not run for president because his father was born an Afghan.

It is no doubt the conjunction of a clerical institution and a state tradition that spared the Iranian Islamic revolution the never-ending logistical questions of political Islam: Who should be the supreme guide? Who is authorized to legislate in matters of religion? Why establish a positive law when we have the *sharia?* Without worrying too much about its conformity with the *sharia,* Iran essentially endowed itself with a genuine constitution, not a mere slogan but one that truly organizes the functioning of an ensemble of institutions; significantly, the legitimacy of the constitution is explicitly founded in its first article on popular will, and not only on the *sharia.* Thus the problem of the amir is settled. The procedures for choosing a guide are clearly defined: the Council of Experts, elected by universal suffrage, designates him. If at a given moment a guide exists, then he is *index sui,* his own evidence, and the people will merely ratify this by voting, conceived of in this case as a show of allegiance *(bay'a).* If no guide is in evidence, then institutions exist to deal with this absence, just as the Shiite clergy have been dealing since the ninth century with the disappearance of the twelfth imam; in this case popular suffrage is a means of legitimation.

We see then that, aside from periods when a guide recommends himself to popular allegiance, the constitution is what organizes power and its legitimacy. There is a political order, which does not efface itself before the implementation of the *sharia*. This is where the Iranian revolution differs from Sunni Islamism.

An Islamic Constitution or a New Secularity?

By adopting a constitutionalist model (even certain strategic safeguards ensure the preeminence of those who fought the revolution), by affirming the legitimacy of universal suffrage, by transforming what should be a theocracy into a presidential system (what I call a "constitutionalist theocracy"), Iran has been able to find a political space, beyond Islamist and revolutionary rhetoric, that does not depend on the impossible virtue of its members, but rather functions on the basis of institutions that survive in the absence of the divine word. A space, in short, that is secular.

In Iran, in fact, the constitution sets the place of the *sharia,* and not vice versa; more precisely, the authorities responsible for reporting on Islamic law exercise their duties in the same way that the French Council of State and Constitutional Council do, that is, within an institutional framework defined by the constitution. The new Islamic state developed a positive law that became "Islamic" by virtue of the sole fact that the state was Islamic: it thus marked the end of the *sharia* as the sole foundation for the judicial norm, an idea that is unacceptable to Sunni neofundamentalists. We are dealing here with a modern configuration, in which the state is the source of law and the source of its own legitimacy. The Iranian model is in fact a "secular" model, in the sense that it is the state that defines the place of the clergy and not the clergy who define the place of politics. Thus, when Khamanei, then president of the republic, announced the primacy of the *sharia* over other laws in a sermon on December 31, 1988, Ayatollah Khomeini issued a public letter of reply, on January 7, 1989, in which he clearly affirmed the preeminence of the revolutionary logic and the laws of the Islamic state over the *sharia*.

It is true that the *sharia* is supposed to be the supreme law and that the parliament incorporated in legislation the most symbolic of the punishments provided for in the *sharia* (*qisas,* retaliation; *diyat,* bloodletting; *hudud,* capital punishment for an offense against God); but the parliament legislates, and judges must refer to the promulgated law and not directly to the *sharia.*

On key questions, Iranian law has remained fairly un-Islamic. The constitution grants equality of rights among men and women (article 20). The discretionary law of repudiation is not recognized for men. There is no legal discrimination on the basis of personal status against Christians, Jews, and Zoroastrians, all of whom perform military service, pay no special taxes, and hold full citizenship; nevertheless, they are prohibited from assuming leadership posts and vote in separate colleges. Similarly, a Muslim foreigner has the same status as a Christian foreigner.[11] In short, Iranian citizenship is not an Islamic notion. Finally, Iran has kept the solar calendar and celebrates the new year on March 21.

The establishment of institutions to ensure that laws passed by the parliament are in conformity with Islam reflects an implicit recognition of a nonshariatic judicial space: the Council of Guardians of the Constitution consists of six ulamas named by the guide and six (secular) "jurists" chosen by parliament from a list provided by the chief judicial authority (article 91, an amendment to the constitution). The Council must verify that the laws voted by parliament are in conformity with Islam (by the majority of the doctors of law) and with the constitution (by a group majority): thus there is a recognition of a constitutional logic that cannot be reduced to the *sharia.*

In fact the Iranian constitution could function in an almost secular manner, insofar as power resides ultimately with universal suffrage and with parliament. The authorities who oversee the conformity of laws with the *sharia* are chosen not by the clergy, but by the political authority. Although the mullahs play an important role, no positions of authority, except for those of guide and half the Council of Guardians, are explicitly reserved for them. Mullahs are named to high administrative functions through political channels. Even the Council of Experts, which is responsible for designating the guide, is elected by the people.

Khomeini: The End of Religious Transcendence

The personal role played by Imam Khomeini complicated matters and drew the high clergy into a political revolution for which it was not prepared. Khomeini was a strange character indeed, both a traditional fundamentalist and a Third World revolutionary: he was able to rally a large portion of young Islamists to the clergy, yet at the same time he broke the rules that had been established among the clergy over two centuries.

The death of Imam Khomeini, on June 3, 1989, brought an end to the logic of the Islamic revolution, according to which the highest authority of the clerical institution coincided with that of the state. Indeed, his successor, Ali Khamanei, previously president of the Islamic Republic and hastily designated the new guide by the Council of Experts (which had itself dismissed its only real dauphin, Ayatollah Muntazari), does not possess the necessary theological qualifications to be the supreme religious leader, a grand ayatollah, a "source of imitation." Khamanei is only a *hujjat al-islam,* who, although he was promoted to the rank of ayatollah the day of Khomeini's death, had neither the seniority nor the diplomas required to compel the recognition of his peers. There is thus a divorce between the supreme religious function (held today by an aged, little-known ayatollah who is not politically active) and the highest political function. The *vilayat-i faqih* is defunct, but it is too late to go back to the old system.

The paradox is that Khomeiniism undermined the Shiite clerical system that had developed over the course of three centuries. Khomeini made the *sharia* subordinate to the revolution; he affirmed, against the tradition, that the *fatwa* pronounced by a grand ayatollah survived that ayatollah (as in the case of the infamous *fatwa* against the writer Salman Rushdie). To his own benefit, Khomeini put an end to the collegiality among grand ayatollahs, whose legitimacy he called into question by "defrocking" Shariat Madari (who died in 1982) and by promoting clerics as a function of their political allegiance and not of their religious rank. The most brilliant clerics gave up their studies to engage in political activism, and today there are no successors to the surviving grand ayatollahs, almost all of whom are over eighty years old. Since Saddam Husayn's execution of the Ayatollah Baqir al-Sadr, all the grand ayatollahs are Iranian: this marks the end of Shiite universalism. The Shiite clergy's system of self-perpetuation and co-optation is dead.

Khomeini eliminated the transcendent, autonomous space from which the clergy spoke: the clergy was brought down to the level of the state, yet without really controlling it, since the political hierarchy is not the religious hierarchy. Today there is not a single grand ayatollah in power. The "Republic of Ayatollahs" is a journalistic invention. But the end of the preeminence of the grand ayatollahs, socially committed scholars who were careful not to compromise themselves in politics, means the end of a certain Shiism.

What Nation?

The dereliction of Shiite legitimacy may have dramatic consequences for Iran. A general rule, valid since the sixteenth century, has it that loyalty to the central state is based on Shiism and not on ethnicity: the Shiites of Iran feel Iranian no matter what their ethnic category (Persian, Arab, or Azeri), whereas the Sunnis do not feel Iranian even if they are of Iranian culture (Kurds and Baluchis). But Shiite solidarity has been badly hurt since the end of the war with Iraq. Tehran's passivity during Saddam Husayn's attack against Najaf and Karbala in March 1991 marked the ascendancy of the concerns of the Iranian state over Shiite solidarity, and thus an end to the legitimation of the Iranian state by Shiism, which alone guaranteed its maintenance as a multiethnic nation.

To make matters worse, since the breakup of the Soviet Union there are national poles of identity for Azeris and Turkomans, something that has not been the case since the creation of modern Iran in the sixteenth century. At the same time, Iran's Sunni population is slowly increasing as a result of the influx of Kurdish and Afghan refugees. Iran's largest province, Khorasan, now has a Sunni majority. The Afghan refugees, although they are Persian speakers, do not assimilate; they have their own educational networks (often financed by . . . Saudi Arabia).

There is a risk that the failure of the Islamic revolution and the crisis in Shiite legitimacy will mark the return of ethnic nationalism.

Radicalism and Nostalgia

The ebbing of political Islam is bringing about a detachment from religion. The fact that the revolution took place means that the flow can run only in the direction of secularization, which has reached its limit with the existing administration; how can a government that is not sure of winning free elections call into question the very element that gives it legitimacy, Islamic symbolism? This is why the issue of the chador is more central in Iran than elsewhere: the obligation to wear the veil is difficult to accept in the postrevolutionary era; it is better tolerated in traditionalist countries like Saudi Arabia. Indeed, daily life is less "Islamic" in Iran than in many Muslim countries. The revolution created a middle ground between certain modern activities and Islamic norms: in sports, for example (Ping-Pong in a chador); in women's right to work (and they do work); in the Islamic wardrobe, which permits denim and raincoats; on television, which shows Islamic female announcers; and in martial music, which is composed in Western fashion.

These areas of compromise are contested neither by the radicals nor by the majority of the clergy. Cultural anti-Westernism is not characterized by the hypersensitivity found in some Sunni neofundamentalist milieus.

But some are nostalgic for this revolutionary heritage—they are the ones who are referred to as "radicals," who seek to retain the gains and symbolism of a revolution that brought them to power, rather than to export an Islamic radicalism whose failure has been evident for years. Having been unable, in ten years of revolution, either to impose or even to conceive of a coherent model for an Islamic economy or society, torn between the strict "fundamentalists," concerned above all with preserving Islamic laws, and the "progressives," preoccupied with developing a state-run, revolutionary model that would break with the previous order, the radicals can only fight a rearguard action. Their weakness lies in the fact that they are in a "conservative" position, guardians of a heritage that is more symbolic than real, and not representatives of economic interests or of structured political forces. They are "against": against opening up to the West, against abandoning the idea of exporting the revolution, against softening the control on mores. The radicals are powerful in institutions produced by the revolution, like the "foundations"— kinds of holding companies that manage considerable funds. These foundations have privileged access to currency at the official rate, which allows them to distribute among their "clientele" consumer goods (refrigerators, mopeds, air conditioners, and so on) acquired at the official rate. We thus find behind the apparatus of the Iranian state the same solidarity and clientele networks as elsewhere, except that the weight of the state in Iran forces them to define themselves through political projects and to work through institutions, even if it means turning the ministries into fiefdoms.

This opposition has little of the conservative neofundamentalism one observes in Sunni countries: its points of contention are neither the *sharia* nor the status of women, but symbols like the *fatwa* against Salman Rushdie, or already outmoded strategies, like the refusal to open up to the West, whether in the form of loans or of diplomatic relations.

All that would be required for the constitution of the Islamic Republic to function in a secular fashion would be a political overture allowing truly different parties to run in elections, the guide becoming a kind of "constitutional theocrat." The final words of Imam Khomeini, like the *fatwa* condemning Rushdie to death, have yet to be administered. The paradox is that in the traditional Shiite system, before the *vilayat-i faqih,* the *fatwa* would have been automatically abolished by the death of its author. But for the legitimacy of the new regime to remain intact, the words must remain valid. It is as if the de facto secularization introduced by the end of religious transcendence compelled the perpetuation of an impossible and symbolic sacred space, in the form of a threat that no one can rescind.

❖ 11 ❖

The Shiite Factor in Iran's Foreign Policy

*I*T IS OFTEN said that Shiism was the nationalist expression of
the Persians who converted to Islam. The story is more complicated: Iran, as we have seen, has really been Shiite only since the
sixteenth century; the sovereigns who reigned over Muslim Iran
from the sixteenth to the twentieth centuries have been of Turkish
origin. Throughout this period, the Persian empire never included
all ethnolinguistically Iranian groups, but has in fact included
immense non-Iranian populations. Even today, barely half of Iranian
citizens speak Persian as a mother tongue.

The Islamic revolution in Iran placed the accent on pan-
Islamism and the support of revolutionary movements of the third
world, while basically, without saying so, playing on Shiism. Interestingly, until 1992 Islamic Iran never played on ethnic and cultural
solidarities among groups of Iranian language and culture, even if
they were Sunnis, like the Tadzhiks, the Kurds, the Baluchis, or even
the Pakhtuns of Afghanistan.

For Islamist ideologues, ethnicity and language are not criteria
for solidarity, for they divide the community; on the other hand,
they see no contradiction between extolling Shiism and pan-Islamic

183

solidarity. They conceive of the Shiite community in the way Marx thought of the proletariat: a particular group that brings about the emancipation of all humanity. Shiism, in thought as in practice, is the avant-garde of the world Islamic revolution. But as a result, universalist discourse notwithstanding, it is to the Shiite communities that the Iranian discourse is addressed and it is among these communities that the revolutionary practice particular to the Islamic Republic has found its best adherents, thereby reinforcing the association between Shiism and Islamic revolution. One of the perverse effects of this association was to allow Sunni Islamist networks, disappointed by Iran, to be wooed by Muslim Brotherhood and Wahhabi movements, until the divorce between these two groups that followed the second Gulf war.

By way of foreign Shiite communities, transformed into a fifth column, Iran has been able to circumvent Arab nationalism, to attempt to destabilize the conservative governments of the Middle East, and to draw from a pool of determined militants to mount operations that a state would have difficulty assuming openly. But at the same time, Iran's foreign policy has boxed itself into the Shiite ghetto without actually controlling this ghetto, as is demonstrated by the allegiance of many Lebanese Shiites to Syria. The Islamic revolution has not included the Sunni world. Iran began to draw lessons from this failure beginning in 1991 by opening up to Sunni Islamists who had broken ties with Saudi Arabia and by engaging timidly, in central Asia, in support of Persian-speaking Tadzhiks, in order to counter both the pan-Turkism and Sunni fundamentalism supported by Saudi Arabia and Pakistan. These maneuvers can no longer be considered ideological: Iran is acting as a regional power, along lines quite similar to those established by the former Shah.

But the role that foreign Shiite communities have played in Iran's foreign policy warrants attention. Among non-Iranian Shiites, the Islamic revolution has had an impact only in communities that have experienced a contemporary process of clericalization (which has occurred only among Twelver Shiites); before this, sociological change had broken the traditionalist and secular framework of these communities, through the effects of rural exodus and pauperization, whether in south Lebanon, in Iraqi cities, or in communities of Afghan Hazaras. More than the actions of Iranian missionaries, it was the resocialization of a destructured and newly urbanized space by native clergy who were educated before the revolution in a very Iranianized environment (as the training sites of all the clergy—Najaf and Karbala—were, despite being on Arab soil) that allowed Iran to establish bridgeheads in foreign lands. At the same time, the Iranian revolution has never been able to move outside this space, which was established before its advent. The impact of the Iranian revolution is thus largely an optical illusion, revealing what already existed but hardly changing the actual situation. The real changes took place between 1960 and 1978, not between 1978 and 1980.

The Iranianization of Middle Eastern Shiism

The theme of the Shiite as an agent from Iran first appeared during the Safavid period (sixteenth and seventeenth centuries). But the various Shiite communities outside Iran remained more or less self-contained until the second half of the twentieth century. It was the clergy and not the Iranian state that would progressively Iranianize non-Iranian Shiite groups, following a strategy that would become that of the Iranian state only in 1979. Twelver Shiites alone were receptive to this clericalization (the other Shiites either have no clergy, like the Alevis of Turkey, or live in closed sects, like the Ismailis or the Zaydis of Yemen). Iranianization does not signify Persianization in the linguistic sense: clergy educated in Najaf and Karbala are bilingual and Arabo-Persian, for often, as we have seen, they are of Arab origin.

Beginning in the eighteenth century, a clergy linked both through kinship and through student-master allegiance, often subsequently transformed into family ties, evolved in Najaf and Karbala; this clergy tended to ensure the monopoly on the ministry of the Shiite world thanks to the practice of investiture *(ijaza)* accorded the student. Certain families, like the Musawis, constitute international networks, with branches in Lebanon, Iran, Iraq, and so on. Najaf and Karbala were the "heart" of Shiism in the sense that these centers attracted, educated, and then assigned posts to students, while maintaining them in a hierarchical network of long-distance allegiance. Young mullahs who came to study were "exported" to countries other than their country of origin. In the beginning this clergy was Arabo-Persian, but beginning in the nineteenth century the disaffection of Arab students caused it to become increasingly Iranian, while a large population of Iranian origin settled at the two sacred sites. In 1957 only 20 percent of the students in Najaf were Arab, compared with 46 percent Iranian.[1] The British, in 1922, then the Ba'thist regime, in 1979, banished to Iran contestant ayatollahs in Najaf and Karbala, which had two consequences: first, beginning in the 1920s the city of Qum could claim the role of the religious capital of Shiism, and as a result the religious center and the political center (Tehran) were closer; second, the high Shiite clergy, until then Arabo-Persian, became increasingly Iranian and identified with the cause of Shiism and of the Iranian nation.[2] The proportion of Arab ayatollahs continued to decline with respect to Iranians, without a subsequent decrease in the influence of the Shiite clergy in Arab areas; on the contrary. In 1980, after the execution of Muhammad Baqir al-Sadr, all the dozen surviving grand ayatollahs were Iranian, including the only one who still lived in Najaf, Ayatollah al-Khu'i. The first Gulf war, which enabled Iraq to put an end to Najaf and Karbala's de facto extraterritoriality, marked the end of a certain Shiism, a Shiism that was Iranianized without being a vehicle for the Iranian state's interests.

One example provides an excellent illustration of the transterritoriality of the Shiite clergy: Imam Musa Sadr, the main force behind the Shiite Lebanese movement Amal, is Iranian, but his ancestor, Abd al-Husayn Amili (who died in 1577), was among the ulamas of south Lebanon who left to join the court of the Safavids.[3] Musa al-Sadr's father was an Iranian ayatollah, but his cousins, who had settled in Najaf, played an important role in Iraqi political life between the two wars. It was the Grand (Arab) Ayatollah Muhsin al-Hakim (who died in 1970 and whose son, Muhammad Baqir al-Hakim, now directs the Supreme Council of the Islamic Revolution in Iraq, located in Tehran) who sent him to Lebanon in 1959. Moreover, a daughter of Ayatollah al-Hakim married a brother of the president of the Iranian Republic, Khamanei. Sheikh Fadlallah, spiritual leader of the Lebanese Hizbullah, was born and lived in Najaf from 1934 until the early 1960s. The examples go on and on.

Iran emerged as a sponsor and guarantor of this policy of Iranianization of Shiite minorities beginning with the Shah, who repressed the Shiite clergy within the country but supported their expansion abroad: he financed the early years of Imam Musa al-Sadr in Lebanon as well as the activist group Al-Da'wa in Iraq.[4] But ultimately it was the advent of the Islamist Republic that gave meaning to the association between Shiism and Iran.

What compelled Shiite minorities to identify with the Islamic revolution? Within their individual national frameworks, they were marginalized and did not identify with the state, but clung to tribal and traditional structures. When the expansion of the state apparatus and the modernization of economic structures obliged them to leave their ghettos (rural exodus in Lebanon and Iraq, temporary emigration in Afghanistan), they identified with a suprastate entity, Shiism, which repudiated the state as tribalism did, but this time from the top: there is a systematic link between the detribalization and clericalization. As it turns out, only clericalization allows the Shiite minority to play a political role on a national level.[5] Claiming a Shiite identity, in fact, indicates a desire to integrate into modern society, and not a rejection of modernity. This shift, from ethnic communalism under traditionalist direction to Shiite universalism, can occur only under the direction of the clergy; they alone (along with the communists) possess a universalist discourse of legitimation. This clergy is very Iranianized. Iranianization is a consequence, and not a cause, of the spread of the myth of Islamic revolution. Both the borders of the Sunni world and the notion of Arabness are repudiated, not in the name of being Iranian, but rather in the name of the Muslim *umma,* of which Shiism positions itself as the avantgarde.

It is important to note that the Islamist radicalization of Shiite communities outside Iran preceded the Islamic revolution in Iran.

Whether through the sociopolitical apostolate of Imam Musa al-Sadr in Lebanon, the preaching of Sayyid Balkhi in Afghanistan,[6] or the political and philosophical activism of Muhammad Baqir al-Sadr in Iraq, the basic Islamist wave swept all Shiite communities worldwide from its core in Najaf and Karbala as early as the 1950s, effecting change on a local basis and through local officers, and was not an aftereffect of the Iranian revolution, which only crystallized and incarnated this movement. The Iraqi movement Al-Da'wa was founded in about 1960, the Afghan movement Sobh-i Danesh at the end of the 1960s. The Iraqi Ayatollah Baqir al-Sadr wrote certain fundamental texts of revolutionary Shiism as early as 1960.[7] It was the victory of the revolution in Iran that transformed Shiite communities agitated by indigenous movements into bridgeheads of Iranian influence. The triumph of the revolution in Iran created an optical effect, hiding from view the autonomous aspects of foreign Shiite communities.

The actors in the Shiite revival are young clerics educated in Najaf and Karbala, united by common allegiance to a grand ayatollah and clustered in local political organizations. This verticality of allegiance counts more than nationality: the Afghan clerics who were disciples of Khomeini would not join the same political organizations as the disciples of Ayatollah al-Khu'i. Imam Musa al-Sadr, an Iranian, is not perceived as a foreigner in south Lebanon, despite his strong accent, since he was sent by Grand Ayatollah Baqir al-Sadr. The term "Shiite" replaces local community identifications (Musa Sadr brought an end to the use of the denomination *metouali* in south Lebanon in favor of Shiite).[8]

The break with traditional society is marked by often violent struggle (the decline in south Lebanon of the traditional notables, the *za'im;* the headway made in the Lebanese Beka Valley by two important clerical families, the Musawis and the Husayns, against the Jaffar clan; the civil war in Afghanistan from 1982 to 1984 between traditionalists of the *shura* and Shiite Islamists).[9]

Thus there has been no exporting of the Iranian revolution, but a prior revolutionary influence on Middle Eastern Shiism, emanating more from Najaf more than from Qum. The Iranians have nonetheless been highly instrumental (Khomeini was in Najaf beginning in 1963; Shamran, the future defense minister of revolutionary Iran, worked and fought in south Lebanon in the 1970s). Many Shiite families of Iraq or the Gulf (Bahrain) are Iranian or of Iranian origin.[10]

Beginning in the 1970s, there was an Iranianization of symbolism among non-Iranian Shiites, in customs (adoption of the *ashura*, the ritual of processions, by the Lebanese in the 1950s and by the Afghan Hazaras),[11] clothing (adoption of the "Hizbullah look": beards, parkas, black chadors), names (adoption of family names ending in *i* among the Afghan Hazaras—Tavasolli, Beheshti, Tavakolli, and so on, instead of the "Mirza Husayns" and "Ghulam Alis" of the previous generation), flags (Iranian for the Hizbullahs of south Lebanon), and language (the educated Afghan Hazaras who speak a very particular dialect, Hazaragi, began affecting Iranian accents and idioms).

This Iranianization of Shiite minorities has its limits, encountering as it does strongly maintained traditional tribal structures (Shiite peasants in southern Iraq), a nationalism that often tends toward secularity despite religious references (the Amal movement in Lebanon), and the resistance of traditionalist clergy (the *shura* in Afghanistan) or secular progressive forces (communist in Lebanon, Benazir Bhutto's PPP in Pakistan, Maoist in Afghanistan), with which the movement maintains ambiguous relations. The theme of the Islamic revolution finds its most fertile ground among the young generations of newly urbanized or emigrant Shiites, cut off from traditional structures and "resocialized" by a politicized and modernist clergy educated in Najaf or Qum.

The Iranian revolutionary state would utilize this growing Iranianization of Shiite minorities to circumvent Arab nationalism, the primary obstacle to the expansion of the Islamic revolution in the Middle East.

The Implementation of Islamic Iran's Foreign Policy

It is thus among foreign Shiite communities that revolutionary Iran had the largest impact. The other points of solidarity (language and culture) have struck few chords. The general rule is that the Shiite connection takes precedence over an Iranian identity (the Azeris are more "Iranian" than the Kurds)[12] or even one's linguistic community (among the Persian-speaking Afghans, only the Shiite Hazaras feel solidarity with Iran). The Sunni groups who are "Iranian" from an ethnolinguistic point of view (Kurds, Sunni Persian-speakers in Afghanistan) receive no particular support from Iran. Only the Shiites identify with Iran.

Despite the universalist and Third World–type dream that motivates Islamic Iran, the revolution is ghettoized within Shiism, as shown by the riots in Mecca on July 31, 1987, when Iranian Shiite protesters were joined only by Pakistani or Afghan Shiites. At the same time, within Shiite circles Iran has an impact only where prior clericalization has occurred and where the theme of the Islamic revolution has encountered a receptive sociological milieu (urbanization and pauperization). This is why the nonclericalized Shiite groups (like the Alevis of Turkey, who, unlike the Azeri Turks, were never part of the Iranian-influenced political circle)[13] are still impervious to Iranian influence.

Iran's foreign policy has thus been able to rely on the support of Arab Shiites (in Lebanon, Iraqi cities, and Gulf emirates), among the Persian-speaking Shiites of Afghanistan, and among the Shiites of Pakistan and, to a lesser extent, of India, even though none of these groups is wholly pro-Iranian. Shiite power outside the Iranian plateau is concentrated in the Persian Gulf, 75 percent of whose waterside residents are Shiite, with bridgeheads in Lebanon and on the Indian subcontinent (from Afghanistan to India). Outside these three points, Shiite universalism's capacity for negating borders is weak, either because there is no Shiite community (Egypt, central Asia) or because the community has not been influenced by the clericalization emanating from Najaf and Karbala (Turkey). One case nonetheless remains ambivalent: former Soviet Azerbaijan, where Azeri nationalism, which rejects all Iranian tutelage per se, integrates the Twelver Shiite identity (many communist party dignitaries are sons of mullahs). But the antireligious repression of the 1920s, followed by Stalin's creation of an independent *muftiyya* in 1941, cut this clergy off from twentieth-century Shiite revivalism; finally,

Sheikh al-Islam Pashazada, the head of the Azeri Shiite clergy, sworn into his functions after Azerbaijan became independent in 1991, is a disciple of Ayatollah al-Khu'i and a former student of Ayatollah Shariat Madari, a moderate opponent of Khomeini, and an Azeri himself, and thus has little sympathy for the Islamist regime in Tehran.

The dominance of Shiism prevents Iran from laying claim to overall Islamic radicalism, for the Sunnis cannot identify with it. The virulent activism of the Muslim Brotherhood and the Wahhabis is openly anti-Shiite (and vice versa). Iran's revolutionary influence extended to Shiism and not to Islamic radicalism. The Gulf states rightly saw their local Shiite communities as an Iranian fifth column, while not being fearful of the activism of the MB.

In what concrete ways did Iran play on Shiism in its foreign policy?

Since the revolution, Iran has made a point of politically integrating foreign Shiite minorities under the guidance of the imam. In a first phase, until 1982, Iran supported all specifically Shiite movements, such as Amal in Lebanon. Then it demanded both radicalization, the abandonment of nationalist references, and integration into specifically Iranian structures (the Revolutionary Guard, the Bureau of Islamic Propaganda in Qum under the direction of Ayatollah Muntazari). This was the moment when "hizbullahs" began appearing, both in Lebanon and in Afghanistan, where a corps of Revolutionary Guards was created among Shiites. The Iranian embassy in Beirut became a sort of Shiite headquarters in Lebanon, where the Hizbullah and the Islamic Amal (created in 1982) opposed the Amal, all the while keeping their distance from the more traditional clergy (Sheikh Shams al-Din). The Iraqi Shiites in exile in Tehran were assembled into the "Supreme Council of the Islamic Revolution of Iraq" in 1982, under the direction of Muhammad Baqir al-Hakim. This control operation sometimes occurred at the price of a veritable civil war (Amal against Hizbullah, pro-Khomeiniites against the *shura* in Afghanistan). This phase ended in 1983. The second phase consisted in launching Shiite groups in pursuit of

Iran's adversaries: here, Lebanon was the primary battlefield against Westerners (destruction of the French and American headquarters in 1983), since an equilibrium was soon established in Afghanistan between the Soviet Union and Iran (no Shiite attacks against the Russians in exchange for relative restraint on the part of the Soviets in the support of Iraq). Iranianization reached its height in 1985–1986, at the time of Fao's victory over the Iraqi army: 1986 was the year of Iranian victory.

But this headway brought about a sacred union of all Sunnis (rapprochement of the MB and the Saudis), caused conflict with conservative Shiites, and did not allow Iran to play on its ethno-linguistic solidarity with Sunnis who speak Iranian languages. The Iranian revolution seemed more Shiite than ever.

Aware of this risk, and despite heated opposition from "radicals" (such as the minister of the interior at the time, Muhtashami) and a segment of the clergy (led by Ayatollah Muntazari), the government of Tehran attempted overtures toward Sunni and even progressive, nationalist, and communist milieus. Beginning in 1986, Tehran developed the habit of rallying those alienated by other Middle Eastern states' policies. The "rejection fronts" gathered at large conferences: "Solidarity Conference of the Iraqi Opposition" in December 1986, "Conference to Safeguard the Sacred Sites" in the winter of 1987, "Conference of Solidarity with the Palestinian People" in October 1991. But the large Sunni organizations were wary of Tehran, which managed to rally only the more compliant Sunnis (like Sheikh Sha'ban in Lebanon or Mawlawi Mansur in Afghanistan) whose power base was purely local. Everywhere the gap grew wider between the Sunni and Shiite communities: in Iraq, Shiites and Sunni Kurds fought in extended order against Saddam; in Lebanon, the Hizbullah was isolated; in Afghanistan, the provisional government of the resistance included no Shiites and was strongly influenced by the Wahhabis. In Pakistan, communal riots opposed Shiites and Sunnis during Muharram 1986 and 1987. The 1987 Conference to Safeguard the Sacred Sites, which was called to condemn the Saudi regime, drew no known Sunnis.

The decomposition of the Soviet empire brought no gains for Tehran: Shiite Azerbaijan adopted the Latin alphabet and turned to Ankara, Sunni Uzbekistan founded itself on more of a nationalist than a Muslim base. Only little Tadzhikistan, which is Sunni but Persian-speaking, seeks in Iran a protector against Uzbeki ambitions, which can only place Tehran in an unstable position with respect to the great mass of Soviet Muslims who speak Turkish. But the defeat of the "Islamo-democratic" government in Dushanbe in November 1992 eliminated almost all Iranian influence in Tadzhikistan.

There is no middle ground between pure Shiite revolutionarism and a nationalist, pragmatic policy. Prisoner of its own symbolism and of its revolutionary legitimacy, Iran was unable to make the strategic choices that would have restored it to its place as a great regional power.

❖ *Conclusion: Tomorrow's Gray Areas* ❖

*I*SLAMISM, NOW FADED into neofundamentalism, is not a geostrategic factor: it will neither unify the Muslim world nor change the balance of power in the Middle East. From Casablanca to Tashkent, the Islamists have molded themselves into the framework of existing states, adopting their modes of exercising power, their strategic demands, and their nationalism. All the states that appeal to the Muslim *umma* nonetheless maintain the concept of nationality and passports; in terms of supranationality, they are far less advanced than the European Union. There is not as much difference between the Algerian FIS and FLN as one might think: the same Third World, anti-Western discourse, the same single-party mold, the same patronage practices; if the FIS comes to power, the opposition to Tunisia and Morocco will merely be reinterpreted in ideological terms. On an economic level, future Islamist regimes will be faced with the same alternative that all governments already face: a weary state socialism offset by a black market, or a liberal neoconservatism constrained to follow the prescriptions of the International Monetary Fund, under the veil of "Islamic banks."

Islamism is above all a sociocultural movement embodying the protest and frustration of a generation of youth that has not been integrated socially or politically.

The Absence of an Islamist Alternative

Today's Islamist movements, like the Algerian FIS, do not offer a new model of society; far from consecrating the return of a conquering, self-assured Islam, they reflect first and foremost the failure of the Western-style state model, which was imported and com-

194

mandeered by single parties and patronage networks. They assemble the outcasts of a failed modernism, mobilizing them around the myth of a return to an Islamic authenticity that never existed. In this sense, Islamism is indeed an agent of integration for the social sectors at once produced by and excluded from the accelerated modernization of Muslim societies (educated youth with no futures, recently urbanized masses). But this integration into politics has not brought into being a new model of society: those who placed their hopes in such a society may one day be amenable to new forms of protest.

There is no concrete political, let alone economic, model inherent in Islamism. Islamism in power will systematize the policies of Islamization "from the top" already evident in officially secular or moderate regimes. In terms of mores and personal status, the distance is not very great between many secular Muslim states and the neofundamentalist enterprise. Henceforth the new motto will be "*sharia* and only *sharia*." This Islamization will target personal law and penal law, leaving intact the traditional or reconstituted solidarity networks, as well as the existing economies, and adopting the political model inherited from the previous regimes—essentially that of the single party.

As we have seen, such a model in and of itself does not generate institutions capable of functioning on their own: the dream of justice and social redistribution can be based only on the virtue of those who implement it. But the transformation of Islamist parties into mass movements and the test of power will produce the same results that it has with all other ideologies: the "pure" will be corrupted or will abandon politics to climbers, careerists, and unscrupulous businessmen.

Any Islamist victory will be a mirage. But the illusion it creates will not be without effects.

The Bleak Society

First of all, Islamization will mean the destruction of the social space between the state and the family. The Islamic society to which neofundamentalism refers never existed. The Islam that the FIS is proposing is (unfortunately) not a return to Muslim civilization: this civilization had its golden age long ago, before its internal decline and the arrival of colonialism, but the FIS, like all neofundamentalist organizations, rejects the very notion of Muslim civilization, which had room for music, philosophy, poetry and, as we have seen . . . a certain secularity. What the Islamists advocate is not the return to an incomparably rich classical age, but the establishment of an empty stage on which the believer strives to realize with each gesture the ethical model of the Prophet. The only place for conviviality here is the family, which is also, but only for men, the only place of pleasure. The resocialization created by opposition Islamist movements cannot withstand the exercise of power.

What new urban space? We see it in Saudi Arabia. It is an empty space, with neither cinemas nor cafés, only teahouses and restaurants. The streets are patrolled by a religious militia, responsible solely for enforcing good behavior and imposing religious practice (prayer and fasting). The only space for retreat is the family. But these are no longer the families of the rural world, in which women participate in the work and there is a popular, living culture. The modern family is mainly a place of consumption: television, videos, and so on. The Islamists will never be able to stop the flow of this consumption, precisely because the *sharia* protects family privacy. And what is circulating in the urban family is the opposite of the Islamic way of life: it is a product of the West. There are no "Islamic leisure activities." The new cultural models (videos) are blossoming into the very heart of the Islamic identity, even though the result is never a Westernization of modes of behavior, but a synthesis, or a juxtaposition, unable to be reduced to one system or another.

Although such a framework may be perfectly suitable to men involved in economic and social activities, in other words, to men of stature or notables, it is hard to imagine how the young generation who vote FIS can benefit from it—first, because establishing a family requires money and housing, and the economic miracle has not yet occurred and is not on the verge of doing so; second, because youth is not puritanical: today it is frustrated and will not tolerate the lassitude and boredom of "Islamic society."

What will imposition of the *sharia* mean? Hypocrisy. For, as the true ideologues of Islamism have always said, from Sayyid Qutb to Maududi and Khomeini, imposition of the *sharia* makes sense only if the society is already Islamic and man finally virtuous. If not, everything is just casuistics, appearance and ruse, the use of which may be perfectly legal (*hile shar'i:* "legal ruse," the kind that allows the believer to get around a shariatic interdiction without falling into a state of sin).

The only model for sociability in Islamism is personal devotion within the framework of the mosque. Why create associations, leisure activities, opportunities for individuals to blossom, when the only model of behavior is devotional? Between the sacred family space (the *haram*), the mosque, and the institution of the state, viewed as a simple instrument of Islamization, there is no structure for the social space, except through traditional or business solidarities, which are obviously not open to the young unemployed generation. In short, what prevents Islamic society from producing totalitarianism (its respect for the family and lack of interest in the social sphere) also prevents it from producing any true social framework: it rejects any space for conviviality and sociability, if only by the strict implementation of the separation of the sexes and, particularly, of the confinement of women to the house (whereas in Iran, and this is the exception, women have the right to work and access to the public sphere). This puritanism is profoundly modern and urban, in the sense that the most rigorous Muslim peasant society (such as the Afghan *mujahidin*, who are as fundamentalist as can be) knows what it means to enjoy laughter, humor, song, and poetry.

The result is not alienation, but social conformity and boredom. A schizophrenia will arise, as it does in all puritan societies: the inevitable transgressions (drugs, alcohol, sex) will take place in hiding and thanks to money. But how long will youth accept being bored, especially when the other model is within arm's reach—on television or across the Mediterranean? The argument for virtue collapses when one can enjoy the goods of this other society, through delinquency, money, emigration, or political power.

The Islam of Resentment

In contrast to Egyptian or Afghan Islamism, contemporary neofundamentalism is not a response to colonial conquest or military confrontation, not a response to regimes that threaten to take action against their own societies, but rather a response to acculturation. But the acculturation has already taken place, and the Islam being used to counter it is a reinvention, an imitation.

Neofundamentalist rhetoric exacerbates the cultural differences between the West and the Muslim world, but in a profoundly asymmetrical way: the Muslim world is in fact already Westernized, but thinks of this Westernization only as alienation. Hence an obvious schizophrenia of behavior in urban environments: the values of consumption, and thus of civilization, are Western; the values that are being trumpeted are those of a recently fabricated authenticity. Islamism is a discourse of protest and adaptation, thus of transition. There are happy Muslims; there are no happy Islamists. Modernity is irreversible, but it has no language. A curious example is music: the first music against which the Islamists waged war was the music of their own culture, classical or popular music (such as the Algerian *rai*); but when they produce music (the martial music of Radio Tehran, for example), it is composed according to the rules of Western music.

There is no Islamist "culture," and the *kulturkampf* of the Islamists against a culture that is an obstacle to pure devotion paves the way for the universal culture: that of Americanization. Was it only by chance that Ali Belhadj, the leader of the FIS, proposed replacing French with English in Algerian schools? For him, there is indeed an international language, and thus, whatever he may think of them, values and models with which one may identify and disseminated by the culture. In making this proposal, Belhadj is in touch with his electorate, which is passionate about the Quran as well as about American series broadcast (in French) on French television and picked up by satellite antennas.

The rejection of Western culture is thus on the order of a curse, a cry, an accusation; but it also has an element of fascination. Neofundamentalist society does not represent hatred of the other, but rather hatred of oneself and of one's desires. The religion of the peasant, of the mullah, of the notable, who are tolerant because they are sure of their vision of the world, is being replaced by the Islam of resentment, which is defensive, which demands recognition.

The Loss of Religion's Authenticity and Space

Islamism is actually an agent in the secularization of Muslim societies because it brings the religious space into the political arena: although it claims to do so to the benefit of the former, its refusal to take the true functioning of politics and society into consideration causes it instead to follow the unwritten rules of the traditional exercise of power and social segmentation. The autonomous functioning of the political and social arenas wins out, but only after the religious sphere has been emptied of its value as a place of transcendence, refuge, and protest, since it is now identified with the new power.

A great deal is said about the return to Islam, but one must nuance this statement. There is a big difference, for example, between Islamist Iran, where one almost never sees a person praying in the street, and the new Islamized neighborhoods of otherwise secular republics (Tunisia, Turkey), where certain streets are practically closed to cars by the crowd of men in prayer. The political victory of Islamism is the end of true devotion. Mosques are packed in places where they have become sites of mobilization in opposition to a state perceived as particularist, client-oriented, and repressive; but they empty out when Islamism takes power. They also fill when it is a matter of bringing immigrants together into a community group, with its own institutions and spokespeople, as in Great Britain. Ghettos are fertile soil for re-Islamization. But in France, the *"beur"* (slang for "Arab") culture of proletarian, second-generation immigrants is a subculture of the dominant culture, and its values (music, consumption, the "look") are in conflict with those of Islam. The protest against French society takes place in the name of the values of this society itself and not those of Islam.

The Return of the Unconsidered

As we have seen, the myth of Islamic society presupposes a casting into sin or a plot of the part of anything that creates social differentiation—whether ethnicity, tribalism, or clans and solidarity networks. Similarly, the corruption and injustice of leaders are attributed to a lack of virtue, and are thus susceptible to eradication through admonishment and counsel. The idea is that in an Islamic society the consensus, obtained in the "silence of passions," as Rousseau would say, must be the rule, the "silence of passions" being the result of the efforts each one makes individually to emulate the Prophet.

Whatever is repressed naturally resurfaces, not as sin, but as a sociological or psychological fact. In most societies in which Islamists militate, the weakness of the state model means that politics, or, more trivially, political games, end up ultimately being based on solidarity groups or "clans," whether they are an expression of family, ethnic, or tribal ties that predate the emergence of a state authority, or the reinvention of communal solidarities in newly urbanized and destructured societies. If social segmentation, individual rivalries, patronage, the lure of profit, and so on are perceived as faults, sins, or plots, then there is no way to understand and combat their unthought-out and ruthless recurrence in the "new" society. This recurrence, as we have seen, is not simply the lingering effect of a tribal and peasant past, but the reconstitution in modern society of traditional modes of loyalty and exercise of power: matrimonial alliances, corporate solidarity, patronage—that is, the exchange of material bribes for political loyalty.

It is true that tribalism *stricto sensu* remains strong in Saudi Arabia and in Yemen, where the fundamentalist party Islah is merely a political outgrowth of the Hashed tribe. But generally the appearance of political Islamism often masks a recomposition of *asabiyya*, solidarity groups, in a manner that is different from peasant tribalism. Michel Seurat shows, in his study of the Bab Tebbane section of Tripoli (Lebanon), how an urban group functions as an *asabiyya* and translates politically into an Islamist party, the Movement of

Islamic Unification, the particularist geographic and sociological base of which its leader, Sheikh Sha'ban, refuses to concede: "The movement is Islam. Does Islam have boundaries?"[1]

Islamism has been unable to move beyond either nationalism or even ethnicity, and this inability has also been blamed on a Western plot. In Sudan, where a regime supported by the Muslim Brotherhood is in power, a former MB, Dawud Bulad, assumed leadership in 1991 of a black guerrilla group in the Darfur that was against the "Arabs" of Khartoum; behind the politics of Islamization, an age-old hostility between Arabs and blacks is also resurfacing. In Algeria, the Arabization extolled by the FIS is to the detriment of the Kabyles. In Malaysia, Islamism is also the expression of ethnic tension with the Chinese. In Afghanistan, the old oppositions between Pakhtuns and non-Pakhtuns is dominating politics.

Finally, as we have seen, the Islamist movements fit into the molds of the nation-states or become the instruments of foreign policy of the large states. Islamo-nationalism wins out over pan-Islamism.

This phenomenon, which is the key to the functioning of politics in societies in which Islamists militate (tribalism, ethnicity, patronage, nationalism), is either denied by them, attributed to lack of faith, or ascribed to a colonialist plot. The myth of unity prohibits thinking about conflict and differentiation, which thus resurface in often uncontrolled violence or in the commandeering of the economy and of state power by patronage networks. Indeed, the fact that one refuses to admit that the sociological reality of differentiation exists does not mean one is unaware of it: on the contrary, it is perfectly mastered as a tactic, but ignored as a concept; hence the permanent gap between the subtlety of the tactical practices and the schizophrenia of the theory. The internal quarrels of the Islamist world—except, no doubt, in Iran—are constantly described as "misunderstandings" among Brothers. The real conflicts are masked behind the palinode of ruptures and reconciliations, such as those that have punctuated the history of the Afghan resistance. Personal ambition and ethnic division will never be recognized as legitimate and will always be attributed to the West . . . except that in private they are constant topics of conversation. Islamism furnishes no conceptual apparatus for thinking about one's own sociopolitical reality; hence its drift toward neofundamentalism.

Solidarity and patronage networks, whether Islamist or not, function and perpetuate themselves because they are plugged into globalized circuits of distribution and circulation of goods: petrodollars, drugs, oil, arms, subsidies coming from other states and distributed to strategic ends, or simply international business (including taxes on freight and imports, the distribution of import licenses, and currency speculation). The globalization of circulation networks is made possible by the weakness, but also by the stability, of the state.

The politics in which contemporary Islamist movements operate is thus a consequence of a new world-space and not of the return to a traditional cultural space. The triumphant neofundamentalism will be incapable of ensuring the insularity of Islamic societies: it depends economically on the world-space in the very exercise of its power; its society is too permeated with Western models, and no one can stop radio, television, cassettes, and travelers.

Islamists and the West

It is no doubt this awareness of the impossibility of insularity that causes Islamists to be obsessed with purity and leads them to fight any Christian presence, even national ones that have always existed, such as the Copts in Egypt, despite the fact that traditional ulamas accept Christians and Jews.

Although the strategy of the neofundamentalists is not based on revolution, it is founded on a stated rejection of all Western values, which wasn't always the case for the Islamists. It was in no small measure paradoxical, for those who have confused all these movements, to see Iran's minister of foreign affairs argue in favor of the right to vote for Afghan women in 1991, against the provisional Afghan government supported by Saudi Arabia and the United States. The political and even cultural models in operation in Iran's Islamic revolution are modern by comparison with regimes like the one in Saudi Arabia, or even by comparison with the debate that animates the neofundamentalists on the virtues of the future "amir" of an Islamic state.

Sunni neofundamentalism applies a wholly religious reading to the North–South opposition: the theme of the new crusade re-awakens that of imperialism, Israel is the bridgehead of the West (or vice versa in the most paranoid versions), Christian missionaries are everywhere. Western culture is judged to be a corrupting influence, and its society is described in entirely negative terms (suicides, alcoholism, depravity, and so on). The neofundamentalist vision of the world is defensive. One point that illustrates this evolution is the Afghan's vision of Jews: before the war in Afghanistan, the Pakhtun tribes boasted of being descended from a lost tribe of Israel; during the war, many traditionalist mullahs could be heard extolling the virtues of the Torah (in opposition, of course, to the atheist communists), but today many Afghan neofundamentalists harp on the Zionist plot.

This cultural opposition to the West is unrelated to the strategic choices made by states. Anti-Christian attitudes and discourse reach their highest pitch among the Saudis, who, strategically, are in the Western camp, but who forbid the erection of churches on their soil, whereas Iran never had an anti-Christian political position and has always accepted a certain Christian visibility (to the point of authorizing the Armenians to make wine).

The defensive rigidity of neofundamentalism therefore demonstrates its inability to incorporate modernity. It has been a long time since Christianity was Islam's other. Even if there is a religious revival among Christians and Jews, it is in no way parallel to that of the fundamentalists. The culture that threatens Muslim society is neither Jewish nor Christian; it is a world culture of consumption and communication, a culture that is secular, atheist, and ultimately empty; it has no values or strategies, but it is already here, in the cassette and the transistor, present in the most remote village. This culture can withstand any reappropriation and rereading. It is a code and not a civilization.

Neofundamentalism is seeking its devil in a different god, but does not see the desert within.

❖ *Notes* ❖

Full citations of sources are provided in the Bibliography.

Introduction

1. See, for example, the case of the political leader in the Bab Tebbane section of Tripoli in Lebanon, in Michel Seurat's *L'état de Barbarie,* p. 142.

2. A movement to reconstruct small communities of the "pure" in remote areas began in Egypt in the 1980s. They include the "Al-Shawqiyya" group in the oasis of Fayum, founded by the Amir Shawqi, who had come from Al-Jihad and was killed by the police in 1990.

3. See Bertrand Badie's analysis of the failure of the modern state in the Muslim world, *Les deux états.*

4. Max Weber, *The Protestant Ethic and the Spirit of Capitalism.*

5. Aside from the writings of Max Weber, one should consult on this subject the works of C. Lefort, M. Gauchet, C. Castoriadis, and B. Badie.

6. In the "patrimonial state" there is no public as opposed to private space; the state is not separate from the sovereign; an *asabiyya* (a term borrowed from Ibn Khaldun) is any solidarity group among persons who consider themselves united by common origins and interests and who aim only to maintain this solidarity.

7. The authority of the Great Mufti, who promulgates *fatwa* that are valid for a specific period and country, is a late creation of the powers in place, who were concerned with religious legitimation—and with controlling the ulamas. Even among Shiites, the *fatwa* pronounced by a *mujtahid* are valid only during the latter's lifetime.

8. This process is well illustrated by the short-lived but brilliant journal *Libre,* eight issues of which were published by Payot from 1977 to 1980.

9. According to Farhad Khosrokhavar's expression in "Du néo-orientalisme de Badie," p. 128.

10. The only contemporary thinker who attempts a true "critique" of Islamic thought from within is Mohammed Arkoun *(Critique de la raison islamique);* Arkoun endeavors to find the original "intention," the "Quranic truth" as opposed to the "Islamic truth." This effort is proof that renewal without denial

is possible. But with regard to contemporary political Islam, Arkoun's thought, although it paves the way for the future, remains of marginal influence today.

11. We find in Arab nationalists the same rejection of existing nation-states, the same mirage of unity, of fusion, the same indifference to the concrete forms of politics, as shown by the enthusiasm of certain Arab intellectuals for Saddam Husayn. This enthusiasm does not stem from a misunderstanding or refusal to acknowledge the facts, as was the case for some Western pro-Stalinist intellectuals. Arab intellectuals (H. Djaït) who supported Saddam Husayn knew that he was a tyrant without scruples, but the prospect of revenge for humiliation and the dream of Arab unity won out over political vision.

12. For a good critique of the phantasm of Oriental despotism, see Khosrokhavar, "Du néo-orientalisme de Badie."

13. A. Laroui, *Islam et modernité*, p. 26.

14. Seurat, *L'état de Barbarie*, p. 131.

15. For a good analysis of the recreation of influence networks in a society profoundly altered by the state, the *dowre* in Iran, see Dale Eickelman, *The Middle East*, pp. 197 ff.

16. Here is one anecdote: reporters on assignment in countries that are poorly understood usually like to begin their series with the opinion of the taxi driver who takes them from the airport. In July 1988, at the Tehran airport, it was the taxi driver who asked me who the next president of the Iranian Republic would be. Noting my surprise, he explained: "You're English; you know better than we do who our leaders will be." He ended by admitting that the French were less well informed than the British.

17. An idea developed in Seurat, *L'état de Barbarie*, pp. 23 ff.

18. For example, in the discourse of an Afghan *mujahidin* leader, Qazi Amin, on the Islamic state in Afghanistan, presented as an alternative to the traditional tribal society ("Conference on Afghanistan," photocopies, Tehran, October 1990).

19. See Chapter 6, "The Islamist New Intellectuals."

20. The thesis of the book by Daryus Chayegan, *Qu'est-ce qu'une révolution religieuse?*

21. These movements were studied by E. Sivan, G. Michaud (M. Seurat) and O. Carré, G. Kepel, and R. H. Dekmejian.

1. Islam and Politics

1. See Chapter 5. See also Dale Eickelman, *The Middle East*, chap. 9.

2. One of the most famous princely advisers was the vizier Nizam al-Mulk during the Seljuk Empire, a good example of what Bernard Lewis calls the "Muslim school of political philosophy," in *The Political Language of Islam*, p. 26.

3. Among them are the *Panj kitab* (Afghanistan), the *Chahar kitab*, the *Haft-o yek* (former Soviet Central Asia), named according to the number of sections of which they are composed. See the remarkable article by N. Shahrani, "Popular Knowledge of Islam and Social Discourse in Afghanistan and Turkistan in the Modern Period."

4. It is a mistake to regard Sufism as systematically opposed to fundamentalism. This theory, which comes out of French studies of maraboutism in the Maghreb, ignores the role of Sufi orders in re-Islamization or conversion, particularly in the Caucasus, Central Asia, and black Africa.

5. E. Kedourie, *Afghani and Abduh.*

6. Ali Mérad, *Ibn Badis, commentateur du Coran.*

7. A. Laroui, *Islam et modernité*, p. 41.

8. For Chinese Turkestan, see K. Karpat, "Yakub Bey's Relations with the Ottoman Sultans: A Reinterpretation." For the Indian subcontinent, aside from the history of the *Khalifat* movement, which cast thousands of Muslims into exile in Afghanistan in protest against the abolition of the caliphate, one should consult the book by Maulavie Mohammed Bereketullah of Bhopal, the French translation of which is titled *Le Khalifat.*

9. Note the absurdity of the expression "Arabo-Muslim": either one is speaking of the "Muslim world" (from Morocco to Indonesia), of which Arabs make up less than 20 percent, or of the "Arab world," where Christians played a considerable role in the establishment of nationalism. What is specifically Arab in Islam has acquired universal status, and what is specifically Arab in the culture of the "Arab world" is not specifically Muslim.

10. Ibn Badis calls on Muslims to forswear the "chimera of the caliphate" in Mérad, *Ibn Badis*, p. 212, which elsewhere (p. 241) quotes an article by Ibn Badis, "Le regretté Mustafa Kémal . . ."

2. The Concepts of Islamism

1. The main reference work on the Egyptian MB is R. P. Mitchell, *The Society of the Muslim Brothers.* For further information about the Syrian MB, see the collection of documents with commentary by G. Michaud (M. Seurat) and O. Carré, *Les Frères musulmans;* and Johannes Reissner, *Ideologie und Politik der Muslimbrüder Syriens.* The primary reference work on the Jamaat is still K. Bahadur, *The Jama'at-i Islami of Pakistan.*

2. On the ties between the two, see E. Sivan, *Radical Islam*, p. 23.

3. For example, Khurshid Ahmed writes, in the foreword to A. Maududi, *The Islamic Law and Constitution*, p. 6, "There is a basic difference between a 'Muslim State' and an 'Islamic State.' A Muslim State is any state which is ruled by Muslims. An Islamic State, on the other hand, is one which opts to conduct its affairs in accordance with the revealed guidance of Islam and accepts the

sovereignty of Allah and the supremacy of His Law." To legitimate this distinction, which tends to go against the tradition, the radical Islamists sought the patronage of the theologian Ibn Taymiyya, who had declared that one could lead the jihad against the Mongols despite their conversion to Islam: see E. Sivan, "Ibn Taymiyya, Father of the Islamic Revolution." But as Sivan notes elsewhere, even the most rigorous canonic jurist, Ibn Hanbal, took exception to this law (*Radical Islam*, p. 91).

4. Hassan al-Turabi, in John L. Esposito, *Voices of Resurgent Islam*, p. 245. See also A. Maududi: "Whosoever devotes his time and energy to the study of the Qur'an and the *Sunnah* and becomes well-versed in Islamic learning is entitled to speak as an expert in matters pertaining to Islam"; *The Islamic Law and Constitution*, p. 209. Muslim social science researchers are the ulamas of today's *umma*, according to I. Faruqi and A. Umar Nassif in *Social and Natural Science: The Islamic Perspective* (Jeddah, 1981).

5. This anticlericalism was present from the start among the Egyptian MB; Sivan, *Radical Islam*, p. 52.

6. Hassan al-Turabi: "[In an Islamic democracy] ideally there is no clerical ulama class, which prevents an elitist or theocratic government. Whether termed a religious, a theocratic, or even a secular theocracy, an Islamic state is not a government of the ulama"; in Esposito, *Voices of Resurgent Islam*, p. 244.

7. Reissner, *Ideologie und Politik*, p. 152. Al-Siba'i wrote a book titled *The Socialism of Islam (Ishtirakiyyat al-islam)*.

8. Thus Hashimi, in *Misaq-i Khun*, a journal of the Jamaat-i Islami Afghanistan, no. 19, p. 39, writes: "In a *tawhid* society, there is no place for *ta'zir* and *qanun*," that is, state legislation.

9. For the MB, see Mitchell, *Society of the Muslim Brothers*, p. 239.

10. For Qutb, see O. Carré, *Mystique et politique*, p. 204; for Yasin, see M. Tozy, "Le prince, le clerc et l'état: La reconstruction du champ religieux au Maroc," in Kepel and Richard, *Intellectuels et militants*, pp. 89 ff.

11. A 1981 article in a women's Islamist journal, *Payam-i Hajar*, anticipating a different blood donation for men and women, carried this title: "First Assure Social Justice, Then the Law of Retaliation"; quoted in Fariba Adelkhah, *La révolution sous le voile*, p. 66.

12. Al-Turabi, in Esposito, *Voices of Resurgent Islam*, p. 246.

13. The fifth MB conference in 1939 explicitly defined the movement as a "political organization"; Mitchell, *Society of the Muslim Brothers*, p. 16. The same is true for the Syrian MB; Reissner, *Ideologie und Politik*, p. 148.

14. A. Maududi: "there is absolutely no scope for making any provision in the constitution of an Islamic State for a non-Muslim to become a ruler . . . to do so would be as irrational and impracticable as would be a non-Communist's becoming the ruler of a Communist state or a Fascist's becoming the ruler of a democratic state"; *The Islamic Law and Constitution*, p. 266. Such reflections,

always made in passing, are nevertheless very revealing about the vision of Islam as an ideology. Islam is sometimes presented as the third way between a Marxism solely turned toward the material satisfaction of human needs and a Christianity preoccupied solely with spiritual salvation. Islam is the religion of total man, thus the religion of equilibrium. This argument is developed by S. Qutb (Mitchell, *Society of the Muslim Brothers,* p. 251) and adopted by the Soviet Tadzhik A. Saïdov (the journal *Sukhan,* no. 18, July 12, 1991, p. 3).

15. The spiritual leader of the Egyptian Muslim Brotherhood, al-Hudaybi, who rejected the radicalization introduced by Sayyid Qutb, emphasized the absence of a Quranic reference for this concept: Michaud (Seurat) and Carré, *Les Frères musulmans,* p. 98.

16. The references are innumerable. On *fikra* among the MB, see Mitchell, *Society of the Muslim Brothers,* p. 207. The term "ideology" can be found, for example, in the introduction (written in English by Khurshid Ahmed, himself a theoretician of Islamism) to Maududi, *The Islamic Law and Constitution:* "Islam is an all-embracing ideology." The term has been so well incorporated in people's minds that after coming to power in Pakistan in 1977, the very conservative general Zia ul-Haqq instituted a "Council of Islamic Ideology."

17. Maududi, in *The Islamic Law and Constitution,* adopts the matrix of modern constitutional law (elections; judicial, legislative, and executive powers; citizenship) and shows how Islam conceives of these categories; but he doesn't start out by questioning them. The same holds for al-Turabi, who speaks of "Islamic constitutional law" in Esposito, *Voices of Resurgent Islam,* p. 249.

18. Thus the famous treatise by the Salafi Muhammad Abduh, *Risalat al-tawhid* (Letter on oneness), refers to this term exclusively with respect to divine unity. "The original meaning of the word *tawhid* is that God is unique and that he has no associate" (p. 4).

19. The references are obviously innumerable; I will cite the Sudanese leader Hassan al-Turabi: "The ideological foundation of an Islamic state lies in the doctrine of tawhid"; in Esposito, *Voices of Resurgent Islam.*

20. On the use of the concept of *tawhid* by the Shiites Ali Shariati and Murtaza Mutahhari, see Said Amir Arjomand, *The Turban for the Crown,* pp. 93 and 96. Among the Sunnis, it was Sayyid Qutb who developed the concept of *hakimiyya;* Carré, *Mystique et politique,* pp. 210 ff. But the terms are often used interchangeably: a series of articles by Abid Tawfiq al-Hashimi, translated from Arabic into Persian and titled *Nizam-i siyasi dar Islam* (The political order in Islam), was published in the Jamaat-i Islami Afghanistan journal, *Misaq-i Khun;* al-Hashimi uses both the term *tawhid* and Sayyid Qutb's expression *hakimiyya.* We find the latter term, among others, in the statutes of another Afghan party, the Hizb-i Islami (*Mas'uliyat-ha-ye Uzu,* p. 93): "The party . . . must cooperate with all organizations and governments engaged in implementing the Islamic *hakimiyya.*"

21. On this basic notion there are again an infinite number of citations available. Here are a few examples. A. Maududi writes: "Islam is not merely a religious creed or compound name for a few forms of worship, but a comprehensive system which envisages to annihilate all tyrannical and evil systems in the world and enforce its own program of reform which it deems best for the well being of mankind"; *Jihad in Islam,* text written (in English) in 1939, p. 16–17. For the use of this term among the MB, see Mitchell, *Society of the Muslim Brothers,* pp. 234–235. The manual of the Afghan Islamist party Jamaat-i Islami, titled *Usul-e Ba'yat va Mas'uliyat-ha-ye Uzu* (Basic principles for the allegiance and responsibilities of the militant) (in Persian), p. 4, says: "Islam is the name of this total and complete order [*nizam-i jami' va kamil*], which organizes everything, all aspects of life"; there follows a list of these aspects: "The state, the homeland, the government, the nation, moral values, death, justice, culture, laws [*qanun*], science, penal law [*qaza'*], that which concerns the material as well as the spiritual, acquisition and wealth, the jihad and preaching [*da'wa*], politics and ideology [*mafkura*]." Such enumerations are common in Islamic texts.

22. Hasan al-Banna, quoted by Mohammed Arkoun in M. Arkoun and L. Gardet, *L'Islam, hier demain,* p. 157.

23. On al-Banna's refusing the idea of revolution while approving the seizure of political power, see Mitchell, *Society of the Muslim Brothers,* p. 308.

24. Al-Turabi, in Esposito, *Voices of Resurgent Islam,* p. 248.

25. On the theme of "modern *jahiliyya*" see Sivan, *Radical Islam;* Carré, *Mystique et politique;* and G. Kepel, *Muslim Extremism in Egypt.* The expression originated with Maududi, who wrote *Islam and Jahiliyya;* even the most rigorous doctors of law, such as Ibn Hanbal, rejected the concept (Sivan, *Radical Islam,* p. 91).

26. This will be the concept of jihad as an absent obligation, the sixth pillar of Islam, adding to the five that are explicitly mentioned in the tradition. This concept was forged by Farag, the ideologue of the group Al-Jihad: see Kepel, *Muslim Extremism in Egypt.*

27. Falling into this category are al-Hudaybi, head of the Egyptian Muslim Brotherhood (Sivan, *Radical Islam,* p. 109); and Muhammad Qutb, brother of Sayyid Qutb(ibid., p. 111). B. Rabbani, head of the Jamaat-i Islami Afghanistan, writes, in a text aimed implicitly at the rival Hizb-i Islami party: "A Muslim who recites the *kalima,* acts according to it, and puts into practice the religious prescriptions cannot be declared an infidel under the pretext that he expresses an opinion or commits a great sin"; *Usul-e Ba'yat,* article 17.

28. Maududi, *The Islamic Law and Constitution,* p. 244. These qualifications are those of the Caliph in the traditional conception of Muslim politics, which we find in the writings of a Salafi author such as Ibn Badis, in the entirely "psychological" description of the leader defined by an ensemble of qualities;

the best solution according to Ibn Badis is "that of a just leader [*imam*], assisted by an assembly of enlightened and responsible men [*jama'at al muslimin*]"; Mérad, *Ibn Badis*, p. 210.

29. The forbidden *(munkar)*, sincerity *(sadaqa)*, equity *(insaf)*, justice *(adala)*, purity *(ikhlas); Mas'uliat-ha-ye 'Ozu*, pp. 105 ff.

30. *Shikl-i yek pishva'i-ye ruhani*, "spiritual," and not "clerical," as the word *ruhani* would mean today in Iran; ibid., p. 85.

31. Carré, *Mystique et politique*, pp. 180–190. This conception of the amir as a charismatic personage appeared from the very start of the MB with Hasan al-Banna (Mitchell, *Society of the Muslim Brothers*, pp. 300–301).

32. For radicals, the manual of the Hizb-i Islami interrogates the militant: "Is the member ready to recognize that his opinion is false if it contradicts the decisions [*faysala*] of the governing authority [*maqamat-i rahbari*] regarding problems of interpretation [*masa'il-i ijtihadi*] concerning daily events?" (*Mas'uliyat-ha-ye Uzu*, pp. 85 and 87). Conversely, the more moderate Jamaat party introduces "safety nets"; an article signed by al-Hashimi envisages two cases, according to whether the amir is a member of the *ahl-i ijtihad*, the body that has the right to *ijtihad*, or not: in the latter case, he must be assisted by a *shura* (*Misaq-i Khun*, p. 38). Maududi also insists on limiting the powers of the amir (*Jihad in Islam*, p. 30).

33. Maududi, *The Islamic Law and Constitution*, p. 240; al-Turabi, in Esposito, *Voices of Resurgent Islam*, p. 243.

34. Qutb, in Sivan, *Radical Islam*, pp. 73–74; Rabbani, in an editorial, "Why Are We Not 'Democratic'?" *Mirror of Jihad*, March–April 1986, pp. 3 and 6.

35. Al-Turabi, in Esposito, *Voices of Resurgent Islam*, p. 248.

36. For the position of Sayyid Qutb, see Sivan, *Radical Islam*, p. 69.

37. A. Maududi writes: "These people [the associates and comrades of the Prophet] thus became the representatives of people and the members of the Consultative Assembly through a natural process of selection, and they enjoyed the confidence of the Muslim people to such a degree that if elections of the type current in modern days [had] been held . . . these and these people alone would have been chosen"; *The Islamic Law and Constitution*, p. 237.

38. Al-Turabi, in Esposito, *Voices of Resurgent Islam*, p. 248.

39. Reissner, *Ideologie und Politik* p. 146.

40. Sivan, *Radical Islam*, p. 129.

3. The Sociology of Islamism

1. For a detailed study of these "new intellectuals," see G. Kepel and Y. Richard, eds., *Intellectuels et militants de l'Islam contemporain*.

2. E. Sivan, *Radical Islam*, p. 51.

3. B. Hourcade, "Iran: Révolution islamique ou tiers-mondiste?" p. 144.

4. Nilüfer Göle, "Ingénieurs islamistes . . .," in Kepel and Richard, *Intellectuels et militants,* p. 171.

5. On the Syrian Muslim Brotherhood, see J. Reissner, *Ideologie und Politik der Muslimbrüder Syriens,* p. 420; and Sivan, *Radical Islam,* p. 119. On the Egyptian MB, see R. P. Mitchell, *The Society of the Muslim Brothers,* p. 329; and Sivan, *Radical Islam,* pp. 22 and 118. In Egypt, a study done on 303 political prisoners, members of the group Al-Jihad, arrested the day before the assassination of President Sadat, shows that one-third were students, 10 percent were university graduates, and 6 percent were high school students; there were doctors, educators, and military personnel, but not a single cleric or peasant; R. Hrair Dekmejian, *Islam in Revolution,* p. 106.

6. These figures are taken from Camille Lacoste and Yves Lacoste, eds., *L'état du Maghreb,* p. 496. This book has a wealth of data and of analyses pertinent to the Maghreb.

7. See Zakya Daoud, "La frustration des classes moyennes au Maghreb," p. 6.

8. Seyyed Vali Reza Nasr, "Students, Islam, and Politics: Islami Jami'at-i Tuleba in Pakistan," p. 72.

9. For Egypt see Sivan, *Radical Islam,* p. 60. In 1971 the student branch of the Jamaat-i Islami, the Jam'iyyat-i Tulaba, carried the elections in the Punjab against the student branch of Ali Bhutto's PPP, the winner nonetheless in the general elections.

10. Hourcade, "Iran," p. 143.

11. These figures are taken from Lacoste and Lacoste, *L'état du Maghreb.*

12. One of the best studies of a traditional Muslim bazaar is that of P. Centlivres, *Un bazar d'Asie centrale: Tashkurgan.* This bazaar was destroyed by the war in Afghanistan.

13. M. Seurat, "La ville arabe orientale," in *L'état de Barbarie.*

14. See Daoud, "La frustration des classes moyennes."

15. On the uncontrolled urbanization of Cairo, see the article by Agnès Deboulet, "Etat, squatters et maîtrise de l'espace au Caire." On Tehran, see B. Hourcade and F. Khorsrokhavar, "L'habitat révolutionnaire à Téhéran."

16. See Lacoste and Lacoste, *L'état du Maghreb,* p. 232.

17. Zaynab Ghazali, in Mitchell, *Society of the Muslim Brothers,* pp. 254–255. On March 18, 1992, the English-language Iranian newspaper *Kayhan International,* which is associated with radical tendencies, published an article protesting the weak participation of women in the workplace.

18. In Egypt, Zaynab Ghazali; see T. Mitchell, "L'expérience de l'emprisonnement dans le discours islamiste," in Kepel and Richard, *Intellectuels et militants,* pp. 193 ff.

19. On the circulation of these themes among Islamist Iranian women, see F. Adelkhah, *La révolution sous le voile,* p. 159.

20. The literature on women in Islam is abundant and often mediocre. The best book on Islamist women is undoubtedly *La révolution sous le voile.*

4. The Impasses of Islamist Ideology

1. Khurshid Ahmed, introduction to A. Maududi, *The Islamic Law and Constitution,* p. 5.

2. A. Maududi, *Jihad in Islam,* p. 19, a position that harks back to a traditional point of view among the ulamas: a Muslim cannot voluntarily live under the rule of an infidel and must therefore, like the Prophet, perform *hijra,* exodus.

3. Maududi, *The Islamic Law and Constitution,* p. 260.

4. This concept is found among the Syrian MBs *(aklaquna al-ijtima'iyya);* J. Reissner, *Ideologie und Politik der Muslimbrüder Syriens,* p. 139.

5. Maududi, *The Islamic Law and Constitution,* p. 218.

6. Ibid., p. 243.

7. Ibid., pp. 238 ff.

8. Hassan al-Turabi, in J. Esposito, *Voices of Resurgent Islam,* p. 248.

9. Maududi, *The Islamic Law and Constitution,* pp. 261 ff.

10. *Usul-e Ba'yat va Mas'uliat-ha-ye Uzu,* Jamaat-i Islami Afghanistan, p. 17.

11. Al-Turabi, in Esposito, *Voices of Resurgent Islam,* p. 245.

12. Hashimi, in the journal of the Jamaat-i Islami Afghanistan party, *Misaq-i Khun,* p. 39.

13. In *Misaq-i Khun.*

14. Muhammad Qutb, in Salem Azzam, ed., *Islam and Contemporary Society,* p. 1. This conversion must thus take place within the militant's very being: "The members of the Jamaat-i Islami Afghanistan must be absolutely certain that their ideology [*ideolozhi*] and their thought is a purely Islamic ideology and thought;" *Usul-e Ba'yat,* p. 2. On al-Banna, see R. P. Mitchell, *The Society of the Muslim Brothers,* p. 234.

15. Al-Turabi, in Esposito, *Voices of Resurgent Islam,* p. 250.

16. G. Kepel, *Muslim Extremism in Egypt.* On the "moderate" Islamist version of *jihad,* see Maududi, *Jihad in Islam,* as well as the JIA journal, *Mirror of Jihad,* "What Is Jehad and Who Is a Mujahid?" May–June 1982, in which jihad is defined with respect to two levels: the political goal ("to establish the supremacy of God ... eliminate oppression ... establish a just society") and the devotional goal ("to purify one's soul and develop oneself morally and spiritually," "to carry out every good action to serve the cause of Islam").

17. See J. P. Charnay, *L'Islam et la guerre,* pp. 15 ff.

18. M. Arkoun, in M. Arkoun and L. Gardet, *Islam, hier demain,* p. 163.

19. P. Vieille and F. Khoshrokhavar conduct remarkable analyses of "martyrdom" in *Le discours populaire de la révolution iranienne,* pp. 160–177.

20. Al-Turabi, in Esposito, *Voices of Resurgent Islam,* pp. 241 and 243. Yet Turabi also sings the praises of the Islamic state, as is clear from his political action.

21. Note that revolutionary Shiism has never had this definition of an elitist party, no doubt because the elite were already defined: the clergy, or rather, the high clergy.

22. I take as sources the text of the statutes of two Afghan Islamist parties (the Hizb-i Islami and the Jamaat-i Islami). According to the HI, the amir must "incarnate in his own personal actions the principles, bases, and foundations [*usul wa muqrarat*] of the party, and, in his leadership activity, he must take into consideration 'the limits of God' [*hudud*], the obligatory principles [*ahkam*] and supererogatory of the *sharia* [*mas'uliyat-ha-ye Uzu*]" (p. 105); interestingly, here the party comes before God.

23. "The members of the Central Council must attempt to incarnate the most perfect model of Islamic virtues in order to preserve the unity of vision and action" (*Mas'uliyat-ha-ye Uzu,* p. 103). "The moral superiority of the members of the Central Council, in comparison with the other members of the party, must be absolutely clear and evident" (p. 104).

24. See Muhammad K. Shadid, "The Muslim Brotherhood Movement in the West Bank and Gaza."

25. See Mitchell, *Society of the Muslim Brothers,* p. 300.

26. The Afghan organizational chart seems to have been based on that of the Arab world's Muslim Brotherhood, in which we find the following degrees: (1) *Halqa* (cell): initiation to the Sunna and the teachings of al-Banna; (2) *Al Usra* (family): give 5 percent of one's revenues and obey the local leaders of the brotherhood; (3) *Active Member:* chosen by the amir; must have studied the Quran; (4) *Majlis al-Shura:* named by the amir among the active members.

27. *Mas'uliyat-ha-ye Uzu,* p. 83. Note the ambiguity of the Islamist movement as compared with Sufism, which is officially banned, but in fact profoundly present in many leaders', including al-Banna's, apprenticeship, as well as in their terminology and vision of the world (Mitchell, *Society of the Muslim Brothers,* p. 14). In this text, the word *ruhaniyat* should be understood in the Afghan Persian sense of the word ("mystical spirituality") and not in the modern Iranian sense ("clergy").

28. Sadat's assassins in 1981 were convinced that their action would be followed by a popular uprising and the establishment of an Islamic society.

29. E. Sivan, *Radical Islam,* p. 86.

30. Muhammad Qutb (brother of Sayyid Qutb), in Azzam, *Islam and Contemporary Society,* p. 1.

31. On the topic of an "Islamic sociology" that claims to be normative and to introduce the values of faith, see the citations by A. Roussillon, "Intellectuels

en crise dans l'Egypte contemporaine," in G. Kepel and Y. Richard, eds., *Intellectuels et militants de l'Islam contemporain*, pp. 237 ff.

32. See Chapter 6, "The Islamist New Intellectuals."

33. On the rejection of a sociological reading of Muslim society, see Arkoun and Gardet, *L'Islam, hier demain*, pp. 166–167.

34. Ibid., p. 162.

35. It is absurd to apply this denial of history to Islamic culture as a whole, since Islamic culture is a product of this history and thereby finds itself negated by Islamism.

36. Mitchell, *Society of the Muslim Brothers*, p. 204.

5. Neofundamentalism

1. On the "Islamist engineers" in Turkey, see Nilüfer Göle in G. Kepel and Y. Richard, eds., *Intellectuels et militants de l'Islam contemporain*.

2. A movement founded in the 1920s on the Indian subcontinent whose sole purpose is preaching in order to bring all "sociological" Muslims back to strict Islamic practice. The Tablighi Jamaat has always forbidden political action. Without being Wahhabi, it favors a reformed, very scripturalist and formalist fundamentalism. The French branch is the "Foi et pratique" association. See G. Kepel, *Les banlieues de l'Islam*.

3. For an example in the municipality of Tipassa (Algeria), see Camille Lacoste and Yves Lacoste, *L'état du Maghreb*, p. 210.

4. See, for Algeria, Ahmed Rouadjia, *Les Frères et la Mosquée*.

5. For a photo of Talmassani, see G. Michaud (M. Seurat) and O. Carré, *Les Frères musulmans*, pp. 116–117, photo 16. During this period the founder of the Afghan Islamist movement, Professor Niazi, also wore a tie.

6. A. Maududi didn't hesitate to attend Hindu ceremonies. Khomeini never proposed the status of *dhimmi* (protected) for Iranian Christians or Jews, as provided for in the *sharia*: the Armenians in Iran have remained Iranian citizens, are required to perform military service and to pay the same taxes as Muslims, and have the right to vote (with separate electoral colleges). Similarly, the Afghan Jamaat, in its statutes, has declared it legal in the eyes of Islam to employ non-Muslims as experts, a position that would undoubtedly be rejected by the neofundamentalists.

7. Seyyed Vali Reza Nasr, "Students, Islam, and Politics: Islami Jami'at-i Tuleba in Pakistan," p. 72.

8. Although, as we have seen, Sufism has left a strong mark on the Islamists; similarly in Afghanistan the Naqshbandi brotherhood joined with Islamist parties such as the Afghan Jamaat. See O. Roy, *Islam and Resistance in Afghanistan*.

9. See the writings of Shérif Mardin. On the renewal of brotherhoods in

Morocco, see M. Tozy, in Kepel and Richard, *Intellectuals and militants,* pp. 83 ff.

10. Christian Coulon, "Sénégal," p. 68.

6. The Islamist New Intellectuals

1. This chapter adapts material from my contribution to G. Kepel and Y. Richard, eds., *Intellectuels et militants de l'Islam contemporain.*

2. In Pakistan, for example, there is fierce competition between Westernized intellectuals and ulamas in the judicial institution: Islamic *qadi* and judges educated in the British tradition struggle for positions through the debate on the Islamization of the judicial system. On the strategies (patronage, sensationalist publications, financial exploitation of the student) that underpaid Westernized professors can use to maintain their social status, see A. Roussillon, "Intellectuels en crise dans l'Egypte contemporaine," in Kepel and Richard, *Intellectuels et militants,* pp. 230 ff. These strategies are disadvantageous to the students, among whom the Islamists eagerly recruit.

3. On the efforts of the Moroccan state to control the unrestrained preachers, see M. Tozy, "Le prince, le clerc et l'état. La reconstruction du champ religieux au Maroc," in Kepel and Richard, *Intellectuels et militants,* pp. 76 ff.

4. The modern educational system is also based on repetition and memorization, without direct contact with the professor, except for those who can afford private lessons; for a study of the situation in Egypt, see Roussillon, "Intellectuals en crise dans l'Egypte contemporaine"; and Judith Cochran, *Education in Egypt,* p. 59.

5. On the autodidactic acquisition of theological knowledge by the new intellectuals, see M. Tozy, "Le prince, le clerc et l'état au Maghreb," in Kepel and Richard, *Intellectuels et militants,* pp. 87 ff.

6. See, for example, the declaration of the president of the Revolutionary Council of Afghanistan, Nur Muhammad Taraki, some time after the coup d'état that carried him to power in April 1978: "The conspiracy under the pretext of entry exams because of which the youngsters could not go beyond the eighth grade was abolished"; "Report of the Five-Month Performance of the DRA" (in English), 1978, Bibliotheca Afghanica, 2099. For Pakistan, see L. D. Hayes, *The Crisis of Education in Pakistan,* p. 173: "Among the most frequent related issues to provoke agitation is the examination system."

7. On one adaptation of the image of the perfect Man, within the framework of a Sufi order, the Bektashis, see A. Gökalp, "Une minorité Shiite en Anatolie: Les Alevi," p. 751.

8. "Westernized intellectuals" define themselves by a social position and a university curriculum close to their Western counterparts, but especially by a theoretical postulate that A. Roussillon formulates as follows: ". . . possibility

of a *controlled acculturation* allowing one to appropriate the knowledge and technologies engendered by the West—but not the values or the philosophical assumptions associated with this knowledge or technology—and to mobilize them in the service of objectives that are 'specific' to Egyptian society (or Arab, or Muslim)," in a talk at the round table "Horizons de pensée et pratiques sociales chez les intellectuels du monde musulman," Paris, CERI, June 1987.

9. *Da'wa* is the call, preaching; *muballigh* is the itinerant preacher, the missionary. Although these are not exclusively Sufi words, they were widely used by the mystical missionary orders, in particular in central Asia and on the Indian subcontinent.

10. An idea developed by Ibn Badis, in A. Mérad, *Ibn Badis, commentateur du Coran,* p. 222.

11. See Roussillon's text quoting Adil Husayn, who distinguishes between "Arab Islamic rationalism" in the human sciences, which incorporates belief in the existence of God as sole creator, and "temporal Western rationalism"; Roussillon, "Intellectuels en crise dans l'Egypte contemporaine," p. 238.

12. See Christian Coulon, "Les nouveaux Ulama et la résurgence islamique au Nord-Nigeria," p. 5.

13. There is a distinct difference between Sunnis and Shiites regarding the notion of *ijtihad:* for the traditionalist Shiites, perfect mastery of the corpus authorizes the practice of *ijtihad;* among the Sunnis, it is to avoid this necessity of mastering the corpus that the new intellectuals reinvent the notion of *ijtihad.* But in the work of an Islamist Shiite author, Ali Shariati, we find the idea that prior mastery of the corpus is not a precondition for the right to *ijtihad.*

14. Thus the Afghan Islamist militants of the Hizb-i Islami always speak admiringly about the encyclopedic knowledge of their leader, the "engineer" Hikmatyar, the author of numerous pamphlets on science, the refutation of Marxism and theology alike. This attribution of encyclopedic knowledge to a leader is a strong tendency in Marxism (the omniscient figure of Kim II Sung, but also the figure of Thorez, whose knowledge was praised by the scholar Georges Cogniot).

15. Coulon, "Les nouveaux Ulama," pp. 7 ff.

7. The Geostrategy of Islamism

1. R. P. Mitchell, *The Society of the Muslim Brothers,* p. 172.

2. On the Palestinian Islamist movement, see J. F. Legrain, "Mobilisation islamiste et soulèvement palestinien," in G. Kepel and Y. Richard, eds., *Intellectuels et militants de l'Islam contemporain,* pp. 131 ff.; M. K. Shadid, "The Muslim Brotherhood Movement in the West Bank and Gaza."

3. *Razvie bolsh'ie niet nieobkhodimosti v religii?* translated by "Ibadi," Institute of Regional Studies (n.p.[Peshawar?], n.d.) (personal collection).

4. G. Michaud (M. Seurat) and O. Carré, *Les Frères musulmans,* p. 98. For more on the thought of Sayyid Qutb, see O. Carré, *Mystique et politique,* p. 139.

5. A. Roussillon, "Intellectuels en crise en Égypte contemporaine," in Kepel and Richard, *Intellectuels et militants,* p. 247.

6. One of the recruitment offices was the PLO bureau in Saudi Arabia, run by a former MB.

7. Note the politicization of all the veterans of Afghanistan, whether Muslims or veterans of the Soviet army (who are also called "Afghans.")

8. Wahhabism is the Sunni doctrine the most opposed to Shiism, and vice versa. Although in 1959 a *fatwa* of Al-Azhar University in Cairo made Shiism the fifth of the judicial schools of Islam, Wahhabis and Shiites consider one another to be heretics. Thus in 1989 the Iranian Ministry of Culture and of Islamic Orientation published the Persian translation of an Arab work by Muhammad Husayn Qazvini titled *Firqah-i wahhabi* (The Wahhabi sect). In 1991 a *fatwa* of the Council of Saudi ulamas declared, to the great embarrassment of the government in Riyadh, that Shiites were heretics. This is an old and weighty matter: in 1801, the sacred Shiite sites of Najaf and Karbala were sacked by Saudi Wahhabis.

9. *Al-Jihad,* no. 56 (June 1989), article by A. Azzam.

10. In a tradition found today in Soviet Central Asia and existing on the Indian subcontinent since the nineteenth century, the term "Wahhabi" is used to designate all reforming fundamentalists and not solely the disciples of the founder of the Saudi sect.

11. M. Hedayetullah, *Sayyid Ahmad,* pp. 144–145.

12. A sign of the religious dogmatism of the Wahhabis can be seen in this excerpt from a Saudi article by Abdullah al-Rifai: "Muslim wise men in the world have a major role to play in enlightening the ignorant Afghans. Non-Islamic customs and traditions have penetrated their lives"; "Afghan mujahadeen fight to defend their faith, country," *Arab News,* September 14, 1985, p. 9; this article also contains criticism of Western humanitarians, termed "Christian missionaries."

13. Hassan al-Turabi, a jurist educated in France, director of the Sudanese MB, and head of the National Islamic Front in Sudan, is the brother-in-law of Sadiq al-Mahdi (leader of the Umma party, president of the Sudan from 1985 to July 1989, a descendent of al-Mahdi, who fought the English during the nineteenth century and founded the Ansar brotherhood); he was named attorney general in 1983 by Numayri during the turn toward Islamism; imprisoned in early 1985, he again became the dominant figure in Sudanese political life after Numayri's fall in April 1985.

14. In March 1988 the newspaper *Jumhuri-ye islami* published a series (the second of its kind) titled "The Wahhabis," in which Wahhabism was defined not as a *madhab* but as a heretical sect created and manipulated by the British secret services.

15. Thus it is common for Saudi Arabia to refuse visas to Pakistani Shiite immigrant workers.

16. M. Tozy, "Islam et état au Maghreb."

17. Should one view the establishment in France by the minister of the interior and of cults of a "Conseil représentatif de l'islam en France" (CORIF, 1990) as an extension of this desire for state control of Islam?

18. See E. Sivan, *Radical Islam,* pp. 135 ff.

19. For excerpts from this text, see Camille Lacoste and Yves Lacoste, *L'état du Maghreb,* p. 223.

20. This was the Shah Bano affair, a wife repudiated at the age of seventy-three who sued her husband for a food allowance; the husband used the *sharia* to refuse her. The supreme court found Shah Bano in the right, in the name of the secularity inscribed in the constitution, but in February 1986 the parliament passed a law forbidding Muslim divorcees from demanding a food allowance. For more on the origin of the affair, see V. Graff, "Islam et laïcité"; see also *India Today,* January 31, 1986. Note that the leader of the organization that waged a campaign for Muslim personal law, the "All Indian Personal Law Board," is the same Sayyid Abul Hasan Nadwi who was a companion of Maududi and of Sayyid Qutb, and Maududi's translator into Arabic.

8. The Islamic Economy

1. The primary work on this subject is Maxime Rodinson, *Islam and Capitalism,* esp. chap. 2.

2. Which is not simply interest on a loan: *riba* (increase) supposes non-equality in an exchange, whether the difference results from the exchange of nonequivalent quantities or from the presence of a risk in which the other contractual party does not share.

3. R. Khomeini, *Tawzih al-masa'il* (The explanation of problems), p. 543. The traditional nature of this book reflects the fact that Khomeini was speaking here as a theologian *mujtahid* and was therefore obliged to give his interpretation of problems traditionally asked of every theologian; he thus readopted the form and the outline of works written by his predecessors.

4. See Ayatollah Baqir al-Sadr, *Iqtisaduna* (Our economy); and Abdul Hasan Bani Sadr, *Iqtisad-i tawhidi* (The unitarist economy).

5. This theme of the third way appears regularly in Islamist thought, on both a political and an economic level. We find it from the Syrian MBs of the 1950s (J. Reissner, *Ideologie und Politik der Muslimbrüder Syriens,* p. 152), to the radical mullahs of Soviet Tadzhikistan (the mullah Abdullah Saïdov, interviewed in the journal *Sukhan* on July 12, 1992), to the Pakistani Jamaat: A. I. Qureshi, *The Economic and Social System of Islam,* pp. 6 and 7.

6. In this category we find Muslim Brothers (Mustafa al-Siba'i; see Reissner, *Ideologie und Politik,* p. 152), but mostly the Shiites: Baqir al-Sadr, *Iqtisaduna;*

Abul-Hasan Bani Sadr, *Iqtisad-i tawhidi;* Ayatollah Mahmud Talighani, *Islam va malikiyat* (Islam and property). This last book begins with an anthropological analysis and continues with a critical review of Western authors, only later addressing the Islamic approach.

7. Bani Sadr, *Iqtisad-i tawhidi,* p. 161.

8. The theme of "Islamic socialism" was developed among the Syrian MBs in the 1950s: Mustafa al-Siba'i wrote a book titled "The Sociology of Islam"; see Reissner, *Ideologie und Politik,* pp. 151 and 152; for the Egyptian MB's notion of "social justice" see Mitchell, *Society of the Muslim Brothers,* p. 251; Sayyid Qutb wrote a short treatise titled *Social Justice in Islam (Al-adala al-ijtima'iyya fi al-Islam).* For the Turks, the concept of Islamic socialism was developed by Nurettin Topçu; see Paul Dumont, "Turquie," pp. 105–106.

9. On this term, for the Syrian MB, see Reissner, *Ideologie und Politik,* pp. 153–154; see also Bani Sadr, *Iqtisad-i tawhidi,* p. 237.

10. See Bani Sadr, "Mahdudiyat-ha-ye Malikiyat" (The limitations of ownership), in *Iqtisad-i tawhidi,* p. 273; see also Abd al-Qadir Sid Ahmed, "Finance islamique et développement," in *Revue tiers-monde* 23, no. 92 (October–December 1982), 882.

11. Bani Sadr, *Iqtisad-i tawhidi.*

12. On primary goods in general, see Rodinson, *Islam and Capitalism;* on the Islamist interpretation, see Bani Sadr, *Iqtisad-i tawhidi,* p. 193.

13. For a "socialist" reading of *zakat* among the Syrian MB, see Reissner, *Ideologie und Politik,* p. 154.

14. Bani Sadr, *Iqtisad-i tawhidi,* p. 392.

15. Ibid., p. 396.

16. Ibid., pp. 336 and 401.

17. For a good analysis of the current Iranian economy and society, see B. Hourcade and F. Khosrokhavar, "La bourgeoisie iraniennne . . ."

18. Ibid.

19. Mitchell, *Society of the Muslim Brothers,* p. 275.

20. See C. H. Moore, "Islamic Banks and Competitive Politics in the Arab World and Turkey."

21. In this category we find Sunni thinkers, generally from the Indian subcontinent and today often close to the Saudis. Among them are the Pakistani Khurshid Ahmed, an economist and distinguished member of the Jamaat-i Islami and a former minister of planning and development, "Economic Development in an Islamic Framework," in *Islamic Perspectives; The Economic and Social System of Islam,* by A. I. Qureshi, who is close to General Zia; Sadiq al-Mahdi, a former prime minister of Sudan, "The Economic System of Islam," and Prince Muhammad al-Faisal al-Saud (founder in 1981 of the Dar al-mal al-Islam holding company), "Banking and the Islamic Standpoint," both in S. Azzam, *Islam and Contemporary Society.*

22. As defined by Imam Khomeini in *Tawzih al-masa'il,* p. 543.

23. See. F. Moini, *Yearbook Iran 89/90,* pp. 11–41.

24. The president of the Pakistani Habib Bank thus declared: "Interest-free banking should not be taken to mean that banks—financial institutions—would neither pay any return on their on deposits nor get any income from their loans, etc."; quoted in J. Esposito, *Voices of Resurgent Islam,* p. 284.

25. See the French newspaper *Libération,* June 24–25, 1989.

26. See M. Seurat, "Etat et industrialisation dans l'Orient arabe," in *L'état de Barbarie.*

27. Grace Clark, "Zakat and 'Ushr and a Welfare System," p. 92.

28. For example, when the MB presented candidates during the Egyptian elections of 1987, the Rayan group denied having financed them. After a standoff between the government and the Islamic financial institutions in 1987, following the bankruptcy of the Al-Hillal company, a compromise was struck and the government endeavored to reduce pressure on these institutions.

29. *Al-Bouchra,* November 3, 1988, p. 8, published in France.

30. Al-Mahdi, in Azzam, *Islam and Contemporary Society,* p. 104; Rodinson, *Islam and Capitalism.*

31. We find this thesis well expressed in the writings of Khurshid Ahmed, who establishes four premises: (1) social change is not the result of entirely predetermined historical forces; (2) man is the active factor in change. All other forces have been subordinated to him insofar as he is the representative of God on earth *(khalifa);* (3) change consists in a change of environment and a change in the heart and soul of man; (4) life is a network of interrelationships; "Economic Development in an Islamic Framework," in Ahmed, *Islamic Perspectives,* p. 231.

32. This is not to say that there is no serious economic or sociological research in Muslim countries, but only that such research occurs outside Islamist rhetoric. See, as an example of high-level sociological analysis, Mustafa Azkya, *Jam'e shinasi va tus'e nayaftigi rusta'y Iran* (The sociology and under-development of the Iranian village) (Tehran, 1365 [1987]).

9. Afghanistan

1. On this relationship, see O. Roy, *Islam and Resistance in Afghanistan,* chap. 1.

2. See Pierre Centlivres and Micheline Centlivres-Demont, *Et si on parlait de l'Afghanistan?* pp. 31 ff.

3. It is not by chance that the greatest Western specialist on political life in Afghanistan for more than thirty years was an anthropologist, Louis Dupree (who died in 1989), who analyzed politics as if it were an extension of anthropology in other forms. One should see this approach not as a case of a specialist

overstepping his bounds, but as a characteristic of political life in this country: Louis Dupree, *Afghanistan.*

4. I have analyzed in my book on Afghanistan the process of politicization through the establishment of Islamist parties. Without rehearsing my conclusions there, let me simply refer to my final question: which process will win, the retention of traditional solidarities or politicization?

5. See Jean-Paul Charnay, *L'Islam et la guerre,* p. 250.

6. For a discussion of this concept of *qawm,* see Roy, *Islam and Resistance in Afghanistan.* The *qawm* is synonymous with the *asabiyya.*

7. See A. Ahmed, *Millenium and Charisma among Swat Pathans* and *Pukhtun Economy and Society;* Louis Dupree, "Tribal Warfare in Afghanistan and Pakistan," in Akbar S. Ahmed and David M. Hart, eds., *Islam in Tribal Societies;* Leon B. Poullada, *Reform and Rebellion in Afghanistan;* see also all the British tales of the "Afghan wars" from 1840 to 1919.

8. See. Roy, *Islam and Resistance in Afghanistan,* chap. 7.

9. As illustrated by the taking of Kabul in 1929 by insurgents from the north directed by Bach-yé Saqqao, after the departure of King Amanullah. The fall of Kabul in April 1992 is based on a similar scenario.

10. See Charnay, *L'Islam et la guerre,* pp. 15 ff.

11. Ibid., p. 252.

12. Ibid., pp. 232 and 250.

13. On the sociological modifications due to the war, see Roy, *Islam and Resistance in Afghanistan,* chap. 10.

14. On all these highly complex elements, see O. Roy, "Ethnies et politique en Asie centrale."

15. M. Seurat, *L'état de Barbarie,* p. 130.

10. Iran

1. On Shiism see Yann Richard, *L'Islam chi'ite.* On the history of Iranian Shiism, see Said Amir Arjomand, *The Shadow of God and the Hidden Imam.* On the Islamist revolution, see idem, *The Turban for the Crown.*

2. Ali Shariati, in his book *Tashayyu-i alavi, tashayyu-i safavi* (The Shiism of Ali, the Shiism of the Safavids), draws a distinction between the original Shiism, bearer of revolt and a social message, and official Safavid Shiism, which is conservative and clericalized.

3. See Pierre Martin, "Chiisme et *'Wilâyat al Faqîh,'*" p. 148.

4. On the *akhbari* and *usuli* conflict, see Yann Richard, *Le Shi'isme en Iran,* pp. 43 ff. This conflict illustrates how a purely theological debate can have geostrategic consequences that are not manifest in the stakes at the time.

5. P. J. Luizard, *La formation de l'Irak contemporain.*

6. Here is an anecdote: during my study of the mechanisms of politicization

of the Afghan ulamas, I asked Professor Tawana, an eminent figure in the Jamaat-i Islami, at what moment he personally felt obliged to get involved in politics. He answered: "When I found Feuerbach on the shelves of the School of Theology library," a sign for him of a communist influence within the educational system itself. In Qum it was the mullahs themselves who ordered, and read, Feuerbach.

7. P. Vieille and F. Khosrokhavar, *Le discours populaire de la révolution iranienne.*

8. Ibid.

9. The texts are clear in distinguishing the difference from Sunnism: "The Islamic state is not a return to the past," says Khomeini in an official collection of his quotations, *In Search of the Path of the Imam's Words* (in Persian), vol. 10 (Tehran: Inqilab-i Islami), p. 164.

10. See E. Abrahamian, *Radical Islam.*

11. In contrast, Sunni fundamentalists want to reestablish the principle of *dhimmi;* A. Maududi, *The Islamic Law and Constitution,* p. 245: "The two kinds of citizenship that Islam envisages are the following: (1) the Muslims, (2) the *Zimmis.*"

11. The Shiite Factor in Iran's Foreign Policy

1. H. Battatu, "Shi'i Organizations in Iraq," in Juan R. Cole and Nikki R. Keddie, eds., *Shi'ism and Social Protest,* p. 189.

2. From 1984 on, Imam Khomeini spoke of the "nation of Iran," whereas previously he had spoken only of the *umma.*

3. Fouad Ajami, *The Vanished Imam,* pp. 39 ff.

4. For Lebanon, see A. Norton, "Shiism and Social Protest in Lebanon," and for Iraq, Battatu, "Shi'i Organizations in Iraq," both in Cole and Keddie, *Shi'ism and Social Protest,* pp. 163 and 179.

5. In Afghanistan, the process of detribalization-clericalization was begun as early as 1892, when Amir Abdurrahman quashed the Shiite Hazara tribes: two groups (which have an important common intersection) the *sayyid* and the *sheikh,* educated in Najaf, filled the void (see L. M. Kopecky, "The Imami Sayyed of the Hazarajat"). On Lebanon, see Cobban, "The Growth of Shi'i Power in Lebanon," in Cole and Keddie, *Shi'ism and Social Protest,* pp. 137 ff.

6. On the genesis of the Shiite movement, embodied in the 1950s in Sayyid Balkhi, see O. Roy, *Islam and Resistance in Afghanistan,* chap. 9; and Edwards, "The Evolution of Shi'i Political Dissent in Afghanistan," in Cole and Keddie, *Shi'ism and Social Protest,* pp. 201 ff.

7. Such as the economic treaty *Iqtisaduna,* which appeared in 1960, as well as the text that inspired the Iranian constitution, *Note préliminaire . . .,* translated by A. Martin in *Les Cahiers de l'Orient,* pp. 157 ff.

8. See Ajami, *The Vanished Imam*, p. 155.

9. See Roy, *Islam and Resistance in Afghanistan*, pp. 141–145.

10. For Iraq, see Battatu, "Shi'i Organizations in Iraq," pp. 179 ff.

11. For the Hazaras, see Kopecky, "The Imami Sayyed of the Hazarajat," p. 91, which mentions the circulation of *muharam* prayers on cassettes recorded in Kabul; and Edwards, "Shi'i Political Dissent in Afghanistan," p. 214, which mentions the novelty of these prayers in the twentieth century. The Iranian influence thus seems to have been important and recent.

12. Two of the great ayatollahs of 1980, al-Khu'i and Shariat Madari, were Azeris, even though both opposed Khomeini. Prime Minister Musavi was also Azeri. The Azeris are well represented among the elite of the Islamic revolution, as they were in the Tudeh party.

13. The secularity of the Turkish Alevis and of their Syrian Alawi counterparts can be explained by the fact that they were never Twelver Shiites. See A. Gökalp, "Une minorité chi'ite en Anatolie," pp. 748–763.

Conclusion

1. Michel Seurat, *L'état de Barbarie*, p. 159.

❖ *Bibliography* ❖

Abduh, M. *Risalat al-tawhid* (Letter on oneness). French translation. Paris: Paul Geuthner, 1978.

Abrahamian, Ervand. *Radical Islam: The Iranian Mojahedin.* London: Tauris, 1989. Also published as *The Iranian Mojahedin.* New Haven: Yale University Press, 1989.

Abdelkhah, Fariba. *La révolution sous le voile.* Paris: Karthala, 1990.

Ahmed, Akbar. *Millennium and Charisma among Swat Pathans: A Critical Essay in Social Anthropology.* London: Routledge and Kegan Paul, 1976.

———— *Pukhtun Economy and Society: Traditional Structure and Economic Development.* London: Routledge and Kegan Paul, 1980.

Ahmed, Akbar S., and David M. Hart, eds. *Islam in Tribal Societies: From the Atlas to the Indus.* London: Routledge and Kegan Paul; New York: Methuen, 1984.

Ahmed, Khurshid, ed. *Islamic Perspectives.* Leicester: Islamic Foundation, 1979.

Ajami, Fouad. *The Vanished Imam: Musa al Sadr and the Shia of Lebanon.* London: Tauris, 1986; Ithaca: Cornell University Press, 1992.

Arjomand, Said A. *The Shadow of God and the Hidden Imam: Religion, Political Order, and Societal Change in Shi'ite Iran from the Beginning to 1890.* Chicago: University of Chicago Press, 1984.

———— *The Turban for the Crown: The Islamic Revolution in Iran.* Oxford: Oxford University Press, 1988.

Arkoun, Mohammed. *Critique de la raison islamique.* Paris: Maisonneuve et Larose, 1984.

Arkoun, M., and L. Gardet. *L'Islam, hier demain.* Paris: Buchet-Chastel, 1982.

Azzam, Salem, ed. *Islam and Contemporary Society.* London: Islamic Council of Europe, 1982.

Badie, B. *Les deux états.* Paris: Fayard, 1986.

Bahadur, Kalim. *The Jama'at-i Islami of Pakistan.* Lahore: Progressive Books, 1978.

Bani Sadr, A. H. *Iqtisad-i tawhidi* (The unitarist economy). In Persian. N.p.: Nashr-i hajr, 1357 (1978).

Bereketullah, Maulavie Mohammed. *Le Khalifat.* French translation. Paris: Paul Geuthner, 1924.

Burgat, François. *L'Islamisme au Maghreb*. Paris: Karthala, 1988.

Carré, O. *Mystique et politique: Lecture révolutionnaire du Coran par Sayyid Qotb, Frère musulman radical*. Paris: Presse de la Fondation nationale des sciences politiques, Editions du Cerf, 1984.

Centlivres, Pierre. *Un bazar d'Asie centrale: Tashkurgan*. Wiesbaden: Ludwig Reichert Verlag, 1972.

Centlivres, Pierre, and Micheline Centlivres-Demont. *Et si on parlait de l'Afghanistan?* Paris: La Maison des sciences de l'homme, 1988.

Charnay, Jean-Paul. *L'Islam et la guerre*. Paris: Fayard, 1986.

Chayegan, Daryus. *Qu'est-ce qu'une révolution religieuse?* Paris: Les Presses d'aujourd'hui, 1982.

Clark, Grace. "Zakat and 'Ushr and a Welfare System." In Anita Weiss, ed., *Islamic Reassertion in Pakistan*. Syracuse: Syracuse University Press, 1986.

Cochran, Judith. *Education in Egypt*. London: Croom Helm, 1986.

Cole, Juan R., and Nikki R. Keddie, eds. *Shi'ism and Social Protest*. New Haven: Yale University Press, 1986.

Coulon, Christian. "Sénégal." In *Contestations en pays islamiques*. Vol 1. Paris: CHEAM (Centre des hautes études sur l'Afrique et l'Asie modernes), 1984.

——— "Les nouveaux Ulama et la résurgence islamique au Nord-Nigeria." Photocopied mission report, Centre d'étude d'Afrique noire, Bordeaux, June 1986.

Daoud, Z. "La frustration des classes moyennes au Maghreb." *Le monde diplomatique*, November 1991.

Deboulet Agnès. "Etat, squatters et maîtrise de l'espace au Caire," *Egypte, monde arabe* (Cairo: CEDEJ) 1 (January–March 1990).

Dekmejian, R. Hrair. *Islam in Revolution: Fundamentalism in the Arab World*. Syracuse: Syracuse University Press, 1985.

Dumont, P. "Turquie." In *Contestations en pays islamiques*. Vol. 1. Paris: CHEAM, 1984.

Dupree, Louis. *Afghanistan*. Princeton: Princeton University Press, 1980.

Eickelman, Dale P. *The Middle East: An Anthropological Approach*. Englewood Cliffs, N.J.: Prentice-Hall, 1981.

Esposito, John L. *Voices of Resurgent Islam*. Oxford: Oxford University Press, 1983.

Etienne, B. *I'Islamisme radical*. Paris: Hachette, 1987.

Gökalp, A. "Une minorité chi'ite en Anatolie: Les Alevî." *Annales*, May–August 1980.

Graff, V. "Islam et laïcité." *La démocratie indienne*, special edition of *Esprit*, 1985.

Hayes, L. D. *The Crisis of Education in Pakistan*. Lahore: Vanguard Books, 1987.

Hedayetullah, Muhammad. *Sayyid Ahmad: A Study of the Religious Reform Movement of Sayyid Ahmad of Râ'e Bareli*. Lahore: Mohammed Ashraf, 1970.

Hizb-i Islami. *Masiuliat-hâ-ye 'Ozu.* Peshawar, n.d.

Hourcade, B. "Iran: Révolution islamique ou tiers-mondiste." *Hérodote,* no. 36 (January–March 1985).

Hourcade, B., and F. Khosrokhavar. "L'habitat révolutionnaire à Téhéran." *Hérodote,* no. 31 (October–December 1983).

——— "La bourgeoisie iranienne ou le contrôle de l'appareil de spéculation." *Revue tiers-monde* 31 (October–December 1990).

Jamaat-i Islami Afghanistan. *Mirror of Jehad* (Peshawar). English-language journal, 1982–.

——— *Misaq-i Khun* (The blood pact), no. 19 (1987). Editorial in Persian.

——— *Usul-e Ba'yat va Mas'uliyat-ha-ye Uzu* (Basic principles for the allegiance and responsibilities of the militant). 10th ed. Peshawar, Hamal 1360 (March–April 1981).

Karpat, K. "Yakub Bey's Relations with the Ottoman Sultans: A Reinterpretation." *Cahiers du monde russe et soviétique* 32, no. 1 (January–March 1991), 17–35.

Kedourie, Elie. *Afghani and Abduh: An Essay on Religious Unbelief and Political Activism in Modern Islam.* London: Frank Cass; New York: Humanities Press, 1966.

Kepel, Gilles. *Muslim Extremism in Egypt: The Prophet and the Pharaoh.* Berkeley: University of California Press, 1986.

——— *Les banlieues de l'Islam.* Paris: Le Seuil, 1988.

Kepel, G., and Y. Richard, eds. *Intellectuels et militants de l'Islam contemporain.* Paris: Le Seuil, 1989.

Khomeini, R. *Tawzih al-masa'il* (The explanation of problems). Merkaz-i neshar-i farhangi-ye rija, 1366 (1987).

Khosrokhavar, Farhad. "Du néo-orientalisme de Badie." *Peuples méditerranéens,* no. 50 (January–March 1990).

Kopecky, L. M. "The Imami Sayyed of the Hazarajat." *Folk* (Copenhagen) 22 (1984).

Kramer, Milton., ed. *Shi'ism, Resistance and Revolution.* Boulder, Colo.: Westview Press, 1987.

Lacoste, Camille, and Yves Lacoste, eds., *L'état du Maghreb.* Paris: La Découverte, 1991.

Laroui, Abdallah. *Islam et modernité.* Paris: La Découverte, 1987.

Lewis, Bernard. *The Political Language of Islam.* Chicago: University of Chicago Press, 1988.

Libre (Paris: Payot). Eight issues, 1977–1980.

Luizard, P. J. *La formation de l'Irak contemporain.* Paris: CNRS, 1991.

Martin, Pierre. "Chiisme et 'Wilayat al-Faqih.'" *Cahiers de l'Orient,* no. 8/9.

Maududi, A. *The Islamic Law and Constitution.* 1955; reprints, New York: Oriental Art, 1969; Lahore: Islamic Publication, 1980.

——— *Jihad in Islam.* Beirut: Holy Coran Publishing House, 1980.

Mérad, Ali. *Ibn Badis, commentateur du Coran*. Paris: Paul Geuthner, 1971.

Metcalf, Barbara D. *Islamic Revival in British India: Deoband, 1896–1900*. Princeton: Princeton University Press, 1982.

Michaud, G. (M. Seurat), and O. Carré. *Les Frères musulmans*. Paris: Gallimard, 1983.

Mitchell, R. P. *The Society of the Muslim Brothers*. Oxford: Oxford University Press, 1969.

Moini, F. *Yearbook Iran 89/90*. Menas Associates.

Moore, C. H. "Islamic Banks and Competitive Politics in the Arab World and Turkey." *Middle East Journal* 44, no. 2 (Spring 1991).

Mortimer, Edward. *Faith and Power: The Politics of Islam*. London: Faber and Faber; New York: Random House, 1982.

Nasr, Seyyed Vali Reza. "Students, Islam, and Politics: Islami Jami'at-i Tuleba in Pakistan." *Middle East Journal* 46, no. 1 (Winter 1992).

Poullada, Leon B. *Reform and Rebellion in Afghanistan, 1919–1929: King Ana-mullah's Failure to Modernize a Tribal Society*. Ithaca: Cornell University Press, 1973.

Qureshi, A. I. *The Economic and Social System of Islam*. Lahore: Islamic Book Service, 1979.

Reissner, Johannes. *Ideologie und Politik der Muslimbrüder Syriens*. Fribourg: Klaus Schwartz Verlag, 1980.

Richard, Yann. *Le Shi'isme en Iran*. Paris: Jean Maisonneuve, 1980.

——— *L'Islam chi'ite*. Paris: Fayard, 1990.

Rodinson, Maxime. *Islam and Capitalism*. New York: Pantheon, 1974.

Rouadjia, A. *Les Frères et la mosquée*. Paris: Karthala, 1988.

Roy, Olivier. *L'Afghanistan: Islam et modernité politique*. Paris: Le Seuil, 1985. Translated as *Islam and Resistance in Afghanistan*. Cambridge: Cambridge University Press, 1986.

——— "Ethnies et politique en Asie central." *Revue du monde musulman et de la Méditerranée* (Aix-en-Provence, Edisud), January 1992.

Seurat, Michel. *L'état de Barbarie*. Paris: Le Seuil, 1989.

Shadid, M. K. "The Muslim Brotherhood Movement in the West Bank and Gaza." *Third World Quarterly* 10, no. 2 (April 1988), 658–682.

Shahrani, N. "Popular Knowledge of Islam and Social Discourse in Afghanistan and Turkistan in the Modern Period." Photocopy of a paper presented at the American Research Seminar, 1985.

Shariati, Ali (under the pseudonym Ali Mozayani). *Tashayyu-i alavi, tashayyu-i safavi* (The Shiism of Ali, the Shiism of the Safavids). N.p., 1973.

Sid, Ahmed A. "Finance islamique et développement." *Revue tiers-monde* 23, no. 92 (October–December 1982).

Sivan, Emmanuel. "Ibn Taymiyya, Father of the Islamic Revolution." *Encounter*, May 1983.

———— *Radical Islam: Medieval Theology and Modern Politics.* New Haven: Yale University Press, 1985.

Talighani, Mahmud, *Islam va malikiyat* (Islam and property). 4th ed. Tehran, 1963.

Tozy, M. "Islam et état au Maghreb." *Maghreb Machrek,* no. 3 (1989).

Vieille, P., and F. Khosrokhavar. *Le discours populaire de la révolution iranienne.* Paris: Contemporanéité, 1990.

Weber, M. *The Protestant Ethic and the Spirit of Capitalism.* Translated by Talcott Parsons. New York: Scribner's, 1976.